White Christmas in April

PETER LANG
New York • Washington, D.C./Baltimore • Boston • Bern
Frankfurt am Main • Berlin • Brussels • Vienna • Canterbury

White Christmas in April

The Collapse of South Vietnam, 1975

EDITED BY

J. Edward Lee
and Toby Haynsworth

PETER LANG
New York • Washington, D.C./Baltimore • Boston • Bern
Frankfurt am Main • Berlin • Brussels • Vienna • Canterbury

41266238
DLC

9-28-00

Library of Congress Cataloging-in-Publication Data

White Christmas in April: the collapse of South Vietnam, 1975 /
edited by J. Edward Lee and Toby Haynsworth.
p. cm.
Includes bibliographical references and index.
1. Vietnamese Conflict, 1961–1975—Personal narratives, American.
I. Lee, J. Edward. II. Haynsworth, Toby.
DS559.5.L42   959.704'3'092—dc21   99-30262
ISBN 0-8204-4538-X

Die Deutsche Bibliothek-CIP-Einheitsaufnahme

White Christmas in April: the collapse of South Vietnam, 1975 /
J. Edward Lee and Toby Haynsworth (ed.).
–New York; Washington, D.C./Baltimore; Boston; Bern;
Frankfurt am Main; Berlin; Brussels; Vienna; Canterbury: Lang.
ISBN 0-8204-4538-X

Cover design by Lisa Dillon

The paper in this book meets the guidelines for permanence and durability
of the Committee on Production Guidelines for Book Longevity
of the Council of Library Resources.

© 1999 Peter Lang Publishing, Inc., New York

Printed in the United States of America

For the Warriors

Sergeant Tyre D. Lee, Sr., Captain Tyre D. Lee, Jr.

Rear Admiral Hugh C. Haynsworth, Jr., and Major General Homer D. Smith

"Out of this war are going to come some of the finest people this country has ever seen."

General William Westmoreland

Acknowledgments

"War is not a sport but a duty, and we should not love it."
William Gilmore Simms

White Christmas In April: The Collapse Of South Vietnam, 1975 would have been impossible without the cooperation and guidance of key people. At the top of our list would be the last two Defense Attachés, Generals John Murray and Homer Smith. More than sixty generous men and women cooperated with this project, giving us their prospective. Four individuals who shared their private collections deserve special recognition: Joseph Gildea, John Guffey, Edwin Pelosky, and Glenn Rounsevell. All of the interviewees were extremely helpful and generously shared their recollections, photographs, and personal collections. They are thanked for, as Richard Armitage told us, "clearly telling the story of the war."

Additionally, one of the Winthrop University History Department's graduate students, Jacqueline Lukich, saw this project as a personal mission and helped us assemble the manuscript.

In everything we do, our spouses are beside us. We thank Ann-Franklin Hardy Lee and Martha Bragg Haynsworth for steadfastly and patiently endorsing *White Christmas In April*. And our children, Elizabeth Ann Lee, Hugh C. Haynsworth, IV, and Samuel M. Haynsworth, who escaped the war but shared our desire to understand how it all ended, are saluted. May they continue to escape such chaos; may they never have to make the sacrifices.

Table of Contents

Preface

*The young dead soldiers do not speak. Nevertheless, they
are heard in the still houses: who has not heard them?*
Archibald MacLeish, "The Young Dead Soldiers."

This book originated over five years ago as an effort to explain the collapse of South Vietnam to college students born, mostly, in the late 1970s and the early 1980s. These students missed America's longest war—even though many of them had parents affected by it. We, as editors, have found ourselves affected by it, also.

The accounts of Saigon's last days, through which we can glimpse aspects of our total Vietnam experience and can serve as a prism, are powerful primary sources. Our interviews are constructed upon the memories of men and women who witnessed the end of America's involvement in Southeast Asia. Sprinkled throughout our interviews are documents which broaden our understanding of the events of the spring of 1975. Together with the interviews, these sources recreate the wide range of emotions which swirled around "Operation Frequent Wind." It is our hope that *White Christmas in April: The Collapse Of South Vietnam, 1975* will answer our students' questions—as well as your own.

Introduction

*Historians will eventually dig it all out. They will perhaps treat
me very kindly, perhaps more kindly than I should be treated.
But there is a hell of a story yet to be told.*

Ambassador Graham Martin

Ron Nessen, President Ford's Press Secretary, says that as Saigon collapsed
under the suffocating weight of the communist assault on April 30, 1975,
our nation's media was told that all military personnel had already been
evacuated from South Vietnam's capital. In the chaos of the moment,
however, Nessen and White House Chief of Staff Donald Rumsfeld
discovered that eleven marines still remained atop our embassy, awaiting
one last helicopter. Rumsfeld told the Press Secretary that the previous
statement should be amended and the truth revealed. As Rumsfeld explained
to Nessen, too many lies and distortions had occurred during America's
longest war, and he wished to end the United States' involvement in that
war with complete truth. Nessen stepped back into the White House briefing
room and informed the reporters that eleven marines still remained and that
a helicopter had been dispatched to rescue them.[1]

Two years after that last helicopter ferried those marines to safety,
Frank M. Snepp, III, the Central Intelligence Agency's former chief strategy
analyst in Vietnam, published a troubling book entitled *Decent Interval*. A
theme of bitterness flows through that book as Snepp shares his anger over
the disintegration of Vietnam that occurred during the spring of 1975. He
argues that America mishandled the evacuation of Saigon and, "as parts of
South Vietnam dropped off the body like pieces of a disintegrating ice
floe," we seemed unable—or unwilling—to honor our commitment to those
South Vietnamese who had stood with us during the war. The promises that
had been made to President Nguyen Van Thieu at the time of the 1973 Paris
Peace Accords had been forgotten. Snepp blames Presidents Richard Nixon
and Gerald Ford, Ambassador Graham Martin, and Secretary of State Henry
Kissinger who, by 1975, had allowed their commitment to South Vietnam to
be erased by Presidential scandals, economic malaise, and problems in the
Middle East.[2]

In his book, Snepp says that 3,000 Vietnamese who had served our
country's various agencies and had been assured, if things ever collapsed,
that they would not be abandoned to the communists, were left behind.
Snepp concludes *Decent Interval* by writing:

Hopefully, with the passage of time and healing of the national trauma inflicted by the war, we will be able to give history its due, a complete and unflinching retrospective, extending beyond platitudes and recriminations that till now have blinded so many of us to what actually happened to Vietnam, and ourselves, in the two years following the Paris peace agreement.[3]

It has been twenty-five years since an ill and disheartened Ambassador Martin, with the embassy's American flag strategically shielded under his arm, headed toward one of the last helicopters leaving the embassy compound. It has been a quarter of a century since Radio Saigon played Bing Crosby's "White Christmas" as a signal to begin the evacuation which would be called "Frequent Wind." It has been a generation since images of frantic Vietnamese civilians, struggling to scale the embassy's wall, flashed across America's television screens. Likewise, it has been over twenty years since Frank Snepp, in disgust, resigned from the CIA and wrote his story of betrayal. It has been over five years since President Bill Clinton lifted the trade embargo against Vietnam which had been enacted on the heels of the communist victory. It has been nearly five years since, with diplomatic relations restored, former Secretary of State Warren Christopher visited Hanoi and declared an end to "a decade of war and two decades of estrangement." Symbolically, our current ambassador, Pete Peterson, was for five and one half years a prisoner of war in North Vietnam. And Baskin Robbins has opened an ice cream shop in Ho Chi Minh City (Saigon). Therefore, the time has come, as Frank Snepp wrote in 1977, to "give history its due."[4]

Our research into the last days of the war in Vietnam is not nearly as pessimistic, accusatory, narrow, or bitter as that offered in *Decent Interval* which, perhaps, was written too soon after the communists had overrun our former ally. We, like Snepp, see the duplicity of past government officials and the paralysis of Ambassador Martin, who required two direct orders from President Ford to evacuate the embassy. We have, however, also documented acts of heroism and courage. The final days of South Vietnam were characterized by chaos, tragedy, indecision, confusion, and bitter memories such as Snepp's. But in April of 1975, we also saw sacrifice, compassion, and a successful mission which saved the lives of over 100,000 endangered people.[5]

Haney Howell, CBS News' last Saigon Bureau Chief, left Vietnam the final week of April. He had covered the horrible C-5 transport plane crash which early that month claimed the lives of thirty-eight American women and 200 Vietnamese orphans, part of the ill-fated "Operation

Babylift." Howell had been "in country" for three years reporting on what he labels "a civil war." Howell recalls a steady "cultural breakdown" within the society. As the South Vietnamese Army evaporated and shed its uniforms, panic struck the country's civilians. His most difficult moment was when he had to refuse to take a couple's child along with him on CBS' airplane. Howell explains the chaos as "White Christmas" played on the radio by observing "no one wanted to be the last person to die in the Vietnam War." Looking back on his service in Vietnam, Howell remembers the horror in the mother's face as he told her he could not allow her daughter to flee with him. And he criticizes the media's coverage of the war, which included Walter Cronkite's comments in the wake of the 1968 Tet offensive that the war was unwinnable. Howell sums up his role in the spring of 1975 by identifying himself as "the last bureau chief of the network which lost the Vietnam War."[6]

Seventy miles off the coast of Vietnam a human drama was commencing. Helicopters designed for a crew of four were carrying as many as fifty Vietnamese to safety aboard American ships such as the *USS Midway*. Some of these aircraft were labeled "Air America" to shield their CIA identity. According to the *Midway's* Commanding Officer, retired Admiral Lawrence Chambers, "our crew did things that I didn't think were humanly possible." Working around the clock on April 29–30, the sailors emptied each incoming helicopter, searched for weapons, provided the dazed refugees with food, comforted the children, and then prepared for the next arrivals. When a CIA officer arrived with a pearl-handled pistol, which he refused to surrender, a naval officer calmly issued a receipt, confiscated the weapon, and tossed it into the South China Sea. The *Midway's* Executive Officer, Larry Grimes, adds that one "Air America" helicopter contained a cargo of Scotch Whiskey. The liquor, like the pearl-handled pistol, was tossed overboard.[7]

On the day the communists overran Saigon, South Vietnamese Major Bung Ly loaded his wife and their five children into a small reconnaissance plane designed to seat two passengers. He aimed his plane toward the *Midway* in a frantic race to freedom. The military command structure had evaporated. As Bung Ly explains, "no one was left over me." He stresses, "I had to take care of my family."[8]

Circling the *Midway*, Bung Ly dropped a note, wrapped around a wrench, which read, "Can you move the helicopters to the other side? I can land on your runway. Please rescue me!" At first, there was skepticism as to whether such a feat was possible. But it became obvious that the young husband and father was determined to make the attempt regardless of the

obvious danger. To try a landing in the ocean in an aircraft with a fixed
landing gear was hopeless. As Major Ly said later, his children would have
had no chance to escape, even if he might have been able to do so himself.
Captain Chambers hesitated no more. He ordered the rain-soaked flight
deck cleared; helicopters worth hundreds of thousands of dollars were
shoved overboard. As the Vietnamese major made his desperate approach,
Chambers shouted "Clear the deck! Bird Dog on final!" The plane, lacking
a tailhook, bounced once, screeched to a halt, and then the officer and his
family were embraced by the cheering crew. The old hands at carrier air
operations marveled at his airmanship. When asked where he had learned to
fly so well, Bung Ly answered with one word "Texas."[9]

Journalist Haney Howell says that "anyone who had a key to a plane"
tried to flee the collapsing nation, either aboard helicopters supplied by our
government or, as the situation deteriorated, in small planes like the one
commandeered by Bung Ly. As the swarm of aircraft came in, *Midway*
officer H. C. "Toby" Haynsworth explains, "we would get the people out of
the helicopters, push the empty helicopters over the side and make room for
the next flight." He adds, "as I watched first scores, then hundreds, and
finally thousands of refugees disembark from the helicopters, it became
clear to me, as it never had been before, that life under a communist regime
must be a terrible life."[10]

Some of the Vietnamese fled by boat and spent weeks looking for
rescue. As the *Midway* lay at anchor off of Thailand onloading South
Vietnamese F-5 aircraft that had been flown there by escaping South
Vietnamese pilots, a small broken-down motor launch loaded to
overflowing with frightened Vietnamese approached the aircraft carrier. The
admiral in command of the task force was reluctant to have these pathetic
souls brought on board as he had no specific authority to permit it. He sent a
message to Pearl Harbor asking for instructions.

Captain Chambers was of another mind. He twisted his ship on its
anchor chain so that it was in "international waters." He sent his Executive
Officer, Captain Larry Grimes to the scene so that he would be able to
provide a firsthand report of the boat's condition. The vessel was in terrible
shape. It became obvious that the Thai government was not going to let the
Vietnamese land in their country and that sending the boat back out to sea
would likely be a death sentence. Captain Grimes did not wait for a reply to
the admiral's message to headquarters. He sent one of his officers into the
flimsy craft with a fire ax and directed him to chop a hole in the hull. As the
boat began to fill with water, the frightened refugees were brought on board
the aircraft carrier. Grimes says, "we purposely scuttled" the boat, saved

eighty-four lives, and rejoiced because "it was the correct thing to do." The official ship's log is a little more discreet; it records, "Forty foot fishing boat approached *Midway* with eighty-four Vietnamese refugees aboard. Indicating boat was damaged and sinking—repairs attempted. Repair attempts in Vietnamese fishing boat unsuccessful. Vessel sank alongside *Midway*. Refugees taken aboard *Midway*."[11]

Meanwhile, back in Saigon the last contingent of marines had been evacuated. At the studios of Radio Saigon, the jammed controls repeatedly broadcast the South Vietnamese and American national anthems until the communists kicked the door down and silenced the tape. At the presidential palace, General Minh, the caretaker leader of the South Vietnamese government, prepared to surrender. The editor of the North Vietnamese army newspaper, a colonel, drove a tank up to the palace's doors. General Minh greeted him by announcing "I have been waiting since early this morning to transfer power to you." Tersely, the colonel responded, "There is no question of your transferring power. Your power has crumbled. You cannot give up what you do not have. Between Vietnamese, there are no victors and no vanquished. Only the Americans have been beaten."[12]

In his *Vietnam: A History*, Stanley Karnow writes that the evacuation "was close to miraculous." He tells us that the original plan was for "White Christmas" to signal an orderly exodus of Americans and South Vietnamese. Buses were to pick up the evacuees and transport them to designated helicopter pads, but as the communists descended upon Saigon, mobs of hysterical citizens wrecked the plans. What occurred was an every-man-for-himself surge whirling in an atmosphere of pandemonium. Thus, it is "miraculous" indeed that ships like the *Midway*, *Hancock* and *Coral Sea*, brave helicopter pilots running on empty, figuratively and literally, courageous pilots like Bung Ly, cooks and supply personnel who provided thousands of meals, and sailors who ignored international boundaries could conclude the war with such grace under pressure.

In our judgment, we find the bitter portraits by Frank Snepp and Colonel Harry O. Summers, Jr., who has written of the evacuation "It was not a proud day to be an American," to be too pessimistic as we survey the events from the vantage point of two decades. In a war which cost 1,000,000 Vietnamese lives and an additional 58,000 Americans, wrecked a beautiful country, produced atrocities like the 1968 My Lai Massacre, and scarred our nation psychologically, "Operation Frequent Wind" had moments of gallantry which should make us all proud.[13]

The evacuation, instead of being viewed as the final chapter of a tragic war, can be considered the first episode in what has become, in recent years, a new relationship between Vietnam and the United States. Such a healthy and complete reassessment allows us to finally proceed with laying the foundation for new inquiry into the historical lessons we should learn from our Vietnam experience which will include an examination of how wars begin—and end. We commence ten thousand miles from Asia with an examination of raw Washington infighting circa 1975. An unavoidable link has formed between an increasingly unpopular war and the political forces which collided in America to accelerate the collapse of South Vietnam. Our instructor is General Alexander Haig, President Nixon's last Chief of Staff.

Chapter 1

Slow Strangulation

As a former secretary of state, NATO Commander, combat veteran, and White House Chief of Staff, Alexander Haig views the collapse of South Vietnam as being closely linked to weakness in our executive branch and the misuse of military power. Too many factors collided for the outcome to have been avoided. President Lyndon Johnson, a master politician, failed to follow his "gut." President Richard Nixon, a skillful student of foreign policy, did not anticipate that he would be drowned by Watergate. And President Gerald Ford, unelected, was reluctant to go to Capitol Hill and demand renewed bombing of North Vietnam.[1]

Haig levels his fire at the timid climate of the era. Until it was too late, Johnson listened to holdover Kennedy advisors like Defense Secretary Robert McNamara. Nixon never dreamed that his administration's scandals would interfere with his ability to enforce the Paris Peace Accords. And Ford, Nixon's pardoner, inherited a presidency that had been emasculated by a public that no longer had the "stomach" for war. In Saigon, President Thieu saw his nation slowly strangled by the dual forces of an impotent former ally and an emboldened North Vietnam, unafraid to invade its neighbor. Thus, Haig suggests that the events of April 1975 were sadly anticlimactic. The die had been cast two years earlier when Nixon had been crippled by Watergate. As Haig observes, "It was all over, for all intents and purposes, by April 1973."[2]

President Nixon believed that our involvement in Vietnam had been a mistake in the way it was conducted. His problem was that he did not take the kind of action he should have taken early in his administration and bring the war to a conclusion. You will recall that Eisenhower brought an end to things in Korea by making it clear to the Russians that we knew that they were behind it and that he would use whatever weapons he had at his disposal to settle it. That began peace negotiations in the Korean case.

Now, what I urged Nixon to do right at the outset, during the first year of his administration, was to seize the opportunity when American planes were shot at in international waters off North Korea and bring the war in Southeast Asia to a conclusion. We would remove all the Russian sanctuaries and we would use all the weapons at our disposal. Now, Eisenhower was thinking nuclear. We were not. Nixon rejected my suggestion at the last minute. There was a split view at the National Security Council on it. Nixon told me—he took it to his grave—that this was the most serious mistake of his presidency, not Watergate. We should have moved on it quickly and decisively, because the source of the problem was in Moscow and not simply in Hanoi. As you will recall, the Vietcong problem disappeared with the 1968 Tet Offensive. They were the proxy of Hanoi which was, in turn, the proxy of Moscow.

By the beginning of Nixon's second term, Nixon had already sent the signal that he was prepared to bomb Hanoi. And, as you recall, he had bombed Hanoi in December 1972. He had done it earlier that spring. On both occasions that got the north to sit down and talk. On the first occasion—the mining and bombing—we didn't really use all the weapons at our disposal like the B-52s and so forth. But they did begin serious discussions. For reasons associated with misjudgments in Moscow, the North Vietnamese toughened their position in November of the election year. They were anticipating a change in the White House. So that is when the president started the bombing. Now, that bombing was decisive in getting the Paris Peace Talks resumed, our prisoners out, and a peace settlement that was about all the traffic would bear.

As the bombing began in December—it happened over Christmas—the Senate was in recess. We were getting hourly threats that there would be an impeachment vote after they got back; or, at a minimum, a vote to cut off all bombing in Southeast Asia. That put a pistol to Nixon's head and to Kissinger's head from the standpoint that they had to accept a less than acceptable treaty that permitted North Vietnamese troops to stay in the south. I was very skeptical of that. I expressed that skepticism. That doesn't mean that I had a better idea because I didn't want Nixon to be impeached. That would have been an even worse outcome and I think he could have been.

The agreement, notwithstanding its flaws, still should have been viable if two provisions had been met. One was a high level of support from the United States for Saigon. As it turned out, when Watergate surfaced, and it began to paralyze Nixon, the support for the war was slowly strangled. Opponents to the war slowly but surely strangled support for the war. Now, in addition to that, the guarantee that was given to Thieu that, in the event of violations, we would react strongly—meaning to bomb Hanoi again—that guarantee was abrogated when, in July 1973, Congress voted a bombing halt. That was a disaster. Never in the history of our nation has Congress removed the implicit sanctions to enforce a treaty. But they did. They passed legislation which exceeded the intent of our Founding Fathers.

In 1973, Nixon had every reason to believe that he would be around for four more years. If the North Vietnamese had launched the attack they did two years later during the Ford Administration, I am reasonably sure that Nixon would have gone up to the Hill and said, "You can impeach me if you want, but I'm going to enforce our agreement."

Ford was a victim of his own circumstances. He had to bind the wounds of Watergate. When I was in NATO in February 1975 I got a call from President Thieu's security advisor, Duc, asking to come see me. He said, "General, President Thieu would like to know, if you had it to do all over again, would you have advised him to sign that peace treaty?" And I said, "I'm not sure that it's a relevant question, because I'm not sure there was any alternative." The lack of support for the war in Vietnam by the American people was due to the fact that they had lost their stomach for it as a result of the mishandling of the thing.

I was concerned that Thieu had sent his emissary because Thieu knew something that I didn't know—that they must be collapsing. I called Henry Kissinger, the Secretary of State, on a secure line, and told him about the experience I had just had. I said, "They must be coming apart very rapidly. The president must go up to the Congress like Harry Truman and call for immediate military action against Hanoi." He said, "Al, I agree with you. It's worse than you think because they are coming down the trail by the hundreds and hundreds. And the South Vietnamese are running out of ammunition." So, I said, "If you aren't going to speak to the President, I will." I flew back and asked for an audience with the President and I told him that he had to act now or he would lose the presidency. And we spent an hour or two together. And Ford said, "I just don't think the American people have the stomach for a resumption of this." Well, I said, "I think that you'll be a one term president." And I got up and left. That is the sad end of that war.

Thieu would have every reason to believe Kissinger and Nixon double-crossed him. And he believes that to this day. The facts are that they were presiding over a nation that had already lost the war in its own mind because of the mismanagement of that war. It was the wrong application of military power. If you decide to use it, you must use it decisively or not use it at all. Lyndon Johnson could have won that war. He should have put the Russians on notice. That is what he told me when I used to go brief him. His guts were usually pretty good.

It was over, for all intents and purposes, by April 1973. Here was a president who was in a fight for his survival. There was a law passed by the Congress that forbade any bombing. And there was the removal of sanctions and the strangulation of the ARVN. There was a constant and steady decline in the level of support being given to Saigon. It was a slow strangulation, so that by the end of the first year of the Ford Administration, it was over.

When I was at NATO, the news of the collapse of South Vietnam was probably the saddest day of my life, especially the horrible way that it was brought to a conclusion. I had told the President that he had to roll up his sleeves like Harry Truman and go up there to the Hill and have it out with those guys. I think that I would have bombed the North Vietnamese and let them impeach me if they wanted. There were a lot of things that worked against President Ford, including the reaction to the pardon of Richard Nixon. He didn't dare do anything else. In Washington, the pardon became an excuse for turning on him by his own party as well as by the Democratic Party. As a result, he wasn't a whole president in his own right.

Chapter 2

More

During his long life, Jack Brady has served his country in a variety of ways. As a young man, he entered the U.S. Army in 1943 and saw combat in Europe as an infantryman from July 1944 to March 1945. After World War II, he earned a college degree and served as an R.O.T.C. instructor at the University of Notre Dame where he received a master's degree. While stationed in the United Kingdom, Brady earned a doctorate from the London School of Economics. Upon retirement from the military, Brady went to work as staff director of the U.S. House of Representatives Committee on Foreign Affairs.[1]

In the following comments, Brady bluntly analyzes the role of politics in the conduct of the Vietnam War. He laments that, "We were in bed with the wrong guys." Brady considers the 1968 Tet Defensive to be the turning point for America's involvement in the war. By 1975, the seventy-five members of the Class of 1974 Democrats who had been elected in the wake of the Watergate scandal had arrived on the Hill. These ideological members of Congress took aim at America's continued support of Saigon just as they had attacked the U.S. Congress seniority system. Brady observes, "They were interesting times."[2]

In 1974, the administration requested one and a half billion dollars in assistance for Vietnam, as I recall. And, after a long fight, the most they could get was 750 million dollars. The mood in Congress was antiwar and the antiwar factions were becoming more and more vocal and more and more numerous. In early 1975, Majority Leader Tip O'Neil sent a bipartisan group to Vietnam led by Representative John Flynt of Georgia. Pete McClosky of California, Bella Abzug of New York, and Millicent Fenwick of New Jersey were members.

So, we went out there. My specific job was to determine whether or not the South Vietnamese needed the additional military assistance. A substantial amount of it was to be used for ammunition. We went to Cambodia first. When the group arrived in Vietnam, it was clear to me that there was absolutely no way they were going to get a report out of that group. They were all over the political landscape. There was no getting them together. Bella Abzug was as radical on one note as the Department of

Defense escort we had was on the other. Anyhow, Graham Martin was the ambassador out there. He wanted the additional assistance. It was largely at his nagging and pushing that this group was sent out there.

Well, we came back, and as far as I know, we never did get a recommendation from that group about what to do concerning the additional assistance. Some thought they needed it. Others felt it wouldn't make any difference. Vietnam was gone. And all we were going to do was just put a Band-Aid on a cancer. Those who supported the war and those who opposed the war didn't trust each other. There wasn't any room for accommodation. Surprisingly enough, the day Vietnam fell, April 30, I got a photo album from Vietnamese military headquarters showing us inspecting their military museum with all this captured military equipment.

U.S. Representative Tom Morgan, the Chairman of the House Foreign Affairs Committee, started out as a firm supporter of the war but he ended up reversing his position. And there were others. The pressures on those guys at that time, from what I call the pacifist wing of the party, were enormous.

I really didn't support the war, but the administration was backing it and I thought we had to support it. I began to change my position on the war in 1965 when we started the bombing. I have long believed you do not win military engagements with bombing, having been an infantryman in World War II, and having been bombed and strafed twelve times, and not once by the enemy. At any rate, that is when I began to change. I thought—and members of Congress who agreed with me thought—that we had two fundamental decisions to make in Vietnam. Were we going to invade North Vietnam? If we invaded, that meant full mobilization. It also meant the possibility—or probability—of China coming in. That led to the ultimate decision: were we willing to use tactical nuclear weapons? Once you answered those questions you came up with "no's." We should have gotten out. But Lyndon Johnson couldn't—wouldn't—say "no" to General Westmoreland. And the one thing about Westmoreland was the middle syllable of his name. "More" described his tactics. "More." "More." "More." And all it did was get Lyndon Johnson further into the hole.

John Kennedy, I believe, would have gotten us out of that war. We had an old saying in the army I was in: "You don't exploit a disaster." And once you've got a disaster you change politics. You change tactics. But the mood in the Congress was nasty. And at the same time, you had the Indochina Resource Center, which was supplying all kinds of information and misinformation to the Hill about what was going on in Vietnam.

One of the reasons the congressional delegation went out there in 1975 was that the bill had aid for Cambodia in it. The group was going to Cambodia one day and all of these human rights groups in Vietnam asked Bella Abzug to go down into the third military region of Vietnam instead and look at the human rights situation. She said to me, "What should I do?" I said, "There are a lot of people back in the States who are depending on your assessment of what's going on in Cambodia, and you have already talked to every human rights person in this country. You owe it to your people and to yourself to go to Cambodia." Well, I talked them into it and we went to Cambodia. And we came back, and the day we got back, there was a meeting that afternoon in a small committee room to discuss the report and what we were going to say. And they were all there. And they agreed to do nothing. And we came out and media grabbed Bella and Millicent Fenwick.

Bella wanted some information from me that I had in my office so she was going down to my office with me. And I was pleading for at least food for Cambodia. I said, "Bella, you can't feed a corpse." She erupted into some expletive and said, "You say that all the time, Jack."

The whole Congress was fractured. This whole town was fractured. And those who opposed the war were a growing number of people. There was a lot of misinformation being put out around town. The fundamental fact of the matter was we never understood that war. Our military never understood it. Our politicians never understood it. As happens so often, you end up backing the wrong side. I was stationed in Korea in 1954. We were on alert to go to Dien Bien Phu to bail out the French. They would take a group down to Seoul and load them in boats. Another group of soldiers would be loaded in airplanes to see how long it would take to get the troops loaded to head to Vietnam. We went through those exercises. My understanding was that the Joint Chiefs of Staff were trying to convince Eisenhower, "It's the wrong war at the wrong time at the wrong place and the wrong enemy."

The one thing you will find out is that politicians are skeptical. All the information was showing that we were winning the war. And along comes the Tet Offensive of 1968. We weren't winning the war much anymore! I think that was the watershed. That's what put Robert Kennedy into the campaign.

Ambassador Graham Martin had grandiose schemes about a lot of things. Everybody knew that if we were going to support an evacuation of Vietnam, we were going to have to provide troops to support the evacuation. But that was subsequent to our being kicked out. We could have gotten those people out while we were still there in large numbers.

The question was, "Where were we going to put the refugees?" Who wants 1,000,000 refugees tied up on your shores? There wasn't a lot of sympathy for the Vietnamese who came. On the other hand, I don't think there has been a group of people who came into this country and became less of a burden and took care of their own people like the Vietnamese did, and have.

Graham Martin was called "the general." In the early 1970s, he was our ambassador in Rome and I was given the job to go to Europe and tell the Congress how we could reduce American troops in NATO by 50,000. I was waiting in the anteroom to Martin's office in Rome. Martin comes to the door, opens it, and my military escort and I headed into the office. The next thing I know the door is closed and my escort is on the other side alone. Martin always became an advocate of the country he was stationed in. He said, "I can tell you how to cut two divisions from NATO." I'm all ears. He said, "Replace them with Italian divisions." Martin always got himself involved in the military aspects of embassy business. He was a hands-on guy. He thought he was a general and he was stubborn.

Martin came back from Vietnam with the congressional delegation in February 1975. On the flight, he bent my ear about how important more aid was for the South Vietnamese. My recommendation was that we give them half of it but even that wouldn't fly. Martin didn't suffer fools lightly. And he thought there were a lot of fools in Congress. I liked him.

Chapter 3

Oil And Money

The war ended in triumph for twenty-five-year-old Tran Trong Khan, a Vietcong officer who was present in Saigon on April 30. Today, Khan is counselor at the Vietnamese Embassy in Washington. His office features smiling assistants and travel brochures. The embassy's conference room is adorned with American and Vietnamese flags. A quarter of a century ago, however, Khan was an insurgent thirsting for victory over the same Americans who he now invites to return to his country— under strikingly different circumstances from those that existed in the spring of 1975.[1]

In April of 1975 I was with the victorious side as it entered Ho Chi Minh City. At the time I was a twenty-five-year-old greenhorn lieutenant, a member of a commission that had been established as result of the 1973 Paris Peace Accords. While I was born in the north, just south of the Sino-Vietnamese border, I spent most of the war in Vietcong areas.

Originally, the commission to which I was assigned consisted of representatives of the governments of North Vietnam, South Vietnam, the Vietcong, and the United States. However, after about sixty days, most of the members from the United States withdrew, as did those from North Vietnam, so we shifted to a two-part commission involving only the Vietcong and the Government of South Vietnam. One component of the original commission, the one tasked with the search for MIAs, survived as the Four-Party Joint Military Team. Its mission was strictly limited to the MIA question.

The breakdown of the parent four-part commission resulted from an important feature of the Paris Peace Accords. That was the fact that the agreement documents were written in both English and Vietnamese, and both texts were considered to be equally authentic. This is standard in any agreement between parties whose native languages are different. The Vietnamese version was written in the language as spoken in the north. A fluent Vietnamese speaker can tell the difference between the language of the north and that of the south the same way that one can tell the difference between "standard" English and the way the language is spoken in Texas. The importance of these different versions of the agreements was that they made possible different interpretations of what we considered to be one of the most important clauses in the Accords. That is the part that, in the Vietnamese language version, declares Vietnam to be one country, independent and neutral. The United States had never recognized that fact, nor did it after Paris in 1973. If it had, the United States never would have committed its troops to South Vietnam. It was the inclusion of this recognition of the existence of a single nation named Vietnam that led to our signing of it.

The Accords also provided for the safe pullout of all American forces and the release of all prisoners held by the VC, the North Vietnamese, and our allies in Laos and Kampuchea.

Once you achieved your main goal of the release of prisoners of war, the fate of the MIAs was your principal concern. Searching for these missing Americans was the charge of the much smaller four-party team so the original commission was then reduced to just the VC and the Government of South Vietnam. It was the view of the government in North Vietnam that the internal affairs of the southern region of Vietnam should be resolved by the South Vietnamese themselves, that is, the Government of South Vietnam and the Vietcong, so it no longer believed that its participation on the commission was appropriate.

This difference of opinion as to whether there was one Vietnam or two was manifested when I first came to South Vietnam. I was asked to sign a visa. I did not do so because I considered it all to be a single nation.

There was another four-party group established by the Paris Accords. It was the International Commission of Control and Supervision (ICCS). At first, it consisted of representatives from Poland, Hungary, Canada, and Indonesia. The Canadians were soon replaced by an Iranian delegation. This group was established to resolve any disagreements arising as the Paris Accords were being implemented. However, the treaty required that all ICCS decisions be unanimous in order to have effect. Since each side in disagreements had advocates on the International Commission, virtually no decisions were unanimous, and the ICCS became ineffective as a resolver of disputes. This leads to the most important thing in the making of foreign policy: force. Basically, if you lose on the battlefield, you cannot get a good agreement at the negotiating table.

One of the problems that you Americans faced in your efforts at nation building in South Vietnam was the unpopularity of the Thieu government.

It was not necessary to wait until Thieu became the head of state in order to identify the root cause of the United States' problems. They began in the 1960s with the assassination of Ngo Dinh Diem in 1963. He was a very nationalistic leader. Even though he was not especially popular, he was very powerful. He was very, very powerful. If you speak to any Vietnamese today, he would say that he has a higher regard for Diem than for Thieu. This does not seem to be well understood in your country. You should read McNamara's book. You should also read those written by Clark Clifford and

Roger Hilsman. You need to realize that those in Washington had already made a terrible mistake by 1963. From the perspective of the South Vietnamese, you have removed the rationale for your commitment. Why, basically, are you there? In theory, you are there to build a free, democratic country. But if you kill the president when he does not obey your orders, I think that is wrong, terribly wrong.

When compared to those who came to power immediately after Diem's assassination, the Thieu government was much better in the sense that it was more stable. Was it corrupt? You know that it was. I had many contacts and meetings with the American-trained officers in the South Vietnamese armed forces. They happened to be much richer than many American military officers that were killed, in spite of their relatively low salaries. Yes, corruption was widespread.

Even though I was a greenhorn lieutenant without any formal military training, I could see that the end was coming for the Thieu government before it actually fell. There were four basic reasons why I believed that it would happen.

The first was that by signing the Paris Accords, the United States demonstrated that it did not have the courage or willingness to continue the war under all circumstances. That meant that the U.S. commitment to the war effort in Vietnam was declining. We were monitoring very closely how much money you were giving to your allies. Were you putting your money where your mouth was? If you gave less money, that meant less of a commitment.

The second reason for believing that the end for South Vietnam was near was the removal of all American forces: ground troops, naval forces, and air forces. We could then see that the end was inevitable. It was now just a question of when. As a military officer, I then believed that a military victory was possible. A significant factor contributing to this view was our conviction that this was nothing less than a struggle for our survival as a nation. We believed that we were in the right. As long as we survived, we would fight. So there was no questioning of bargaining about who would be the winner. If we were not to succeed, it would be simply because we were unable to win. There was no limit to our commitment. When the Americans left, we concluded that the first phase of the war was over and now was the time to make it happen. While I was not a decision maker, I am sure that was the attitude of the leadership.

Third, your South Vietnamese allies made many strategic mistakes. The end result then became clearer and clearer. For example, the evacuation of the Central Highlands, which they began without consulting the United States, was a great mistake. While I was not aware of that at the time, the leadership in North Vietnam was fully aware of what was going on. They realized that this provided them with a great opportunity.

In previous years whenever we attacked in the Central Highlands, we would target the most important objectives. Two factors prevented a military victory. One was the fact that the South Vietnamese still had American air and naval support, and there was a high commitment to the war on the part of the United States. If we were able to capture an objective, you would then reduce the target to rubble, and we had to withdraw. In other words, we figured out that by trying to capture the most important objectives, we were inviting massive retaliatory air and/or naval bombardments. You would then destroy the target "in order to save it."

In 1974, it was decided to use a different approach. We provoked in the east, but attacked in the west. That is how we came to attack at Ban Me Thuot. Even though it was impossible to hide our creation of extensive road and supply networks in advance of our offensive, it was not possible for our enemy to know what was in the minds of our commanders.

And fourth, while it is easy to praise heroes, I believe that the military leaders on our side may have made the best plans in the world. While they did not plan to take the whole of South Vietnam until sometime in 1976, these plans were flexible enough to permit adjustments as the operation developed. In addition, the leadership tested their plans and carefully observed the developments within South Vietnam. The battle for Phuoc Long in December and January was one such test. The question was whether or not the loss of this provincial capital some ninety miles north of Saigon would provoke a reentry into the war by the United States with its B-52s and other forces. Would the Enhance Plus effort you left in place to increase the South Vietnamese military capabilities be enlarged? We were closely monitoring the volume of military equipment that you were supplying to your allies, but the one item that we monitored most closely was the quantity of oil held by our enemy. While you had left thousands of aircraft, tanks and other weapons systems, they all needed fuel. The South Vietnamese had thousands of airplanes, but only a few liters of oil. The other item that we were watching closely was the amount of money being provided to the cause by your Congress. Oil and money were measures of your commitment.

When the end came, and you sent a small contingent of marines to secure the evacuation zone at Tan Son Nhut on April 29, we knew that they would not be there long. In my opinion, there was a kind of "gentlemen's agreement" to allow the evacuation to go forward. We just stopped fighting and shelling a few hours. We didn't shoot much. Then you were gone.

Chapter 4

Dunkirk

Vietnam was not Colonel Pelosky's first war. He joined the army air corps in 1943, fought in the Pacific theater, participated in the occupation of Japan, was wounded in Korea, and served three lengthy tours in Vietnam. During our interview, Pelosky, an engineer, expressed admiration for "the Asian mind." He genuinely liked the Vietnamese people— playing with their children, dining with them, and having tea with village chieftains.

By late 1974, however, Pelosky, chief logistician for the Defense Attache's office, noticed a breakdown in South Vietnam's ability to wage war. Division commanders "were desperate" because problems and "diversions" sidetracked supplies. Even bandages were scarce; medics washed and reused them. Graft was alarming, and Pelosky suggests that Vietnamese officials were "taking half of it [supplies] and selling it [on the black market]." Compounding the problem were distracting visits by American Congresspeople hostile to continuing a high level of support for South Vietnam. And at the American Embassy there were layers of bureaucracy and a surreal social scene in which aides enjoyed a series of parties. That is why, Pelosky stresses, "I loved to go out in the field."[1]

In March 1975, Pelosky ventured to Danang to survey the critical supply situation and to investigate a disruption in the radio relay system. Quickly, he realized the imminent collapse of the South Vietnamese military. Soldiers with their families streamed through the city. Pelosky found himself under mortar attack from the approaching communists. On the coast, "thousands and thousands of people in rafts" frantically sought to escape the enemy. On the highways, "you never saw so much humanity. Bodies were everywhere." These are his memories of the convoy of tears.[2] Additional details are provided in the accompanying memorandum which Pelosky submitted to his superior, General Homer Smith on May 21, 1975.

The purpose of my visit to Military Region I (MR I) was twofold. First, we wanted to find out why the LORAN (radio relay) at Tam My (a port just east of Hue) had been evacuated by the contractor who had been running it. And second, I was to evaluate the logistical situation north of the Hai Van Pass, an area that included Hue and Phu Bai, as well as the conditions in the region surrounding Danang.

Due to Air Vietnam having difficulty keeping good flight schedules, my ARVN liaison officer, Colonel Trong, and I arrived in Danang at approximately 1100 hours, 20 March 1975. We were met by Lieutenant Colonel Cu, Chief of Staff of the 1st Area Logistical Command (ALC), and taken by jeep from the airfield to the China Beach Area, or East Danang, where the 1st ALC headquarters was located. Driving there, we passed the crossroads where one can either turn into the City or head east to China Beach or go south to Hoi An, Tam Ky, and Quang Ngai. I observed that there was continuous heavy traffic of civilians and military vehicles loaded with household goods and piled higher yet with civilians and ARVN military personnel. MPs were directing traffic and the majority of the vehicles were sent across the river into East Danang.

At the 1st ALC Headquarters, Colonel Chau, 1st ALC Commander, had his staff assembled for a situation briefing. Since I had been the Senior Advisor to the ALC in 1970–1971, most of the officers were still there and were personal friends. They had been informed of the purpose of my visit, so we sat down immediately to discuss the Tam My LORAN site and the logistics posture north of the Hai Van Pass.

It was obvious that Thua Thien Province was about to fall and elements of the North Vietnamese were closing around Hue to cut further movement to the south. By this time, the Airborne Division had departed, and most of the Marine Division had pulled out north of the Pass. Elements of the 1st ARVN Division, Rangers, and Regional Force (RF) units were the blocking force. The discussion centered around how many LCM-8s, LCUs, and other watercraft were available to evacuate materiel through the Port of Tam My. Since Tam My was silted in, no LSTs could be used. The 1st ALC had already ordered ammo, POL, and other high-priority items to be moved from the Direct Support Groups (DSGs) to Tam My. This was required since the railroad was inoperative and the main north/south highway, QL-1, was choked with traffic.

That afternoon I visited the Consulate General's Office and found that Mr. Francis had not returned from convalescent leave. His deputy, Terry Hull, was anxious to talk to me. The conversation centered on the evacuation by the contractor of the LORAN site and the fact that she had approved it. She had done so based on the best intelligence available and on recommendations from her staff in Hue. It was decided that I should go and make an on-the-spot inspection and report my findings.

Since my journey to the Consulate General took me through the part of the city bordering the riverfront, I gained my first insight into what the refugee problem really was. The population had swelled to twice its normal size. People were living on the sidewalks in makeshift tents; cooking was done in open fires; and when people relieved themselves, it was right in the gutter. There was a stench in the city that almost overwhelmed you. I also saw a number of bodies of older people that had died. One of the reasons that they were just left there was that once the people departed the inner city, they could not return, so it was easier to wrap the bodies and leave them, hoping that the public works or sanitation department would pick them up.

After seeing this horrendous problem of sanitation, I asked the ALC staff what provisions had been made for setting up a refugee camp like was done in the 72 offensive. The answer was that neither the Danang mayor nor the MR I Commander had given any instructions. My next move was to visit the Consulate General's office where I was told by the USAID officials that a Dr. Dan from President Thieu's cabinet would arrive on 22 March with a plan. I was shocked and angry that it was probably too late, and an epidemic could happen at anytime. Nobody seemed to care!

Upon return to the headquarters, the ALC Commander called the ARVN Associated Depot Commander and we sat down to determine what relief items might be available for the refugees (e.g., tents, cooking pots, lime, water purification equipment, etc.). I understand that this equipment was offered later, but never used.

At 0800, 21 March 1975, a Vietnamese Air Force chopper landed on the 1st ALC pad and staff elements from the ALC, Colonel Trong and I flew toward Tam My. No sooner had we started to climb toward the Hai Van Pass than I noticed that one-third of the way down the slope of the pass, vehicles were blocked bumper to bumper. We made several passes over the area and saw that a culvert had been blown and that repairs were being made. A half mile away a fire fight was in progress and we assumed that it was the ARVN fighting with the sappers or North Vietnamese elements trying to cut the pass. Since the top of Hai Van Pass was fogged in, we dropped down and followed the coastline north. The further we went, the lower we flew, until we were fifty feet over the water. Then, to my amazement, I noticed the large number of small watercraft in the water. It reminded me, as we progressed up the coast, of the motion picture "Dunkirk" where every available watercraft was used to evacuate the beachhead. At first, the small boats were in small groups and many were being pulled—even rafts! Also on the beaches we could see where the people had camped overnight. Further north, there were more boats, and they were all flying the South Vietnamese flag.

We landed at Tam My inside the confines of the LORAN site. Just before landing, I noticed the Vietnamese Navy (VNN) a short distance away where they were busily loading their small craft. The Tam My port itself had six LCUs, about five LCM-8s and other small boats. The holding area was filled with equipment and ammunition which was being loaded onto these craft.

I inspected the LORAN site and my first thought was to try and save the large diesel motors that were still operating, even though the site had been abandoned. A squad of ARVN engineers were guarding the area, and although the individual trailers were locked, there had been some vandalism.

I would estimate that there were between two and three hundred refugees on the road between the LORAN site and the post trying to get in. Inside the post were soldiers' dependents waiting to embark on the ARVN and VNN watercraft after the equipment was loaded. I talked to several commanders from the Marines, the 1st Division, and the Rangers. They were surprised that I was there but most happy to see that the U.S. had not abandoned them completely.

One observation that boggles my mind yet to this day is what some believe to be the most important possession to take with them when they are abandoning their homes. I saw ducks, dogs, pigs, bed frames, old clocks, etc., along with the normal pots and pans and bundles of firewood.

We flew to Hue at about 1000 feet, and little traffic was moving toward Tam My. As we circled part of the city at a higher altitude, the fog had lifted, I could see that very little traffic was coming into the city from the north—only walking stragglers pushing carts and bicycles heaped high with earthly possessions. Off to the west, south, and north, incoming artillery could be observed, and an occasional round fired from the city (probably 122-mm. rockets). From there we flew into Phu Bai and landed at the basic training camp there. We talked to the Camp Commander and found out that all of his new recruits were on the line holding back the enemy and all that he had were a few guards. We were provided jeeps for the trip to the Direct Support Group approximately two miles to the south. This camp is astride QL-1 running north and south to the pass to Danang. The road, which is a two-lane macadam highway, was clogged with jeeps, trucks—both civilian and military—bicycles, pushcarts and just families with their possessions on their back. They were not walking—they were running! It took considerable time to traverse the two miles because of the one-way traffic and the occasional supply truck or ambulance heading north to Hue while driving at a snail's pace and dodging people. At the Direct Support Group, I met the Commander and his staff and he briefed me on how he saw the situation, which, I must admit, left a lot to be desired. I have known him, and his capabilities for five years, but he was not aware of the tactical and enemy situation. In the logistics area, he was loading CONEX containers with high-priority repair parts to be evacuated to Danang through Tam My.

Since we had the ALC principal staff with us, I recommended they start issuing rice, "C" rations, and other commodities, including barrier equipment. This was started within two hours and prior to my leaving. There were many supply trucks there from units looking for supplies, which were not to be forthcoming since the order to issue them had not been given. (The lack of orders or communication was evident throughout my visit.) While at the Defense Support Group, we came under artillery attack and we hit the bunkers. It was quite apparent that they were trying to hit the airfield only a short distance from us.

Several rounds hit in the depot complex, however, and a number of soldiers and dependents were wounded. The soldiers and officers were completely demoralized and fear was written all over their faces. All the dependents that I talked to said that if they could get to Danang, all would be saved. I hated to disillusion them but it was obvious that Danang could not hold out under a prolonged attack. We finally received word that the 325th North Vietnamese Army Division had cut QL-1 in the vicinity of Phu Loc and everything had stopped right in the middle of the road. It appeared that the only thing that could move was helicopters. Since I had known the Direct Support Group Commander and his staff for five years, all my suggestions were taken as orders and immediately carried out. (The Commander and his staff were all killed on the 25th of April.)

We started back north toward the helicopter, winding our way through the mass of people, when we came under attack. The enemy must have had excellent observation since the exploding shells bracketed the road. This caused sheer panic—people, animals, and vehicles—went in all directions, and I dove out of the jeep into a gully. After fifteen minutes the shelling subsided and we made our way to the camp entrance. Since they had barricaded the entrance, I dismounted and talked to the guards and civilians there—especially the wounded in the guardpost. After another passing shelling attack, we made our way to the helicopter and took off back to Tam My.

We were gone for about three hours in all, but by this time the main road and each footpath was jammed with refugees heading to Tam My. There, the place was wall-to-wall people and all evacuation of equipment had stopped—there was no way to hold them back. Even when the craft were departing, people were trying to climb aboard. They were even hanging on the sides outside of the craft. After seeing this, I realized that we could not dismantle any of the LORAN site and ordered it blown. (Note: On the 25th I found out from Central Logistics Command Headquarters that it was left intact to the enemy.)

Since we were being fired on, we flew back to Danang following QL-1 and skirted Phu Loc. We observed the human misery of people running, trucks burning, and just plain chaos. The whole pass was still clogged—nothing moved. We observed several firefights along the ridge lines and the ARVN were really being pushed.

Back in Danang I reported my findings to the Acting Commanding General. Passing through the city, it appeared that it had swelled in size with refugees. Roadblocks were set up at all entrances to the city to stop refugees from entering.

Back at ALC headquarters, several civilians were there to meet me—many from the 2nd AAD who had worked for me in 1970–1971. They reported the shortage of rice in the city. Fresh food was scarce and each family member had 10–15 relatives in his home. My heart went out to them and my piasters were rapidly depleted. The price of rice had doubled each day.

We stayed up most of the night on the 21st making evacuation plans and moving APCs and other high-cost items from the depot to the pier where LSTs were waiting. Due to the mobs of people using the bridges, the only available time to move heavy equipment was from midnight till dawn. Several calls were taken from Chief of Staff General Khuyen on the logistics posture. I even talked to him about placing more emphasis on moving materiels. He agreed and directed Colonel Chan to do so.

I tried to see the Logistics Officer of MR I several times during those few days but he never returned my calls or the messages that I left for him.

On the morning of the 24th I woke early and went outside my billet, which was alongside the river. I could see the Consulate General across the river and also into the main part of Danang. Approximately fifty meters from me were several LCUs, and I recognized the numbers from the day before. It had taken approximately fifteen hours for these refugees to come the seventy miles or so from Tam My to Danang.

Air Vietnam could not guarantee me a flight to Saigon, but with assistance from the Consul General, Air America could. Since I had several hours remaining, I went to the depot to see how the movement of supplies had progressed, and to review the demolition plan they supposedly had.

The demolition plan, or contingency plan, was there and it was translated to me, but no effort had been made to set charges. I also found out that they really had nobody that could make up a charge. We then had a class in demolitions.

By this time, the Consulate General, Mr. Francis, was back. We had lunch and talked the situation over. He was very optimistic about holding Hue and Tam My, and was in contact with the field commanders. He even discussed a counterattack. This never materialized and all territory north of the Hai Van Pass was lost in about two more days.

Upon my return to Saigon late on the evening of 22 March, most of my Army Division Staff was available for discussions. I had been in contact by phone, and had given the order to alert all available ships to be ready for the evacuation of ammo, POL and supplies, and then refugees.

We had five tugs with six barges immediately available. These had been previously used in support of Cambodia. They were placed on charter to us for the evacuation. During the period March 25–29, 1975, three additional Military Sealift Command cargo vessels; the *Pioneer Contender*, the *Pioneer Contractor*, and the *Trans Colorado*; and the Korea Registry LST *Boo Huong Pioneer*, were also committed. To cover the cost of these charters, we had to reprogram some funds. On March 29, USAID recognized its responsibility and accepted all costs for the evacuation effort.

On Monday, March 24, I sent Mr. Earnest G. Hey of my Transportation Branch to Danang to coordinate the evacuation of materiel. Mr. Hey wrote a well-documented report which is part of the Army Division Final Report. The lack of rear area control of both military personnel and refugees prevented any orderly movement of materiel and prevented many personnel from being evacuated from the Danang area.

EMBASSY OF THE
UNITED STATES OF AMERICA
DEFENSE ATTACHE OFFICE
SAIGON, VIETNAM
(RESIDUAL)
APO San Francisco 96558

AOSAR   21 May 1975

FROM: CHIEF, ARMY DIVISION

TO: MAJOR GENERAL H. D. SMITH

SUBJECT: Historical Documentation of Vietnam

REFERENCE: CINCPAC Memorandum 04, Ser 1052J, 5 May 1975

1. The Army of the Republic of Vietnam (ARVN) had been
postulated logistically and tactically to fight prior to
the anticipated NVA offensive. Beginning in October 1974,
a conscious effort had been made by the Defense Attache
Office (DAO) and the Central Logistics Command (CLC), ARVN,
in allocating resources from the FY75 DAV Program to insure
that sufficient materiel was on hand to sustain intense combat
for a period of 60 days. Materiel stocks in each Area Logistics Command (ALC) had been balanced to the degree possible,
since historically in a general offensive situation the lines
of communication (LOC) had been interdicted by either local
VC units or NVA main force elements.

2. Materiel stocks in the Central Highlands were at the
60-day level for most critical supply items. ARVN had implemented a policy for dispersal of artillery ammunition to
division areas to provide additional security, reduce the vulnerability of materiel from sapper attack, and to provide
materiel to sustain combat in event the LOC's were cut. This
dispersal program was applied country-wide with 83 dispersal
sites being established for ammunition in addition to the 19
depots; 28 stagefields for POL in addition to the base depot
and 21 sub-depots; repair parts at DSU/GSU level; and major
items positioned at the GSU's and Medium Maintenance Centers
to replace combat losses.

AOSAR   21 May 1975
SUBJECT: Historical Documentation of Vietnam

3.   The attack at Ban Me Thout and its subsequent loss to NVA
forces was accomplished in the classic tactic previously used
in the fall of ·Binh Long Province -- pin down ARVN main force
units, attack weaker local force units, interdict the lines
of communications, isolate the objective area, and then apply
sufficient combat power to take the objective.

4.   The decision to evacuate the Central Highlands and the
subsequent unplanned execution of that decision took no consideration of the time, distance, and order of magnitude
factors involved in a retrograde action.   No apparent consideration was made of the stockpiles of equipment, supplies,
and facilities to be moved or destroyed.   Perhaps the most
significant factor overlooked was the impact of the retrograde
action on rear area control, the reaction of the local population, the role that the regional force/popular forces would
take, and the refugee influence on the evacuation.   As an
indication of intentions known to DAO and CLC in the month
prior to the evacuation from Pleiku, the CLC had resisted
efforts of the MR II Commander to position stocks in the
Central Highlands for 90 days of intense combat.

5.   ARVN materiel losses in the Central Highlands were significant.   Major items of equipment on hand in units in the
Pleiku/Kontum/Ban Me Thout areas that were lost totalled
$253.5 Million; general supplies $30.7 Million; medical supplies
$3.2 Million; ammunition 17,855 short tons U.S. worth $36.5
Million; POL valued at $1.3 Million; and extensive military
facilities.   Six military hospitals were abandoned with a 3,000
bed capacity with a value of $2.1 Million.   Little, if any,
materiel was destroyed although the VNAF did bomb the ammunition
storage areas at Ban Me Thout and Pleiku.   The logistics installations had detailed plans for destruction; however, they could
not be executed except on the order of the Military Region (MR)
Commander.   The hasty relocation of the MR II Headquarters left
no decision authority and the destruction order was not given.

6.   The withdrawal for defense of the coastal areas was frustrated by NVA interdiction of Highway 19 and the principal withdrawal took place to the southeast on Highway 7A towards Nha
Trang.   The refugee situation frustrated any effective ARVN
combat action in the retrograde and the concern of RF/PF units
for their families further reduced the ground combat capability
by their complete collapse as a fighting force.

7.   Indications were that the ARVN plans were to relocate to
the coastal areas, establish defensive positions, reconstitute
their forces, and to counterattack to retake Ban Me Thout near
the end of March 1975.   This is supported by plans to establish

AOSAR   21 May 1975
SUBJECT: Historical Documentation of Vietnam

an ammunition supply point to the west of Nha Trang to support
the operation.

8.   Prior to the complete loss of MR II, intense pressure was
placed on the forces in MR I.   Significant combat activity and
assaults by fire were placed on forces to the north, west, and
south of Da Nang.   For some time, the vulnerability of lines
of communication north of the Hi Van Pass (north of Da Nang)
had been a matter of concern.   Efforts had been taken to insure that the Tan My waterway was open.   A total of 12,648 S/T
of ammunition was stored in depots north of the Hi Van Pass
on 24 February 1975.   In addition, 13,899 S/T were stored in
the Da Nang area and 8,523 S/T at Chu Lai.   POL stock in MR I
was principally maintained at Da Nang.   Storage distribution
of product was as follows as of 15 March 1975, for MR I:

(BARRELS OF PRODUCT)

LOCATION	JP4	AVGAS	MOGAS	DFM
DA NANG	16,900	6,900	8,800	24,700
TAN MY	2,500	-	6,100	9,200
PHU BAI	-	370	1,800	3,000
CHU LAI	2,600	700	3,600	7,100
TOTAL:	22,000	7,970	20,300	44,000

9.   The decision not to defend the provinces north of Da Nang
was executed in a manner no better conceived than the withdrawal from the Central Highlands and the results were the same.
There was great difficulty in extracting tactical units with
any significant amounts of unit equipment; sizeable stocks were
left in storage depots and support unit locations; refugees im-
peded organized movement of forces; and limited destruction of
materiel was accomplished.   In the south, NVA pressure cut the
LOC from Chu Lai to Da Nang, isolating forces in that area, and
applied intense pressure to units to the southwest of Da Nang.

10.   Da Nang became the center towards which all evacuation by
both ARVN and refugee columns moved.   The JGS announced that
Da Nang would be held at all costs; however, in reality, the
combat power available to ARVN was disorganized, stripped of
much equipment, and engulfed by an estimated one million
refugees.   Concerted efforts to evacuate materiel were initiated
in early April 1975, with the first priority being given to the
major items of equipment located at the 2nd Army Associated
Depot at Da Nang.   Under the cover of darkness, weapons, self-

AOSAR   21 May 1975
SUBJECT: Historical Documentation of Vietnam

propelled vehicles, and armored vehicles were moved to the
pier area for evacuation. It remained there even until the
loss of Da Nang. Retrograde was halted with the announded
"defense to the death" order. Later efforts to evacuate
equipment were futile because the refugee situation was completely out of control. Even POL tankers which were dispatched to the POL terminal could extract only limited quantities of product before refugees prevented any removal and the
ships were moved out of the harbor. The losses in MR I were
significant and are summarized below:

MR I MATERIEL LOSSES

TYPE MATERIEL	DOLLAR VALUE (MILLIONS)
AMMUNITION	$ 73.0
POL	2.0
GENERAL SUPPLIES	79.8
MAJOR ITEMS	249.8
MEDICAL SUPPLIES	2.4
HOSPITALS (3); BEDS (3,200)	2.0
TOTAL:	$409.0

11. In early March, as the tactical situation in MR I and
MR II was becoming critical, DAO inquired through the Joint
Petroleum Office, CINCPAC to MSC-FE, checking on the avail-
ability of a T-1 Tanker for use in Vietnam. MSC-FE Yokohama,
Japan advised the tanker RINCON was available. Arrangements
were finalized with MSC to have the RINCON assigned to DAO
Saigon for 45 days. Initial plans called for using the
RINCON to evacuate product from Qui Nhon and Nha Trang, then
to utilize the vessel as a floating storage base to extract
or inject product at up-country locations as required. The
RINCON arrived in Vietnam on 12 April 1975, too late for
evacuation of product from Qui Nhon and Nha Trang. In early
April, commercial oil companies advised, due to the tactical
situation, they could no longer guarantee delivery of POL
to Nha Be (Saigon). It was planned, at this point, to utilize
the RINCON for ship-to-ship transfer of product at Vung Tau
for transport to Nha Be (Saigon). In addition, contingency
planning was to send the RINCON to Singapore should the oil

companies exercise their forced majure clause in the supply
contracts. The RINCON was loaded on arrival with 20MB JP-4,
5MB MOGAS, 5MB DFM. The initial assignment was to lay to
off Phan Rang and transfer product to tank trucks in LCU's
for supply to the VNAF at Phan Rang. When Phan Rang fell,
the vessel was programmed for the same type operation to
support VNAF at Phan Thiet. Neither of these operations
were completed. Loss of airfields in MR I and MR II posed
severe question to continued evacuation of refugees by C-130
and helicopter means. A quick look was taken to determine
the feasibility of establishing a staging point at An Thai
on Phu Quoc Island for refueling C-130 aircraft and helicopters. On the spot assessment of facilities at An Thai confirmed that, with minor modifications to the pipeline receiving point, JP-4 could be made available for refueling operations.
The RINCON was dispatched to report off An Thai and standby
for this operation. VNAF was tasked to airlift two refuelers
and crews to An Thai. ARVN POL Division was tasked to modify
the receiving line to enable discharge direct from the RINCON
to the refuelers. The rapid deterioriation of the tactical
situation presented finalization of this operation, and on
1 May 1975, after evacuation from Saigon, the RINCON was
advised, through MSC Subic Bay, to proceed to Subic if the
ship had not received other orders from MSC. On 2 May 1975,
CO MSC FE Yokohama advised by message they were assuming
OPCO of the RINCON.

12. On 24 March 1975, five tug boats with six barges previously used in the Cambodia support effort were placed on
charter to DAO for use in the evacuation of MR I. During the
period 25 - 29 March 1975, three additional Military Sealift
Command cargo vessels (PIONEER CONTENDER, PIONEER CONTRACTOR,
TRANS-COLORADO) and the Korea Registry LST BOO HUONG PIONEER
were committed. After 29 March, USAID recognized their
responsibility and accepted all boats for the evacuation effort.
These vessels and others, under the operation control of the
Evacuation Control Center, Saigon, were used almost exclusively
for the movement of refugees and military personnel from
Da Nang, Qui Nhon, Cam Ranh, Nha Trang, Phan Thiet, Phan Rang
to Vung Tau and Phuc Quoc Island. Approximately 600 MT of
cargo consisting of 1/4-ton vehicles, ammunition and medical
supplies lifted from Qui Nhon to Newport is the only cargo
known to have been evacuated.

13. The order to destroy materiel in the depot facilities in
Da Nang was not given, as in the Central Highlands. Plans for
destruction were available in each of the logistics facilities,
but required approval of the MR Commander to execute. In the
case of the 2nd AAD, the Depot Commander personally visited

AOSAR   21 May 1975
SUBJECT: Historical Documentation of Vietnam

the 1st ALC Headquarters and MR I Headquarters in an attempt
to gain approval for destruction. The depot was not destroyed
although the depot personnel were some of the last to leave
and had to swim to a ship to be evacuated.

14. As Da Nang was being evacuated, the Qui Nhon area was
being held at the Anh Khe Pass by the Rangers and the 22nd
Infantry Division. Refugees began to arrive from the Highlands' area to join those who had moved from the surrounding
village. With the evacuation from Qui Nhon the following
total equipment/materiel from MR II was lost:

MR II MATERIEL LOSSES

TYPE MATERIEL	DOLLAR VALUE (MILLIONS)
AMMUNITION	$ 71.5
POL	3.2
GENERAL SUPPLIES	30.7
MAJOR ITEMS	253.5
MEDICAL SUPPLIES	3.2
HOSPITALS (6); BEDS (3,400)	2.1
TOTAL:	$364.2

15. ARVN plans for defense of the remaining vital areas of
South Vietnam included the area south of a line from Nha Trang,
through Da Lat to Tay Ninh. Forces returning from Pleiku via
Highway 7A arrived in the Nha Trang area and were to be reconstituted in the Lam Son and Duc My National Training Centers
north of Nha Trang. Forces evacuated from Da Nang were initially moved into Cam Ranh to be reconstituted for this defense.
Additionally, a significant number of refugees were also placed
at Cam Ranh. Refugee centers being planned for location at
Nha Trang for 100,000 refugees from MR II; in Ninh Thuan for
150,000 refugees from MR I; and at Binh Thuan for 100,000
refugees from MR I.

16. Medical planning included the activation of military
hospitals at the following locations:

AOSAR   21 May 1975
SUBJECT: Historical Documentation of Vietnam

LOCATION	NO. OF BEDS
CAM RANH BAY	1,000
VUNG TAU	1,500
LONG BINH	600
TOTAL:	3,100

Limited equipment was available from on hand stocks to meet
these hospital equipment needs, having been provided in 1972
in anticipation of the 1972 Spring Offensive.

17.   The subsequent evacuation of Cam Ranh Bay and Nha Trang
resulted in the loss of much of the equipment that had been
retrograded from the Central Highlands and MR I.

18.   The decision to relocate refugees to Phuc Quoc Island
helped prevent many congestion problems in the Vung Tau/
Saigon area.   As the NVA offensive spread, the psychological
impact transmitted by the refugees, the RF/PF forces, and
ARVN soldiers without visible organization or leadership, had
disastrous affects on those areas being defended.

19.   After withdrawal from the Central Highlands in MR II and
subsequent loss of MR I and the major population centers in
MR II, large numbers of ARVN soldiers were returned by vessel
to Vung Tau, and many as stragglers.   Almost without exception,
there was little unit integrity.   Most personnel were returned
as individuals and required identification, re-equipping and
organization/assignment into units.

20.   In a last ditch effort to bolster the capability of ARVN
to defend Saigon, an ambitious project was undertaken to fill
critical shortages of combat units already committed; reconstitute combat capability of any unit returning with sufficient
organization integrity to be made combat ready by providing
filler personnel and equipment, and provide for initial equip-
age of additional combat units in accordance with an established
force reconstitution plan.

21.   There were two Marine Brigades, the Airborne Brigade, and
a brigade of the 2nd Infantry Division which returned with
enough organization integrity to be re-equipped and brought
up to combat strength with filler personnel.

22.   A planning message was fully coordinated with ARVN and

AOSAR   21 May 1975
SUBJECT: Historical Documentation of Vietnam

dispatched to CONUS outlining the equipment requirements, necessary program changes were made calling forward defined lines,
requisitions were submitted for all other equipment and airlift
was requested with specific required delivery dates.

23.   Controls were established to monitor receipt of materiel;
expedited handling, distribution and accountability techniques
were implemented as a joint DAO/ARVN effort, and the Tan Son
Nhut Aerial Port operation work force was supplemented as
necessary.

24.   The initial airlift delivery was requested on 20 March
1975, and first equipment consisting of 14 Howitzers 105MM
M101A1 was received on 1 April 1975, by C5A transport.   Final
air delivery was received 27 April 1975.

25.   This joint DAO/ARVN undertaking resulted in filling
critical shoot, move and communicate shortages to reconstitute
decimated units.   Over eight regimental sized infantry units
and four artillery battalions were reconstituted and deployed,
primarily in defense of the Saigon area.   Combat capability varie

26.   The increased capability to provide Saigon defense was
completed within a four-week period, indicative of the US
military resolve to assist and the ARVN logistical element's
dedication to support their combat forces.

27.   In the last days prior to the evacuation from Saigon,
the ARVN logistics system was still functioning.   Ammunition
issue   support was active to include redistribution of stocks
from the depots at Long Binh and Bien Hoa to a new storage
area at Vo Gap Training Center, a planned storage area at
Vung Tau, munitions loaded on barges for redistribution in
the event land LOC's were closed, and the off-loading of
ammunition materiel at Vung Tau to barges (this action was
terminated 28 April 1975, due to enemy action).   POL support
was continued from storage at Nha Be and Tan Son Nhut, the
30th QM Base Depot, and product onboard POL ships off the coast
of Vietnam.   An accelerated maintenance system provided materiel
for replacement of combat losses and to reconstitute ARVN
forces.   Work hours were extended in all maintenance units and
a double shift employed at the Vietnamese Army Arsenal.   The
1st AAD was on a three shift operation, and showed a real sense
of urgency along with the Army Supply Center in providing
materiel support.   Major items of equipment were dispersed
from the depots to the Direct Support Groups and Medium Maintenance Center in the Saigon area for rapid issue to using
units and to reduce the vulnerability to enemy action.   Trans-

AOSAR   21 May 1975
SUBJECT: Historical Documentation of Vietnam

portation support was taxed to the limits during the entire
evacuation process and in meeting materiel delivery requirements; however, responsive support was provided.

28. The summary of ARVN equipment losses is shown below:

TYPE MATERIEL			DOLLAR VALUE (IN MILLIONS)
AMMUNITION (95,104 S/T)			$ 246.0
POL			19.9
GENERAL SUPPLIES:			
MR I & MR II		$110.5	
MR III & MR IV (ESTI- MATED)		350.0	460.5
MAJOR ITEMS:			
MR I & MR II		503.3	
MR III & MR IV (ESTI- MATED)		1200.0	1,703.3
MEDICAL SUPPLIES			15.5
HOSPITALS:	NO.	BEDS	
GENERAL	2	6,000	
STATION	12	8,800	
FIELD	44	5,500	
NAVAL & AF	2	300	
TB	2	1,800	
CONVALESCENT CENTERS	6	3,600	
DISPENSARIES & CLINICS	264	5,720	
TOTAL:		31,720	(VALUE 20.0 ESTIMATED)

$2,465.2

29. In the month of April 1975, the personnel assets of the
Army Division were progressively reduced to where at the time
of the evacuation on 29 April 1975, there were only five
US military, eight US civilians, and four US contractor personnel
incountry. All were evacuated safely. A considerable number
of the LN DAO Army Division employees and their families were
also evacuated in the last week of April 1975. Evacuation
planning and coordination consumed much of the time of the US
personnel remaining during this period, particularly during
the last week.

AOSAR   21 May 1975
SUBJECT: Historical Documentation of Vietnam

30. In retrospect, from the complex "cause and effect"
relationships that emerged, the following appear to be some
of the most significant and conclusive factors affecting the
turn of events in South Vietnam:

    a. The RVNAF Joint General Staff did not have the
leadership nor did it function equal to the planning and
directive challenge that it faced.

    b. ARVN was postulated to fight in the Central Highlands
and in MR I. The decision to evacuate and the manner in which
it was planned and executed did not consider or include the
impacts on the retrograde of forces, the population, and the
magnitude of the logistics task in an evacuation -- not with-
standing an aggressive, well armed, and capable enemy.

    c. The reconstitution of forces was limited by resources
but more acutely influenced by the amount of time in which to
execute the plan and reorganize the units for combat.

    d. A lack of rear area control of both military personnel
and refugees prevented any orderly evacuation of materiel and
prevented many personnel from being evacuated from up-country
locations.

    e. The ARVN dependence upon additional US support per-
meated their planning and psychi. In the last month of the
conflict, when it was evident that Congress would not act on
a supplemental appropriation, it was difficult, but necessary,
to make every visible evidence of US support to the ARVN
leadership -- principally in the use of the FY75 Program, in
the return of assets from repair and return in CONUS and PACOM,
and major items called forward. This was done.

    f. ARVN reached an acceptable level of self-sufficiency
to cope with the tempo of the war experienced since the cease-
fire. It had not reached the maturity to adjust to the conventional force strength committed by the NVA in March 1975,
complicated by the untimely decisions, indecision, and
the lack of control that followed.

                        E. F. PELOSKY
                        Colonel, USA
                        Chief, Army Division

Danang Falls, the Refugees Move South

Chapter 5

In The Alleyway

As CBS News' Saigon Bureau Chief, Haney Howell reported throughout Southeast Asia. Regularly, he traveled to Cambodia, Thailand, and across much of Asia. In Vietnam, Howell developed numerous sources, some of whom had ties to the communist insurgents.[1]

While reporting the news for three years from his Saigon base, Howell covered the deterioration of Cambodia, the steady erosion of South Vietnam's ability to wage war, the tragic crash of the C-5 "babylift" flight, and the human side of a conflict which changed everyone it touched. In the following interview, Howell, now a professor at Winthrop University, recounts his impressions of the last days of the Thieu government.[2]

I lived about a block from the central part of Saigon; we're talking about Saigon blocks so I was pretty close. To get to my apartment, you got off the boulevard and walked down this alleyway. Right off the street was a restaurant and probably eight or nine of the people who ran it lived in the alleyway. It was a very popular restaurant. At night, after everybody had eaten, they would fold up the restaurant's tables and stoves, and sleep in the alleyway. There were four or five children there and the grandmother of that matriarchal society took care of the children.

There was a girl who was born after I arrived there. I covered Vietnam, Cambodia, Thailand, and most of Asia. I would be gone three weeks at a time. Every time I walked by this kid was getting bigger so it got to be a game. And the grandmother was proud of her, handing her to me. I would play with her and bring treats to her.

Some time around 1974, the grandmother stopped me. They were having problems with head lice. I went to the doctor and I got them some ointment. We rounded up the children and threw them in the shower and washed them from head to toe. This became a weekly ritual even after the head lice went away.

As the wheels started coming off about the time Danang fell, I decided that I was heading on out. About two nights before I left, the movers had already come and my stuff was in crates. The whole family from the alleyway came in. The mother, who looked as young as her children, kind of handed me the baby. They wanted me to bring that child back to the states. I really struggled with that. The problem would have been getting her in anywhere else. If I could have gotten a plane and gone directly to Honolulu, I would have done it. I think she was better off staying with her family. I had observed that family and they were as solid as a rock. In the context of that family, the one that lived in the alley, I don't think they were in any jeopardy. But that was one of the toughest things—to leave that child behind.

The first time anybody said to me directly, "It's over. It's going to end." was when the Central Highlands collapsed. President Thieu was going to stop the communists in the Highlands but he had either run off, imprisoned, or neutralized the Montagnards, who were such brave fighters for his government. They had come to despise Thieu.

The embassy, the government, well-meaning people were being hand fed stuff. I dished out as much as I could from both sides, but I did my very best to report the truth. I had two very solid sources on the communist side. I probably met the highest ranking communist in the south right across the street from the National Assembly in Saigon. I think he would get up in the morning out in the countryside, eat his rice, put on his civilian clothes, and come to downtown Saigon. He told me they were coming in January and I reported it. So, everyone was waiting for the train and, finally, it came.

When you have opportunities in front of you, you keep coming. And they got to Saigon three months before, in their wildest dreams, they thought it would be possible. They were thinking about, perhaps, the fall of 1975. That's why you had the craziness of the wrong units coming into the city. That's why there was a lull in the fighting in the last twenty-four hours; the communists were sorting it all out because their units had just come on down the road. There was nothing in the Highlands to stop them.

Tactically, the worst mistake made by the South Vietnamese was when they allowed families to accompany the troops. That was the only way they could keep the army together. The wives, children, and babies were with the army. As they retreated, it ceased to be an army. The roads were absolutely jammed. They couldn't be an army because there were carts, family belongings, and bicycles everywhere. The scene we saw in Danang was repeated time and time again. They said, "To hell with this war. I'm going to get my family out." I think at its core the South Vietnamese Army was much better than this. Certainly, the marines were.

The ambassador was very courtly. He and I never had a harsh word. I did one on-camera interview with him. It didn't go well. He had nothing to say. I believe around January or February he lost sight of what was going on. Certainly, by March it was obvious to everyone else. We flew all the network employees out six weeks early. My boss, Brian Ellis, put together a very elaborate plan for getting our folks out. It was very quiet. He chartered planes. The employees were sworn to secrecy.

Looking back, it is unbelievable that we would hire Vietnamese to do our country's dirty work; and when the wheels came off, leave them. We left thousands and thousands of people behind. The French didn't do that to their Vietnamese supporters in 1954.

Our network's employees were only allowed to carry one bag with them. So, many of them left their cameras behind. The communists collected the cameras and sold them.

Our parents won the Second World War. To them, the enemy was very clear cut. In Vietnam, it was much more ambiguous. Before 1963, before the coup against Diem, we had done all that we could do. We had destabilized the communist insurgency in the south. The Vietcong couldn't get anything sustained going as we saw with the 1968 Tet Offensive when the Vietcong were defeated. I remember hearing, though, after 1963, people saying, "It's the only war we've got." So people got in line. People headed over to get promoted.

I hope we have learned things about rotating American troops. You can't fight a war in thirteen months and then leave.

When Mr. Kahn, who worked for me, left on our flight out, he left his mother behind in Saigon, sitting in her living room. Mr. Kahn got in a taxi and headed to the airport with five others. Within five minutes, his brother, a full colonel in the North Vietnamese Army, came in to check on their mother. I knew Mr. Kahn had close ties to the North Vietnamese Army.

The people I feel the most sorry for were the women who lived with American men. They were promised that they would be gotten out but they were the ones abandoned by their lovers. They were the ones we saw trying to get over the walls of the embassy.

Vietnamese working on our computer main frame, when it became obvious what was happening, took the computer tapes, listing everyone who worked for us. They went to the other side and said, "Here is what I have. Cut me a deal." These are the people we should have gotten out, but Graham Martin refused to get the wheels turning. If CBS had depended on the U.S. Government, all of our employees would have been lost. Graham wouldn't let any major planning for the evacuation of Saigon take place. He wasn't going to evacuate. He felt that he could pull off a political solution. That's where he was blind. By the time Danang fell, it was hopeless. You know, he lost everything. He had a gorgeous house with lots of things he had collected during his diplomatic career. He and his wife lost everything.

The Coming and Going

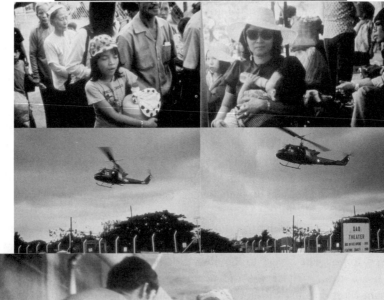

Chapter 6

Setting The Record Straight

The senior military officer in Vietnam in 1975 was Major General Homer D. Smith, the last Defense Attaché. Smith had assumed command of his office in September 1974 and found himself immediately walking a tightrope. On the one hand, he had to get along with Ambassador Graham Martin and navigate the choppy waters of the embassy's political environment. Smith also had to preside over a scaled-down American presence (i.e., fifty uniformed and 1200 civilian administrative personnel) while also trying to reassure President Thieu that the United States remained committed to South Vietnam's ability to wage war.[1]

In his observations below, Smith comments on the collapse of the South Vietnamese military and shifts blame away from the soldiers in the field. By and large, Smith argues, the men in uniform fought courageously with an ever-dwindling supply of American aid. Responsibility for the end of South Vietnam as an independent entity might be better placed on the shoulders of an inattentive and uncommitted Congress which abandoned our ally.[2] Contemporaneous photographs of Ambassador Martin, General Murray, General Smith, and South Vietnamese General Phu can be found at the end of this chapter.

It is most unfortunate that the authors of various articles criticizing the South Vietnamese have drawn the conclusion that their Armed Forces lost their will to fight. Nothing could be farther from the truth. I suspect that the conclusion is based on conjecture, or a simple lack of knowledge. It is for this reason that I have chosen to record some of my thoughts—the thoughts of an individual who served in a responsible position in South Vietnam until the evacuation on April 29, 1975.

To set the record straight, one has to go back to the closing months of 1972 at the time the Paris Peace Accords were being negotiated. I do not intend to discuss again the agonies associated with those negotiations. Instead, let me just say that the leaders of the Armed Forces of South Vietnam were definitely left with the impression that the United States would (1) continue to provide them with the military hardware required to defend their nation and (2) would intervene with military force if the North

Vietnamese Army (NVA) did not live up to its part of the bargain, i.e. refrain from introducing additional military equipment and personnel into the Republic of Vietnam (RVN). There was a proviso whereby military equipment lost, damaged, destroyed or worn out in the course of military activities could be replaced. The introduction of new troops was prohibited. The agreement provided for normal replacement of equipment losses. It did not provide for the escalated introduction of new types of hardware, stockpiling ammunition and other supplies over and above the quantity that existed at the time of the cease fire, nor the introduction of new integral units or individual replacements. In other words, provisions were made for maintaining the status quo—for insuring that both sides had no more and no less than at the time of the agreements.

Since the United States was the provider for the South Vietnamese, we scrupulously managed the input to insure that the supply levels at the time of cease fire were not increased. We selectively called forward replacement items such as tanks, armored personnel carriers, artillery pieces and so forth only to maintain the quantities in the hands of troops at the required level. The Republic of Vietnam Armed Forces (RVNAF) understood this and even subscribed to it because they had been told they would receive, as required, the differences between their losses and the supplies existing in country at the time of the cease fire.

Not so, the North Vietnamese. Almost from the beginning, the North began to stockpile ammunition and other supplies and, in addition, brought into the country large quantities of antiaircraft weaponry (both surface-to-air missiles and radar-supported air defense artillery), heavy artillery, tanks and armored personnel carriers. To provide adequate storage for this materiel the North erected a significant number of facilities. Additionally, the North improved the minor port of Dong Ha on the Cau Viet River just north of Quang Tri City, built several hundred miles of pipelines for moving fuels down through the country, and constructed or improved several hundred miles of highways in order to reduce transportation times in country. This was done over a span of eighteen or so months in South Vietnam—not the North. It was an invasion of which the world was perfectly aware. Further, it was in direct violation of the Peace Accords and all the signatories thereto certainly knew that it was going on. The U.S.A. chose to do nothing but watch.

The Defense Attaché Office (DAO) in Saigon was established to manage the materiel program in support of RVNAF. It was our job to insure that the monies appropriated were properly utilized and the materiel procured was used for the purpose for which intended. I want to make it clear at this point that not one U.S. dollar, as such, ever entered the hands of a single Vietnamese through the DOD management of the materiel program. No soldier or officer was paid with these funds. With the exception of minor procurements in country, by far the bulk of the funds appropriated were spent in the United States and thereby provided jobs for American citizens.

Jointly with the Vietnamese we computed the requirements to maintain an Armed Force of 1,100,000, consisting of Army, Navy, Marine and Air Force elements. These requirements, translated into dollars at prevailing costs, provided the basis for the DOD requests to the Congress. For fiscal year 1975, the original request emanating from the DAO was around $1.6 billion. When you think about it, this is not unreasonable in the day of inflated costs—around $1000 per member of the RVNAF for materiel costs. Our costs for materiel support to our own Armed Forces are considerably higher.

By the time the request for funds reached the Congress, it had been reduced to $1.4 billion. Committee action within the Congress finally produced an authorization bill of $1 billion. But the Congress only appropriated $700 million.

This action came as a distinct shock to senior military leaders as well as the civilian hierarchy of RVN. They had observed our inaction with respect to the continued overt shipment of large quantities of Chinese and Russian furnished war materiel into South Vietnam. While there were the stirrings of apprehension, the rude awakening came at the instance of the $700 million appropriation. Yet, together the DAO and the senior staff of the RVNAF, the Joint General Staff (JGS), aided by the staffs of the separate services, worked out an austere program within the limitations of the $700 million. By far the bulk of the monies went to the ground forces— principally for ammunition and fuels. The next largest portion went to the Air Force to support a flight program with emphasis on close air support, medical evacuation, reconnaissance, and troop and equipment transport. The Vietnamese Navy received just enough funds to barely exist—and this required the deactivation of a significant number of Navy craft. And while the South was being forced to cut back, the North continued to bring increasing quantities of materiel into South Vietnam!

The principal role of the RVNAF was to defend the people and the territory of the nation. The bulk of the population could be found up and down the coast and in the major cities of Saigon, Danang, Qui Nhon and Nah Trang—and, of course in the great Mekong Delta. There are extensive lines of communications—roads and navigable rivers—used by the populace to move back and forth while carrying out normal commerce. To adequately secure these thousands of miles of roads and rivers, not to mention bridges, requires an inordinate number of men under arms. Thus, the bulk of the RVNAF was tied down carrying out these local security responsibilities. Here was their home and here was where they expected to stay. The remainder of the Armed Forces consisted of the Army—nine Infantry Divisions, one Airborne Division, fourteen Ranger Groups and associated combat and combat support elements; the Air Force six Air Divisions; the Marines one Division; and the Navy consisting of a blue water fleet charged with maintaining the security of the coast and contiguous waters and a brown water fleet charged with maintaining the security of the inland waterways which exceeded 2,000 miles in length.

In contrast to the strength of the RVNAF, the North Vietnamese had nineteen Divisions or Division equivalents arrayed throughout South Vietnam. Additionally, there were independent artillery, antiaircraft artillery, and sapper regiments and battalions. The NVA also had seven strategic reserve infantry divisions in North Vietnam and an eighth in Laos. The training base for the NVA was in the North. Their main logistical base was in the North. During the period September 1, 1974 through the end of April 1975, the NVA introduced 178,000 additional troops into South Vietnam, to include six of their eight strategic reserve divisions. Theirs was a mission of attack—attack at such time and location as they saw fit. They did not have to devote troops to defend roads and bridges. They were an expeditionary force designed for invasion and deployed to take over another sovereign country with military force. That this was contrary to the provisions of the Peace Accords apparently was of little consequence to anyone other than the South Vietnamese.

When I arrived in Saigon on September 5, 1974, the appropriation bill for FY 75 had not been passed—but, the handwriting was on the wall. The JGS had already begun to initiate the directives necessary to constrain the expenditure of ammunition and fuels. Other programs, such as contractor support to the Vietnamese Air Force (VNAF), were being whittled down. Both the DAO staff and the JGS were searching for ways and means to cut expenses—to do more with less. VNAF set aside over 225 aircraft of seven different makes and models because they could no longer afford to operate them. The Vietnamese Navy (VNN) set aside over 200 small craft for the same reason. The Army of Vietnam (ARVN) reduced its operating motor fleet by nearly fifty percent by restricting fuels for use by combat and transport vehicle use. Ammunition was rationed by establishing an available supply rate—so many rounds per weapon per day or so many grenades per individual.

This would have been no problem had there been even a semblance of peace. But, in a time when enemy activity was growing, when enemy tactics were becoming increasingly sophisticated and conventional, it was difficult for the soldier in the field to understand why he was being given less rather than more ammunition with which to fight. It was difficult for him to understand why the combat ration he had been given before was no longer available. It was difficult for him to understand why he could no longer get a poncho with which to protect himself from the weather during the rainy season. It was difficult for him to understand why he could not replace his combat boots when they wore out.

The controls placed by the JGS were as detailed as possible from that level. The execution depended upon the lowest level of command. The whole point of the matter is that $700 million was insufficient to sustain RVNAF for the fiscal year under the combat conditions in which they found themselves. Having had this initial jolt to their morale, it is little wonder that they began to question what might happen with respect to the $300 million differential between the authorization and the appropriation bills. Certainly the Executive Branch of our own government recognized that the shortfall was untenable and let it be known that a supplemental request for funds would be supported. The usage of ammunition and fuels was the driving factor which necessitated additional funds. The cost of ground ammunition alone increased by over twenty-six percent as the fiscal year progressed. The costs of transportation and stevedoring also increased significantly. Our joint forecasts on the size of ammunition and fuel reserves as of the end of the fiscal year showed that RVNAF would have little or no staying power against a massive attack unless current usage was further critically reduced or unless replacement stocks would be forthcoming through additional funding. The reduction in ammunition usage was heroic. They did much better than we had any right to expect. But it was not enough.

In December 1974 the pace of combat picked up markedly, particularly in the Delta. In January the NVA invaded and captured Phuoc Long province. This was most probably their testing ground—an overt invasion to test the response of the United States. There was none. After a valiant effort, but without reinforcements and fighting alone, the RVNAF defenders lost the province. Questions have been asked as to why they did not reinforce and drive the NVA out. The facts are that they could no longer logistically support the operation. The JGS so advised President Thieu and he made the decision not to expend further effort—men or materiel. It was a tough decision, but a necessary one. That same month the NVA introduced the 968th NVA Division from Laos into Pleiku province—another overt invasion into South Vietnamese territory.

February was the month of Tet, the celebration of the Lunar New Year. Although the South was ready for increased activity on the part of the NVA, there was no appreciable upswing. The NVA was preparing for a strategic blow in the vicinity of Ban Me Thuot (BMT) in the highlands of Dar Lac province.

During this period the administration was engaged with the Congress concerning the $300 million supplemental. The news from Washington was not good. Several Congressional delegations arrived in Saigon during this period. Their reactions were mixed. Most saw the need for additional support. Several congressmen traveled into the outlying provinces to make personal assessments concerning the fighting capability and will of the ARVN soldiers and their leaders. I found none who expressed other than praise—even amazement—as to what they found.

By early March it was apparent to the South Vietnamese that additional materiel support was not forthcoming for FY75. Indeed, the light was beginning to dawn that there was little chance for much, or anywhere near the required support in FY76. This assumption was supported by a delegation of South Vietnamese congressional representatives who visited the United States in late February and early March.

Since the beginning of reductions in U.S. support, the South Vietnamese leadership had entertained thoughts of reducing the territory to be secured if and when it became necessary. The decision, on or about March 14, 1975, to withdraw from Kontum and Pleiku provinces stemmed from earlier thinking on the matter coupled with the increasingly obvious fact that materiel constraints would require such action. The loss of Ban Me Thuot also contributed to the decision since the President and others believed that this city was of much more importance to the nation than were certain other provinces. The idea behind the withdrawal was sound. Forces would be withdrawn while not engaged, would be moved to a suitable location and would be employed to retake BMT. The timing of the withdrawal and its execution were disastrous and irreversible.

The Military Region II Commander, Major General Pham Van Phu, had been appointed to command in November 1974. General Phu had a good reputation as a division commander but was untested in the command of a much larger element—a corps consisting of two divisions plus support elements. He apparently had little concept of the logistics of large troop movements, particularly under conditions which would introduce large masses of civilians into the problem. He arrived back at Pleiku City, his headquarters, on March 14, 1975. The withdrawal began the following day. His subordinates had no forewarning—no time to do those things necessary to insure a reasonable chance of successful completion of the mission. The main withdrawal route, highway QL-19, which ran east from Pleiku to Qui Nhon on the coast, was cut by the enemy in two locations. The decision was made to withdraw south and east over a little-used road, LTL-7B, through Cheo Reo and out at Tuy Hoa on the coast south of Qui Nhon. This entailed bridging a major river.

The column was organized properly, initially. At the head moved the engineers to improve the road, bridge the river and other streams and to prepare fords where possible. Next came a nondescript mass of civilians in vehicles of all types. Artillery units were interspersed. Finally, bringing up the rear were several Ranger battalions. South Vietnamese Rangers were light Infantry. The NVA 10th, 316th, and 320th Divisions, which had participated in the Ban Me Thuot campaign, were available for new missions. It is interesting to note that the 316th had only recently been introduced from the strategic reserve of the North. Once the column bogged down at the main river crossing, the 320th NVA Division moved against it and just about decimated the entire lot. The remnants, which arrived at Tuy Hoa in early April, were no longer capable of fighting as a viable force. This debacle left only one ARVN division in MR II—the 22nd Infantry Division engaged against the 3rd NVA Division on QL-19 west of Qui Nhon.

I suspect that President Thieu rightly sized up the situation and decided that it was necessary to reconstitute some type of reserve in the Saigon area. At that time, the Marine and Airborne Divisions, which normally were in reserve in the Saigon area, were both engaged in Military Region I—the northern five provinces of RVN. He chose to remove the Airborne Division from its area of operations south and west of Danang. Lieutenant General Ngo Quang Truong, probably the most able Army general officer in service, commanded MR I. The Presidential decision made his already difficult job almost untenable. He journeyed to Saigon in an effort to turn the decision around—he was not successful. Reportedly, he advised the President that loss of the Airborne Division would force him to move the Marine Division, then defending south of Quang Tri City, to replace the Airborne Division in the defense of Danang—the second largest city in the Republic.

The Airborne Division was withdrawn and Truong moved the Marines. He placed several Regional Force battalions and a Ranger Group in the lines at Quang Tri. Once the Marines left, the local population began to move south along the main north-south artery, highway QL-1. As they moved out of Quang Tri City, the NVA attacked and retook the city. The Regional Forces and Rangers withdrew south to a new defensive line north of Hue. The refugees continued moving south and as they passed Hue they were joined by more and more refugees from that city.

In addition to the Marine Division, General Truong had the ARVN 1st Infantry Division north of the Hai Van pass, a major topographic feature which effectively separated the upper two provinces from the remainder of the country. The South had one small port at Tan My just east of Hue near the mouth of the Perfume River usable only by small craft. The primary means of transportation was by convoy up and down QL-1. As the column of refugees, beating its way south, grew larger, it effectively closed off any chance of using QL-1 south for convoy operations.

Truong's plans called for the defense of Hue—the establishment of an enclave which would include Hue and Tan My at a minimum. At this time, late March, he still had available north of the Hai Van pass one Marine brigade plus the 1st Infantry Division. The 325th NVA Division then drove east out of the mountainous area and cut QL-1 north of the pass in the vicinity of Phu Loc city. There remained no means of egress for the refugees or anyone else other than by sea. Scores of refugees moved eastward to the sea where they were extracted by small boats. The route to Tan My became choked with other refugees as did the port itself. All retrograde actions involving the movement of materiel were of necessity suspended in order to use the available boats and barges to move people.

As the situation worsened a different phenomenon manifested itself. The Marine and Airborne Divisions, as noted before, originally constituted the strategic reserve. As such, their bases of operations were in the vicinity of Saigon. Thus, their families resided in the Saigon area, although for the better part of two years the divisions were committed in MR I. This had caused some morale problems, particularly when the constraints in flying hours became effective, thereby reducing air transportation between MR I and Saigon. The ARVN divisions, on the other hand, had their families collocated with them in their various areas of operation. For the most part, these divisions, or elements thereof, were committed to fixed areas throughout the country. They would be moved here and there as the situation demanded but their bases of operations were relatively fixed. It was in the vicinity of these bases that dependents would settle.

The dependents of the 1st Infantry Division were north of the Hai Van pass with their sponsors. As the means for escape were suddenly closed, the situation with regard to evacuating families became untenable. It was at this point that, what I have chosen to call the "family syndrome," first manifested itself. Men and officers set out to save their families. It was that simple. Who else was going to do it? There had been no particular plans made for the evacuation of families because there was no consideration of losing that part of the country. The plans had all been oriented to resupply in case the Hai Van pass was cut. To my mind, the " family syndrome" has been wrongly designated as a lack of a will to fight!

It is difficult for the average American to conceive of a situation where a soldier's overwhelming desire to save his family—wife, children, mother, etc.—would cause him to leave his post. Not in this century, at least, has a single American soldier been faced with the choice. We have always fought away from our own soil and our own families. Our families have remained safely at home. It is interesting to note that the Vietnamese Marines remained together as a body and as a viable fighting force constantly throughout all of this. Their families were safe in their base camps in the vicinity of Saigon.

I don't chose to belabor the point. We saw the " family syndrome" reassert itself time and again for the next several weeks. Yet, we never saw the lack of a will to fight. As the lines around Saigon tightened there was plenty of evidence of hard and skillful fighting.[3] There was plenty of evidence of the NVA breaking in combat—much less so of the soldiers of the South. I know of no case where a member of a regular unit of the South failed to fight when his family was safe.

So, let us as Americans try to understand what really happened. Let us try to place ourselves in the same positions and then make judgments—if we then deem ourselves qualified to do so. But, before we accuse the Armed Forces of the Republic of Vietnam of no longer having had the will to fight, let everyone know for sure what we are talking about.

Chapter 7

"Their Country, Their War"

More than a year before South Vietnam's demise, General John Murray had visions of the end. As an attorney by training, Murray was able to slice away the confusing rhetoric and expose the raw truth: "We forgot history."

While he served as Defense Attaché (June 1973–August 1974), Murray lobbied the Joint Chiefs of Staff the "four disinterested sadists in the Pentagon," to unleash America's military might.[1] It was too late, Murray suggests. The 1973 Paris Peace Accords, in effect, signaled the slide toward the end of America's commitment to Vietnam. While the document may have pledged America's desire to see South Vietnam be given a chance to defend its sovereignty, it was only a matter of time— an interval—before the communists launched their bold offensive. Just as the American navy had not been used effectively in the early phase of the war, we would not, in the political turmoil of 1973–1974, be willing to send in waves of B-52 bombers.

In the following comments, Murray reflects on a variety of topics including order of battle, failed military intelligence, and the reluctance of the U.S. Congress after President Nixon's resignation to stay the course in funding the South Vietnamese military. As Murray observes, "When Nixon tumbled, the Republic of Vietnam fell with him"—eight months before "Operation Frequent Wind" occurred.[2]

When the grunts said "Naked Fanny" in Vietnam they weren't talking about physiology but Nakhon Phanom, the HQ of the 7th AF, in Thailand, and one of the Headquarters, Agencies and authorities both *dejura* and *defacto* that DAO reported to.

For you are digging into the depth of an historical labyrinth that is as horrendous as the need to fill it. Keep in mind that General Smith and I, with a few stalwarts—as forlorn hopes—were put in a straitjacket of a mission statement, termed a TOR (Terms of Reference), clumsily tailored by four disinterested sadists in the Pentagon, a.k.a. the Joint Chiefs of Staff.

The Chairman of the JCS, Admiral Thomas Moorer said to me, "Defense Attaché is a cover. Your job is to support a million alien folk in battle."

History has a long love affair with *Deja Vu*. Vietnam, for America, was a fiasco factory. Mass producing ridiculous failures with the prodigious skill of the wealthy world power of Persia under Xerxes, invading weak (and fortunately not meek) little Greece. The last one, with South Vietnam in extremis, was known by that Kissinger blighted oxymoron, the "Cease Fire" War.

It occurred after all the American ground troops left. When division and corps sized battles were fought. Fought by the ARVN as American troops never had to. Against a larger, stronger, enemy with home field advantage. Fought with weapons American troops never faced there: with the Strella missile that denied airspace under 5,000 feet. An enemy that fought with fleets of T-34 Russian tanks. That fought with a Chinese pipeline of fuel over the Ho Chi Minh Trail. And fought—as American troops never fought—without what the North Vietnamese Army (NVA) and Vietcong (VC) prisoners reported they feared the most: the B-52s and Navy Gun Fire. (Note, the King of Battles is the Artillery. The Infantry is the Queen of Battles. Giap, as his idol Napoleon, was an artillery man. That Russian 130-mm. gun in counter-fire outranged our basic 105-mm. artillery piece. And with the battleship *Wisconsin* withdrawn, only a single cruiser, the *Newport News* [later withdrawn] had guns that outranged that devastating, mobile, Russian 130-mm. gun. [The Vietnam border near the DNE was only 50 miles wide.])

Our Navy, with audacity and the right ships and long-range guns, could enfilade and virtually control the place. But our Army in Vietnam, unlike that of WW II and Korea, never seemed to grasp how deadly the Navy could be in a country that was a peninsula, with the Mekong on one side and the South China Sea on the other, with the Mekong Delta a waterland for riverine warfare exploitation. Looks like our generals in that civil war forgot about our generalship in our own civil war and never heard of Shiloh, Forts Donelson and Henry. Nor knew of the Cumberland, the Tennessee and the Mississippi. Or of how flag officers like Foote and Farragut were the instruments of fame and glory as the salvation of generals.

It is a fallacy to voice the bromide that "Generals always fight the last war." In Vietnam we didn't. And we should have. We forgot history. In WW II it was the U.S. Navy destroyers at Omaha Beach that enabled the infantry to get ashore. And in Korea, it was MacArthur's master stroke at Inchon that turned that war around with battleships a thousand yards offshore placing a protective arch of steel over the 1st Marines and the Army's 7th Division; that was the shelling architecture of that depiction of warfare as an art.

We didn't even have the sense to adopt the French General de Lattre de Tassigny's use of destroyer gunfire up the Day River in the interior of North Vietnam to defeat Giap.[3]

But this is another story. Another one, other than intelligence, to look into is the lack of the application of a principle of war—Unity of

Command—which may start another volume leading to other questions that you may pass on to your students looking for a Master's thesis subject.

Among the factors that heretofore have curiously been perennially exasperating is intelligence failure. We inherited that fatal failure factor; it seems as an eternal recurrence aspect of lost causes. It may also be an enduring feature of human nature, extending to such stupid tragedies that result in the tearful exclamation, "I didn't know the gun was loaded." Yet that is the kind of unforgiving bloody blundering that reason bluntly rejects. Mothers Against Drunk Driving have a tax-deductible organization that obtains them a living out of dying, like undertakers and soldiers (who survive). It is all part of the travesty of our existence. LBJ says, "How the shit did we get mixed up in this place, anyhow?"

I, among many others, have puzzled about and worried about our intelligence, including such an intelligence insider as Colonel Bill LeGro, who have at times been as exasperated with it as today's Army's foremost authorities collecting and analyzing information from satellites, stool pigeons, and Peeping Toms, who are about as reliable as a fly in the ear. I will try, in a rambling way, to touch on the topic of intelligence failure. That is with the understanding that you understand that intelligence failure is not a Vietnam War novelty. In fact, intelligence failure is commonplace. I suggest, if you haven't, you look up an article in *World Politics*, titled "Why Intelligence Failures are Inevitable." You may want to talk to General Walt Woolwine, who was J-4 during my time. When it was all over, and we were both retired, I asked him why they weren't accepting our intelligence. He said, "Johnny, we didn't believe you."

I think, also after the American troops left the country, our military was just disinterested. I went to the tank with General Vien and attempted later to talk to General Creighton Abrams, and Abrams walked away from me. The puzzle was, according to Generals Woolwine and Heiser and Assistant Secretary of Defense Shillito, who selected me, with CINCPAC approval, that Abrams, along with Weyand, was the pivotal approval. Abrams was notably a Patton protégé. I think he may have been more than that, as happens with protégés, they are copies. S.L.A. Marshall says Patton was "about half mad." Ladislas Farago thought Patton, "if not actually mad, was 'at least highly neurotic'." John Eisenhower, a keen observer, who grew up with the Patton family, thought of Patton that "there had to have been a screw loose somewhere." Applying these comments on Patton to Abrams would be right on the mark. After I left Vietnam, I went to address a joint session of the National War and Industrial Colleges. Can you believe it, they didn't even have a map of Vietnam that I could show up on a vugraph or post on the stage! And this was the only live war that was going on and we were supposedly supporting it with our DAO contingent and the promises of three presidents.

In my first quarterly report (June 73; that Homer followed consistently and which I think are the core of historical research) as DAO I deplored the immediate depreciation of the objectivity of intelligence sources with the sudden loss of advisors—the hundreds in the field and on the Military Assistance Command, Vietnam (MACV) staff and with the Army. Navy, Marine and Air Force Commands summarily vanished. Reliance on what was going on was dependent on the South Vietnamese Forces. We had very little in place to check, and cross-check. And as is most important, to triple check on reports, or on gaps in them. If truth, the RVANAF thought, was going to hurt our feelings, there was a pronounced inclination not to give, or to waffle it.

While intelligence failures are not unique, they may be somewhat different, even bizarre as they were in this war. They include, but are not by any means limited to:

1. A lack of understanding of what intelligence is, to be illustrated by a lieutenant colonel of the DAO staff who testified before the Pike Committee about how lousy I handled "intelligence."

We had Vipers in our DAO nest, but maybe not. Colonel Shockley's letter to the Pike Committee stunned me. I, unfortunately, do not have his letter—I may have ripped it up—but you can grasp the gist of it in my letter to General Danny Graham, who fortunately was a friend of mine. I wonder if there is something in my personality that repelled, or made others fear to unburden themselves to me. I suspend judgment on that. Maybe the first book on intelligence should be that of Socrates: "The unexamined life is not worth living." And the first rule is introspection. Maybe the most important feature of intelligence is one's own intelligence to have a good deal of intelligence about oneself. I can say that winning wars may include winning people and while it never occurred to me to include *How to Win Friends and Influence People* on the soldiers' bookshelf, maybe it's an idea worthy of Clausewitz.

2. The farcical dry-run briefing for the JCS in the Pentagon, presented by the DIA on the situation in Vietnam. It was as close to the truth as flat earth protagonists and the nuts who pontificate on the live existence of Elvis Presley and Bigfoot.

3. The CIA vs. DAO versions of what was going on.

4. Order of Battle (OB).

5. Congressional testimony, especially that of Ambassador Martin, that was, at worst a lie, and at best a distortion which misled the Congress.

6. How the RVNAF's own lies about itself contributed to false intelligence about its own OB.

Lieutenant General (then Colonel) Ben Register was with me at the Pentagon and sat in on a rehearsal briefing for the Joint Chiefs of Staff on the war situation in Vietnam. It was a DIA presentation. The Deputy DIA, an Air Force Major General at that time (Gene Tighe), who later became promoted as the Director, presided over the briefing. (I suspect it was because he promoted the politically correct way of presenting the war.) The briefer's presentation was as believable as reverse gravity. I kept my silence. In fact, I asked for it to restrain myself from insane rage. (I've seen more deranged people in the Pentagon dispensary than in a triage tent, and visualized myself there.) In my silence, as I often do, I consoled myself with a homicidal fantasy. I surmised that I was in power enough to direct that all DIA briefing charades be written in vanishing ink and poured over the briefers.

Tighe afterward did assure me the briefing would be changed to conform to reality. I didn't grasp that the reality Gene Tighe spoke of was the reality of political correctness and plausible denial.

Tighe personifies a disastrous ten-year war-long intelligence predicament. The dominance of a disastrously wrong selection of unfit Air Force officers assigned to key intelligence slots until, and thereafter, the war folded.

When MACV was established under CINCPAC there was a big debate among leading characters such as Harkins, Curtis LeMay, Admiral Felt and McNamara. This was an infantry war. Harkins and the Army's Assistant Chief of Staff for Intelligence (J-2) entered the fray and lost. The J-2 at NMCV, as the J-2 at CINCPAC, and the Director of the DIA, (established during the Vietnam War) were all Air Force generals. At CINCPAC, when I was the J-4, I attended intelligence briefings and was later excluded when I challenged some of their simplified conclusions. For instance, I recall one conclusion that the enemy was not growing in strength as replacements were on hold or declining. But my point was they were being strengthened by the growth in inventories and major weapons along with a reduction in casualties. This established the pattern. Can you believe it? The first J-2 under Harkins in this ground war had an extremely limited intelligence background solely with SAC (Strategic Air Command)! (Tighe's claim to his assignment was as a photo intelligence expert. Give him credit. He could detect substance where I saw shadows.)

Order of Battle was a convoluted subject in Vietnam. It is far more than the number of the enemy. OB basically divides the hard-core professional army and the paramilitary or the regional and provincial categories, including the ununiformed. It includes type of units from corps to platoon. It encompasses all kinds of weaponry (maintenance, upkeep and condition); location, size, inventories, and unit history, including status of leadership (their bios) and condition of troops (health, esprit, readiness, age: septuagenarians and subteenagers).

The precise strength of the NVA and VC was always crucial for American military planners in command in the field, as well as politicians in Washington. For it involved money. And that is why OB uncertainties and contradictions so disturbed McNamara.

The rule of thumb was, customarily, that it took ten defenders to handle one guerrilla. (General Bob Kingston, the most prominent Special Forces leader, who had four tours in Vietnam, says "it takes about six to one".) Whatever the ratio, we were committed to support the South Vietnamese. So, if the enemy had 10,000 soldiers we were committed to support from 60,000 to 100,000. No wonder McNamara flipped when he had kept his notes of a previous MACV meeting and wanted to know why in one month the enemy strength had doubled.

The ineptitude of the CINCPAC and assembled big brass, including Intelligence Chiefs that McNamara exposed, was their embarrassment of a high order, even comic, invoking thoughts of Catch 22, military morons, and almost certainly adding to McNamara's doubts about military intelligence and adopting Groucho Marx's depiction of the words as oxymoronic.

I will sort out first of all, the elements of intelligence: collection, analysis, covert action, and counterintelligence; and then to the varieties of collection: HUMINT (use of spies); SIGINT (intercepting the enemies' electromagnetic messages), that includes COMINT (describes how the interception is interpreted, originally or encrypted; FLINT (military hardware interceptions such as radar); and IMINT (collecting intelligence from pictures (sometimes termed PHOTINT) taken from airplanes or space platforms). Remember that the electromagnetic spectrum is a treasure trove for enemy revelation. Sonar, seismic and radar waves can all be intercepted and read. But there is a caution, forgotten at our peril. The Tonkin Gulf over-reaction, and misinterpretation triggered Lyndon Johnson's impetuous macho avalanching way to war. Sonar, radar and communication intercepts can be unreliable, even highly questionable circumstantial evidence, deceptive as the Siren's song that Ulysses listened to.

There is also what the military and CIA, NSA and NSC put in the category of "Open Source Intelligence"—technical journals, ordinary magazines, newspapers. I picked up enemy intelligence from a gutsy reporter who got himself captured (I recall it was McCombs of the *Washington Post*), and *New York Times* and *Wall Street Journal* reporters who were good observers. I took sources where I could find them. Keyes Beach, an ex-Marine who I knew in Korea, and knew war, and won a Pulitzer for his Korean reporting, roamed about the battlefields and picked up insights that put matters in perspective. The *Manchester Guardian* was particularly unbiased, as many of our press and TV were. Our guys customarily told me that the South Vietnamese "loved Americans." But I had some doubts about this when my wife (who learned Vietnamese) went to market with a maid to buy some of their great fruits and vegetables and heard a woman selling at the market saying to the maid, "You hit her over the head and I'll take her pocketbook." (Tough love, eh?)

What I heard and read after the final days coincided with what Martin confided in me about the "superficiality" and "fragility" of the local CIA product. (But knowing Martin, he may have had less kind words for us in DAO, for it must be said that sarcasm was his long suit.) However, he did have faith, as I did, in the CIA's best performer, Charley Timmes. While he was loyal to the station chief, it was obvious that Charley was a professional among neophytes. Charley's piece in *Army* magazine on the last days, refutes Snepp. The wife of one of the CIA types used to give the briefings at the weekly Mission Council meetings. She didn't know the difference between an APC as an armored personnel carrier, and an APC as a headache pill. She twitched with nervousness like the puppy dogs that crawl and wet the floor, causing pity for her plight in lacking self-control and awareness of it. Martin, always the southern gentleman politely ignored her distraught condition as we others took the clue from him. I would look at Bill LeGro and hoped I proved as good an actor as he did. If body language ever revealed my thought, I'm afraid I would have been out of today's Army with its super sensitivity toward gender bias.

I confided in Charley, who was a former Chief of the Military Assistance Advisory Group (MAAG) in Vietnam before MACV was set up. He was also highly respected among the ARVN. Charley and I had a similar background. We were New Yorkers. We were lawyers, he from Fordham, and I from St. John's and New York Law School. But Charley was far ahead of me in war experience—not only in Vietnam. He was an infantryman and paratrooper who jumped with the 82nd into France over the Omaha and Utah beaches before that assault. We used to play tennis together, and we kept our confidences. For as you may have gathered, generals have their own club that others are suspicious of. Especially those members of snobocracy that cluster within State. Charley and I used to laugh about the subtle nervousness about our friendly association, or we wondered, was it? Maybe there was a blend of deceptive elitism within us that wasn't there.

The CIA, in Vietnam, as I knew the group—by the way—when it came to intelligence sources, were addicted to HUMIN. But unbeknownst to Polgar (who was hoodwinked by the Hungarians and persuaded Martin to fall for their dissembling dribble that he passed on to Martin; but which Bill LeGro in his Monthly Intelligence Summary and Threat Analysis (MISTA), and Homer Smith tacitly scoffed at). The CIA had little fellowship with the

ARVN and virtually none with the Navy and Air Force and what they had was bought—always a questionable method among allies. Our friends confided in us as to their doings. Timmes, for instance, was paying the G-2 in III Corps for information. The G-2 submitted to Colonel Lung, the RVNAF J-2, his proposed input, which was then submitted by Lung to LeGro, who edited and corrected each submission. There were two advantages to this. It helped us to monitor what the CIA was saying, thus avoiding contradiction and questions, and it also helped raise the morale of soldiers with such prodigal stipends as would support an army of Lilliputians on a starvation diet. The rather disregard of SIGINT and PHOTINT by the CIA was coupled with disinclination to go through the ordeal of sorting out wheat from the chaff. Also they do not have the extensive training or field experience, nor rapport with the military, in these techniques that the military has. Also, we, the military, spend more time, as we usually have more access and are trained in obtaining intelligence from PWs, the *chien hois,* and enemy letters and diaries, maps and official papers.

This concentration on HUMINT may have been due to Ambassador Martin who had been a military intelligence officer in WW II in the Pentagon, with wide experience, but in the narrow specialty which he was good at: writing staff studies, letters, editing, digesting, and making one-pagers out of lengthy jargon-loaded products from the field. He seemed unaware of our NSC stuff, and looked at high-resolution photography like a Rhorsach test that he did not want to take.

The CIA operators, with the exception of Charley Timmes, were not comfortable in the field with the ARVN. And vice versa. Nor were the Consuls in the Corps areas, and as my Back Channels reveal, the ARVN did not cotton to them. Polgar had no one, except for Timmes, to compare with LeGro, the intelligence pro, with command of infantrymen in combat, and the G-2 for the Big Red One in his background. I must hand it to that most complex of contradictions that was ever assembled within the genes of one person, Martin, that he appreciated the unsurpassed quality of LeGro.

Bill will fill you in on Martin's lying denial that he did not fall for Polgar's Hungarian ploy. Polgar was fluent in that language. But if he picked up the language he didn't read between the lines. It was all hogwash and Bill LeGro, who wasn't reading tea leaves, was reading what the massing enemy strength said. It surely didn't say they were interested in a kindly compromise. But Martin bit, and even dictated and signed an amendment to the last DAO MISTA that bought that bogus Polgar naiveté. It exposes Polgar as inconceivably amateurish. Also the reason why Martin said he "should have gotten rid of Polgar and [for other reasons] von Marbod." Martin also put it this way, "I told Polgar I'd cut off his balls and stuff one in each car if he did something like that again."

The enemy did its own OB of the RVNAF. And we did our own. You would think it would be easy for us to get an accounting of how many troops they had. Not so. They routinely lied about it. Not the brass. But the rank and file. And mostly the company commanders who paid the troops. For they paid the troops, in piasters, as we used to do monthly, in dollars, in our Army. And more important than that, the troops received rations in kind. Rice was more valuable than rapidly inflating money. This was the source of the "ghost and flower" soldiers.

That is, the ghosts that didn't exist. And the flowers that existed, but were not present for duty. Dead soldiers were kept on the rolls alive as their commanders collected their pay and rations, and put them to their own purposes. So too the deserters were kept on the rolls. They were reported for duty as a way to adding to the commanders' stipends. With as high as 1,000 KIA a week; reported as alive, not dead, to pick up the pay; and as many as 30,000 deserters at any one time, this amount could add to the rice and hot noodle soup that fed large families. This ghost and flower business took on the form of charity. It was tolerated or even anticipated, when one was promoted to captain, as a fringe benefit. That was the good side. The bad side was that we never were sure just what the strength of the ARVN was.

Even without these perks, our Army, as Abrams complained when I was there, had a half million men, but was always short of infantry. Infantrymen were odds on favorites to breathe their last there. But they too went AWOL there; they were hospitalized there; they were promoted out of there; sent to school or special training there; went on emergency leave from there; regular leave; R&R; are placed on TDY elsewhere; are siphoned off as dog robbers; are malingerers there; are court-martialed and put in jail there; are listed among the unknowns; and while they do not disappear as ghosts or flowers, Americans, as other soldiers, make an art at being elusive.

Do the SECDEF and DEPSECDEF talk to one another? Another part of the intelligence foul-up was, as is often the focus of SNAFU, the matter of personalities. It was then, at the same time as the debacle with the DIA and the JCS staff, I talked to SECDEF Schlesinger in his office. He agreed with, and seemed to be well aware of my assessment, to such an extent he took his pipe out of his mouth, turned with the hot bowl in his hand, stem pointing, the stem close to my eyes, and then turned to his staff, to give us both emphatic direction. "You," he said, and "he should talk to the Hill and to the Press." (This was after I had received a message in Saigon from the SECDEF's Public Information Officer to keep my mouth shut, and a phone call from Martin that was ditto, and a message from CINCPAC that was more of the same.)

The result was nil. It disclosed once again the powerlessness of the people in power. The only press to talk to me was the *Washington Post*. Not exactly noted for its devotion to the truth. On the Hill, Mike Mansfield then figuratively shut his door in my face with, "I don't want to talk to any more army generals."

Another aspect of the puzzle was a call after retirement when Saigon fell, from the DEPSECDEF, Clements, former Governor of Texas, wanting to know why I didn't inform them in the Pentagon about the disaster about to befall Vietnam. I learned again that the E-ring has invisible walls, that Schlesinger and Clements were not bosom buddies, but that they were so far apart from what we were reporting and forecasting that they could be nose to nose and not see eye to eye.

As the DIA was undergoing denial with accustomed ease and DEPSECDEF Clements was wallowing in ignorance, the Commander-in-Chief was writhing in despair. Richard Nixon declares "When I resigned the presidency on August 9, 1974, I was profoundly frustrated with the situation in Vietnam." And Nixon cites immediately before that sentence his reason for it. A message I had sent from Saigon he, Nixon, describes as "a prophetic cable."

The President then goes on to cite my easy-to-make forecast that the country will die as its budget does. "You can roughly equate cuts in support to loss of real estate."

Starting with our rock-bottom FY 75 budget of $1.126 billion, I degraded it in hundred million dollar, country killing, increments. I ended my cable with this: "$600 million level—write off RVN [South Vietnam] as a bad investment and a broken promise. GVN [Government of Vietnam] would do well to hang on to Saigon and Delta area."

Nixon wraps up the *coup de grace.* "On September 22 and 24, 1974 the House and the Senate approved only $500 million in actual military assistance for South Vietnam. Antiwar congressmen and senators had written off our ally."

If you wonder why Nixon was so well informed, even better informed than his underlings, keep in mind that General Al Haig was his Chief of Staff in the White House. He visited Saigon when I was there and we thereafter exchanged back channels. (When we both retired, we kept in contact when he was the SHAPE commander and as Secretary of State.)

Unless you can shift your profession, keep to numbers, and write like Euclid, you can't expect to get things straight. The various stage settings at different times and places results in Vietnam War history as a theater of the absurd. At MACV, the Five O'clock Follies was the most popular daily farce. Less renowned, there was a series of visitations by dignitaries and "experts" such as McNamara and Taylor and LBJ, with contradictory findings. In September 1963 when JFK received such reports at an NSC meeting of two such experts who took the same whirlwind trip together as representatives of State and Defense, JFK tartly questioned "You two did visit the same country, didn't you?"

The contradictions you will most certainly run into may be somewhat explained to you by Colonel Herb Tiede, a sharp neutral observer of the Marine Corps, who was at MACV when Charley Cook made what is known as, guess what, *The Charley Cook Study,* in 1973, which was presented to Creighton Abrams. Colonel Tiede discloses how the intelligence briefings were warped to favor Abrams' optimistic opinions, and how Abe took to bad news as something to regurgitate and denunciate, with his own venom, on the unfortunate individual who had the audacity to honestly deliver, however gingerly, the unpalatable truth. Cook was from the State Department, an Annapolis classmate of Tiede's, and discovering Tiede at MACV, had put Herb on as an unlikely member of his team. Established by Kissinger, Cook's mission did not receive a welcome from a headquarters that was noted for its social graces.

The personality of Graham is important. I had briefed him in 1974, to top off Bill LeGro, and he thought that I was fixed up. But when he called, and I found out about his testimony before the House Foreign Affairs Committee, I had my doubts. Martin called me in Vietnam from Washington. I said, "How did it go?" hoping for at least an indication that we were going to get more money. Martin said, "They never laid a glove on me." His interest was obviously on himself and not the plight of the ARVN with one foot in their impoverished grave and the other on a politically dependent U.S. banana peel.

There were other hearings, including those involving Fulbright and Hubert Humphrey, that were critical, in which Martin gave misleading testimony that tick both Homer and me off. For it was probably the basis of a statement in Bruce Palmer's book about Homer's and my inadequacy in handling a war that could be better directed by combat types, completely ignoring the fact that the deficiencies that developed had nothing to do with the combat performance of the RVNAF, but rather the Congressional failure to understand and perform other than as Scrooges.

Martin's steeped-in-lies testimony a year after the fall, as Wolf Lehman, Homer Smith and Bill LeGro can assess, was duly worthy of a modern Machiavellian model. Answering close questions, Martin blatantly denied that he had anything to do with General Baughn's relief, stating that it was entirely General Smith's doing. Homer told me that it was entirely Martin who wanted Baughn sacked. (Wolf Lehman emphatically supports Homer.) Bill LeGro's statement, supported by the record, that Martin signed to the MISTA to which Bill attests, as does Jim Wink, adds another lie to the Martin litany of whoppers that ironically accord with his epitaph which he appears to be dictating for the record in his last official testimony. There is

acclaim accorded him by some of the congressmen and disdain by others—
naturally along party lines. For tidal currents of vitriol ebbed and flowed
during that Watergate time. Nixon was but a month away from resigning in
disgrace.

Nixon was never inclined toward small effects. When he tumbled, the
Republic of Vietnam fell with him.

It might interest you to know that Homer Smith had the same
approach from the beginning of our experiences with the war, which was
before it was over for American troops, and before we turned the war over,
in the name of Vietnamization. We had the same, you might say parent-
child, basic philosophy toward our Vietnamese allies, that being tough on,
and spanking them, hurt us more than it did them, but was to their benefit.

Homer and I weren't among the activists, altruistic visionaries trying
to remake the Garden of Eden out of South Vietnam, let alone its military.
Although we knew that there were a lot of talking snakes about, for me the
most volatile serpent wore striped pants. But we did have something in
common with Martin. With him, we would both nuke Utopia if it was in the
interest of the United States.

Homer and I worked for some great, now legendary, logisticians
(Heiser, Woollvine, Besson), and had, as the Air Force historians portrayed
us in their history, the same view of intelligence and observations about the
war. The concept of both of us as *merely logisticians,* sometimes considered
as a pejorative, disclosed no background with our backgrounds. I had my
basic training as an artillery man, served in combat as a corporal in WW II,
later as a captain in Italy, where the *Lluftwaffe* dive-bombed with their
Stukas; and under the British, where I had, among other assignments, that of
intelligence, which included reconnaissance under fire. Brigadier Waghom
said, "You Americans blew up the bridges, plugged up the tunnels, wrecked
up the track where we plan to advance, so you Americans must restore our
right of way." In the Korean War, I was in places at machine gun sites where
no one knew where the front was, and one appreciated that the barrel of the
M-60 could swing quickly around 360 degrees, because nobody knew where
the front was. My first tour in Vietnam, on the first light of the first day, I
was at Vung Ro Bay, where the troops of one of my battalions had just taken
thirty casualties. But tactics is simple compared to logistics. Tactics is
simple as basic arithmetic and two plus two equals four. Logistics is as
complex as calculus and there is always an X and Y factor with formulas
that Einstein's associates inspired. Tacticians are Little Bo Peeps that leave
their sheep for the logisticians to find them. Our greatest generals were
schooled as logisticians. Lee and MacArthur were engineers; Grant was a
quartermaster. In WW I, history notes that George Marshall was a
transportation officer on the Western front. We had some lunkheads as

generals in Vietnam that were out of their league, and elsewhere, as in CINCPAC (Admiral Gayler thought we could fight the war in Vietnam with bows and arrows). Of course whether the DAO was stereotyped as a logistician or a combat type is beside the point. The TOR and the political and sanctuary design of the war, with the elimination of the promised support of U.S. air and sea power, put together with that brilliant Kissinger permitting Le Duc Tho the Trojan Horse that left 250,000 North Vietnamese Army troops in South Vietnam was as ludicrous as it was shameful idiocy. We might have just as well had Benedict Arnold at the Peace Table.

Our philosophy had a practical precedent from a notable predecessor in an earlier war, who rode on camels, not helicopters, but was in a quagmire based on politics and sucking sand as ours was on muck, mountains, and jungle; and the most formidable intercontinental sucking obstacle of all, Capital Hill. Our fabled historic predecessor put it into words for us, that the local artists on To Do Street put on plaques made of artillery brass. It's from the *Seven Pillars of Wisdom.* We both took Lawrence of Arabia's advice as a driving force:

> *Better they do it imperfectly, than you do it perfectly.*
> *For it is their country, their war, and your time is limited.*

Chapter 8

"A Done Deal"

Within the context of the Cold War and America's determination to contain the spread of communism, Colonel William LeGro believes that "drawing the line in Vietnam was the smart thing to do." As the former chief of intelligence for the Defense Attaché Office, LeGro served two tours of duty in South Vietnam, the final one beginning in December 1972 and ending with the evacuation. He adamantly states that one lesson of the war is that, "When the United States makes a commitment, it should honor that commitment." Unfortunately, after the Paris Peace Accords, America reneged on that commitment, LeGro argues. The South Vietnamese military fought heroically until the end, but the supplies we made available to them were "cast-off" ships and "secondhand" equipment. By 1975, America's attention had turned elsewhere and the commitment became stained by dishonor.[1]

I'm one of the few who genuinely liked Graham Martin. I got along with him very well. In fact General John Murray and I talk about it a lot. He has an entirely different view. His might be more accurate. Some people think Martin was using me as kind of a foil against the CIA station chief. I don't believe that. I think Martin genuinely wanted to do the best job he could. Murray doesn't think he did enough in getting military assistance for Vietnam. He couldn't change things, anyway. It was a done deal. When we left in 1973 after the peace treaty was signed, the die was already cast. We weren't going to rescue Vietnam if it came under severe attack.

They had made that decision, "they" meaning Congress. Still, President Nixon was determined to defend Vietnam. But he lost all of his influence because of Watergate and became virtually powerless to change anything. I don't know how much impact Watergate had on the communists' strategic plan. They were going to attack anyway. The timing was probably influenced by Watergate.

There was no doubt in the minds of the leaders of the South Vietnamese Army, and probably President Thieu as well, that the North Vietnamese were going to continue the war and they weren't going to wait around for the Vietcong to rise again. They were going to come in with their main force. We were tracking them; we knew where they were.

All of our intelligence did go to the highest levels here in America. Either they didn't believe it or they suspected we were right and didn't want to do anything about it. Or they knew we were right and couldn't do anything about it. I think, really, they didn't care. I think that was true of the Department of Defense and of the services, as well. They were focused on Europe, again. There was a great draw-down of forces in Europe during the Vietnam War and now they were concentrating on rebuilding those forces. They didn't want this distraction in Indochina. They had written it off.

Certainly, the communists had some agents in headquarters here and there. But I don't think they turned any significant numbers of the ARVN anywhere. The problem wasn't people being turned. The problem was the Vietnamese had no reserve. They had committed everything. So, when they had to face a situation like Phuoc Long in 1974, and later at Ban Me Thuot, they had no reserve and no way to get it there in any case.

The communists decided to take Phuoc Long and, depending on our reaction, make the next move. Our reaction was to protest—a couple of messages. That was it. Very clearly, it was a coordinated operation. I like to think of the operation at Quang Duc Province, west of Ban Me Thuot on the border, as the last successful ARVN response to the North Vietnamese. The south was able to airlift a regiment into Quang Duc and counterattack and drive the North Vietnamese away. They drove them out but it was a costly operation. That was in the summer of 1974. Basically, the South Vietnamese were not able to deploy or to use artillery the way they should have. They were rationing ammunition. Their trucks were up on blocks.

The attitude of the members of Congress who came over in March 1975 was "Let's find out how bad the Vietnamese are running this thing. It's their fault. They aren't doing a good job." Despite the fact that Congress had cut the budget to $700 million from a budget of $1.2 billion.

I took Representative McCloskey of California to the Delta, Can Tho, the headquarters of IV Corps. I introduced him to the corps commander. McCloskey said, "I want to see a Vietcong prisoner." He wanted to see if they were treating them well. We were just about to be overrun, and he wanted to see if we were treating prisoners well. So, I took him to the jail. McCloskey asked, "Are they political prisoners or military?" Then, he wanted to see one of the regiments. So, I took him up to the parrot's beak. And he did the same thing: "Do you have any prisoners of war?" Then, McCloskey wanted to go up to II Corps. There was action going on. I asked McCloskey if he wanted to go up on the hill where the artillery was. He said he didn't want to do that. It was kind of an attitude of "it's all over." And Bella Abzug came on that trip, too. Abzug spent her time visiting what she called "political prisoners" in Saigon. To go over there and expect that the U.S. Bill of Rights was being observed in a time of war was silly.

The South Vietnamese fought awfully well everywhere. When they were overwhelmed up around Hue, by four or five divisions to their two divisions, they broke. The airborne had been pulled out. Three divisions came in on one regiment of ARVN at Ban Me Thuot. During the retreat, several ranger battalions fought heroically.

There was corruption among a number of leaders of the Thieu government. Some of them were incredibly rich and they shouldn't have been. Some of the generals weren't corrupt. One general came here with nothing and got a job cleaning toilets in a hotel. A lot of them were in that shape.

Corruption was not the cause of the collapse. The reduction to almost zero of United States support was the cause. If we had kept our material support at the level necessary to fight a major war, and remember we had told them that we would, they could have withstood that final offensive for a while. The South Vietnamese would have needed, however, the promised United States air support to continue to defend their country because they didn't have the opportunity to choose the battlefield. The initiative was always with the other side. The communists knocked out the outposts on the border, in the outlying areas, and then they closed in. The North Vietnamese were very clever, and they attacked at the place where it would have the most effect.

We did a terrible thing to the South Vietnamese. We had promised to be ready to reintroduce American military force if the president gave the order. We had planes stationed nearby. This whole thing makes me very sad.

In November 1974, 1 brought two Vietnamese intelligence specialists to America. I was concerned that the people in Washington weren't reading our reports. So, I brought these two guys to the states. In Washington, we met with the deputy director of CIA, Vernon Walters. And he was gracious, speaking French to the Vietnamese. We had lunch in his private dining room—waiters in white coats. We tried to get the conversation on to what was going on in Vietnam, but Walters wasn't interested. Then we went to meet with an Air Force general. It wasn't high on his priority list, either. Before we could start talking, he launched into a lecture on the Soviet missile threat. They had already decided that Vietnam was lost.

We really started the evacuation around the fourth or fifth of April 1975. General Homer Smith approved. He put out the word to our women, asked them to leave first. He asked them to take care of the orphans. I lost fifteen employees in the terrible C-5 crash. I went to Ambassador Martin around the second week in April and I asked to send my aide's wife and baby out. He said okay. That was the first movement of Vietnamese. Martin showed no resistance.

Chapter 9

"Nobody Told Martin"

As the Central Intelligence Agency's Saigon Station Chief, Thomas Polgar methodically assembled information which he found few policymakers in Washington wished to receive. In Polgar's biting assessment, the intelligence gathering was "almost faultless"; it was the policy that was flawed. Washington was "unwilling to act or unable to act." The government was paralyzed by Watergate and President Gerald Ford's Administration "could never organize itself to move specifically in any direction."[1]

In this interview, Polgar offers a sympathetic snapshot of Ambassador Graham Martin. The diplomat seems to have been abandoned by politicians and military commanders who, by the spring of 1975, had decided to step away from America's commitment to South Vietnam. Unfortunately, Polgar explains, "nobody told Martin."[2]

I thought that the Paris Peace Accords were a reasonable compromise, and I think that had the North Vietnamese observed the agreement, we could have lived with the situation for a long time to come.

We considered the possibility that they would not live up to the agreement, and for that reason we moved the 7th Air Force from Saigon up to Thailand to Nakhon Phanom. It was called the United States Special Action Group. And the idea was that, as Henry Kissinger put it, if we find that the North Vietnamese violate the substance of the agreement, our retaliation, and I quote, "would be instant and brutal." The only trouble was, that as, more and more, the Nixon Administration got bogged down in Watergate, the U.S. threat had lost its credibility. The intention to retaliate was there, but after the Watergate affair, as I said, in the summer of 1974, and even earlier with the election of a Democratic Congress in 1972, the Vietnam War became so unpopular that it was inconceivable to Congress that after the Paris Agreements we would re-engage. It wasn't incredible to Kissinger when he entered into that agreement, but, you know, the pillars upon which he built his edifice just collapsed.

Although, in all fairness, after the Paris Peace Accords, 1973 was the most peaceful year we ever had in Vietnam. And although it was not free of hostilities—we never had a period free of hostilities in Vietnam—the hostilities were below a threshold that we could tolerate. And, again, our side wasn't squeaky clean either. Because we also kept pushing to retake marginal territory.

Both sides considered in 1973 that there's a cease fire; there's a quadripartite, or four-nation international commission that is going to supervise and control the cease-fire terms—and that, incidentally, never proved to be a viable proposition—and the whole proposition was based on the assumption that the United States would continue resupplying South Vietnam item for item. And, similarly, that the Russians and the Chinese could resupply their forces. Mr. Kissinger's expectation was that as a result of his agreements with Brezhnev the Russian resupply would gradually cease, and North Vietnam's forces in South Vietnam would sort of wither on the vine. And South Vietnam's forces would be kept viable by one-for-one replacement of equipment lost or damaged. Well, that also never happened, because, in fact, we stopped our resupply to the South Vietnamese for budgetary reasons. Congress wouldn't pass any appropriate legislation. The supplemental appropriations disappeared, and Thieu, instead of living off income, so to speak, had to start living off capital as far as his military activities were concerned. But certainly, as I said, 1973 was a relatively quiet year, but it wasn't a totally quiet year, because there was some military activity going on, both along the Cambodian border in the delta area, where we had Viet Cong forces, and up in the northeast corner of MR I, where the South Vietnamese Marines were trying to take back some territory. And also, similarly, the Phoenix Program and its successes domestically continued with their countersubversive measures which was also a form of warlike activity.

On paper, the South Vietnamese were stronger, but the disposition of the forces was entirely different. You remember the map of Vietnam, which is sort of long; and the South Vietnamese Army was sort of evenly distributed on a territorial basis. The North Vietnamese could always concentrate their strength where they wanted to attack, because they had the guarantee that the south would not be allowed to attack the north. So the North Vietnamese could concentrate at the key points where they wanted to bring strength. The South Vietnamese intelligence was never so good as to anticipate any possible attack. So they had to try to defend everything all the time. And the situation was a little bit different in that in any given city you have more police, speaking of the United States, than you have bank robbers, but from time to time banks get robbed, because the bank robber knows where he wants to go and the police don't know that is where he's going to go. So, if you do not have to fear retaliation, the North Vietnamese were tactically a lot more mobile than the South Vietnamese.

I think that the only part of the American effort in Vietnam that really worked was intelligence. I think that the intelligence was almost faultless. But, as I learned from the course of history, good intelligence cannot compensate for bad policy.

The South Vietnamese knew where the North Vietnamese were concentrating, but knowing something and doing something about it is a little bit different. Now there was a real problem on the South Vietnamese side. It was that things were completely centralized in the person of President Thieu. So even though Colonel William LeGro and General Homer Smith, who talked to their counterparts in the Joint General Staff structure, and I think that Colonel LeGro's relationship with his South Vietnamese counterpart was particularly close, there were problems of getting information, particularly bad information, or—by bad I mean "unpleasant" information—up to the level of Thieu. And it wasn't until we were deep into the North Vietnamese offensive of 1975 that I managed to arrange my briefing for Thieu personally on the military situation, and I was accompanied at that meeting by Ted Shackley, my predecessor in Vietnam; and at the time he was the Chief of the East Asia Division of the CIA. And he came out with that last-minute mission that General Weyand headed, and it was the presence of Shackley that gave me the excuse to go and brief Thieu personally, because Ambassador Martin was very jealous that only he could talk personally to the president. But anyway, we briefed President Thieu, and we brought him to tears when we gave him, without any cosmetics, the truth of the situation. He just didn't realize things were that bad.

This was after the fall of Danang. I would say it was probably during the first week of April. And I had personal access to the Prime Minister, and I briefed the Prime Minister regularly on how bad the situation was, particularly after the collapse in the Central Highlands. In fact, that things were that bad was news to the Prime Minister, too, although he was a four star general and you would have thought that he would have had access to all information. But there is something about their society that prevented the truth from reaching the top. Of course, I wouldn't say that is unique to their society. There were many factors which prevented the South Vietnamese from moving, and one of the things was that there was extreme concern about loss of equipment which wasn't going to be replaced. So even though, when we started in 1974, with the North Vietnamese nibbling away in the northwest corner of Military Region Three, Thieu was very hesitant in letting his aircraft engage at a practicable altitude. And I remember that very vividly. And he said, "If I lose one of my C-130s, I have lost nine percent of my entire force." Also, the collection of planes that we left behind, was really not the best that we had. Now there were a lot of factors at play there in 1973–74. We had the Arab-Israeli War which caused a lot of American equipment destined for Vietnam to be diverted to Israel. I remember talking to one of the Hungarian Air Force colonels who was on the Hungarian mission, and he said he asked for assignment to Vietnam, to this international commission, because he was a professional Air Force officer and he wanted to see the latest in American equipment. And he said he didn't expect that he would find an air museum.

The whole American military effort, as you will remember, was always based on unlimited logistics. And they were always going to use quantity instead of using human lives. We were going to fight a resource war. We did it in World War II. We tried to do it in Korea. And we were going to try to do it in Vietnam. We were able to do it in Vietnam as long as we were there. We probably expended more ammunition in Vietnam than during World War II. Now the American Army trained the Vietnamese Army in its own image, and the Vietnamese were trained to fight a rich man's war. They had the tanks, the armor, the airplanes, and the artillery; but as the Americans' resupply dried up, in effect they were forced to fight a poor man's war for which they weren't equipped. And they lacked the mobility toward the end, which was absolutely essential. Now the mobility, of course, was also affected by the very poor infrastructure in Vietnam. There were very few roads where armor could move effectively, or at least so the South Vietnamese thought. Also, toward the end there was that catastrophic decision of Thieu's to reverse the evacuation of the Marine Division from Hue which completely bollixed up Route 1. And so, basically from the lack of resources and the lack of reliable logistics resupply, a lot of ills developed.

You have to think of the 1973 Middle East War and the Arab oil embargo. And oil became scarce and became very expensive. And where you thought $1 million could buy X gallons, suddenly $1 million could buy X minus Y. And it was constantly changing. And not only that, the idea that our people were waiting in long lines at gas stations in the United States, and they were going to ship oil to Vietnam was very unpopular. There was never actually an oil shortage in Vietnam. They could get the oil from Saudi Arabia, and then refined from Singapore. The problem was that the money that was available to buy that oil was less and less sufficient to the needs.

Although Thieu was an elected president, I would never say that he had the kind of identification with the Vietnamese people that, say Ngo Dinh Diem had in earlier years. Not for very long, but he had it for a number of years. But basically, the authority of the Government was not at issue. The Government was able to fulfill the normal functions of government as long as there was no massive military attack against them. It was not a very efficient government and there never really developed a civilian government structure in Vietnam. All the province chiefs, for example, were military people. And the province chiefs represented both the military power of the province and the civil administration. Now there are legends on how corrupt some of these province chiefs were, and I wouldn't doubt it. But they could have survived with a corrupt South Vietnamese Government just as the Philippines survived with a corrupt Philippine Government—or South Korea does—or Thailand—or anywhere. In any country where you do not pay your Civil Service adequately, you can expect corruption. It's a way of life. That was not the trouble. The trouble was that there was just no margin in the resources of that government to cope with a military invasion.

I was in Vietnam fairly recently, and I don't think that things have changed that much, although things clearly are much better. I mean, Vietnam today is a rapidly developing nation, and they are at peace. But they still pay their Civil Service nothing. On the other hand, the government doesn't expect its civil servants to starve. The philosophy is that if you hold the position, you are smart enough to survive. As is the case in Mexico. So, I think that corruption is a problem, but it wasn't corruption that resulted in the downfall of Vietnam. Because in some cases, for example, at the last stand of the 18th Division, around the middle of April, they were just as poorly paid as anybody else, yet they had good leadership. And they gave a good account of themselves.

Now, they always have had a leadership problem in the Vietnamese Army because of two factors. First, most of the general officers started their careers as noncommissioned officers in the French Army. Therefore, everybody was, maybe, three or four ranks above his capacity. No Vietnamese General ever had the experience of fighting divisional level combat. While the Americans were there, they had the military advisors, and if truth be told, these military advisors were the de facto commanders. So they weathered the 1972 offensive because you had some very good American officers at the division and at the corps level "advising" their Vietnamese counterparts. But there was a sort of curious detachment in the Vietnamese officer corps from what was going on, and I remember on the day after the fall of Pleiku; and, you know, there was this big argument, did you order the evacuation of the highlands or not, and that is a separate story, but what I want to say is, that on the very following Sunday—the front is collapsing—they sent a guy to Second Corps headquarters down in Nha Trang, and there is nobody on duty; and "Why aren't you on duty?" "Well, its Easter Sunday." And on that critical weekend, again, when Pleiku fell, and they tried to get in contact with people in the military, and in the Joint General Staff, there was only one general officer on duty. They didn't know that the Second Corps was evacuating. So their communications completely broke down at that point. Which, incidentally, gives lie to the theory that they tried to pull an evacuation and keep it as a surprise from the Americans. In fact, Lieutenant General Quang, who was the President's military advisor at that point, was very surprised when we told him that there was an evacuation going on. So that was one of the great, and never completely clarified incidents in the war. How could General Phu, who was the Commanding General of the Second Corps so misunderstand Thieu's instructions that he pulled the evacuation without any sort of staff preparation?

Well, it became complete chaos, because they didn't even know that the road that they were taking had no bridge across the river.

The CIA had no contingency plans for the invasion by the north and a complete breakdown in the south because it was just not permissible. To give the American Government a framework to plan for defeat. That just isn't done.

There was never any collapse in the delta. There was never any collapse immediately around Saigon, but as the events in the highlands unfolded, the chief of Vietnamese intelligence—you know, and they had two parallel intelligence structures—in everything they imitated the Americans—or followed our advice—there was the Vietnamese Central Intelligence Office, which was headed by General Binh, and then there was the J-2 of the Joint General Staff. And General Binh told me that the evacuation from the Central Highlands, or the collapse in the Central Highlands, was the end of South Vietnam as we know it. The structure that the Americans built up in Vietnam is finished. Now, this was not accepted by Washington. And certainly not accepted by Ambassador Martin. But not accepted by Kissinger either. And, in fact, several weeks after that, when the Weyand mission came out, the whole idea was to try to prop up everything. To try and form a defensive line in Military Region Three around Saigon, and hang on to Saigon and the delta, which economically speaking would have been a viable proposition, but you cannot separate your economics from your overall psychological situation.

You know, after the fact it is easy to say the communists were going all the way anyway. There was, in fact, a planning document of the Politburo to which we had access. It said that the next year was going to be the great victory. They didn't think that they could finish it in '75. But clearly their policy changed in the fall of 1974. In 1974 they reassessed their policy, and that is clearly reflected in the North Vietnamese documents, when they said that the exit of Nixon caused them to re-evaluate the situation. And with Nixon, they couldn't be sure, even though the Congress passed the bombing ban. The fact is that the President remains Commander-in-Chief. And if President Nixon had ordered the B-52s to take off from Saigon, the North Vietnamese couldn't be sure whether the pilots would go to the bombers or to the lawyers. My guess is that the pilots would have executed the orders that came down the chain of command.

The North Vietnamese were afraid of Nixon. They were not afraid of President Ford. And President Ford, unfortunately, made a couple of speeches which the North Vietnamese interpreted as meaning that he wasn't really serious about defending South Vietnam. He never really pushed that hard. It wasn't as emotional a thing with him as it was with Nixon.

We had a very crazy chain of command in Vietnam. We had CINCPAC (Commander-in-Chief Pacific) who was responsible for the naval operations; we had a four star general in Saigon who was responsible for the local operations; and his command authority overlapped with CINCPAC; then we had the JCS taking a very active role from Washington; then we had Kissinger's ties to the Ambassador, and only the Ambassador could see President Thieu, as I previously mentioned; even the four star general couldn't see Thieu without the Ambassador's presence. And one day when General Creighton Abrams came out he told us a little story, that it was the custom for the mothers of the generals to get together for sort of a quilting session during which, one night, they took a little bit more sherry than usual, and really put together the craziest quilt you ever saw. One of the big generals saw it and said, "This is it. This is going to be the chain of command for Vietnam." So the thing is, that on any given day, we had conflicting advice from not only one place in Washington, but several places in Washington, including Kissinger; the JCS; the Secretary of Defense, personally; the CIA; Kissinger to the Ambassador and me; and the subordinate military through their separate chains of command. And I don't know whether you read McNamara's own account of what happened in the Gulf of Tonkin. You know, where he gets on the phone with the four star Admiral McCain and says, "Are you sure that this has happened?" And the Admiral says, "No. I'm not sure."

And strictly speaking, there was no one really in charge. There was no one really in charge in Washington. There was no one really in charge on the ground. Occasionally, Admiral Gayler (CINCPAC) thought that he was in charge. Ambassador Martin always thought that he was in charge. And there were also conflicting motivations. The Ambassador was absolutely convinced that the moment that the word gets out that we are leaving, we are going to have a Danang-type collapse with people trampling on each other, and killing Americans, and what have you. The military, who clearly saw the situation as hopeless, after, say the fifteenth of April, they wanted to get an orderly evacuation underway, taking out no more than one thousand Vietnamese. And that was the plan.

General Richard Carey, the Marine general who was charged with the actual tactical operation, flew in and out of Saigon a couple of times, and they talked with each other, and what they had in mind was the same kind of evacuation they had in Cambodia. You know, that was called "Eagle Pull"— the other's called, "Chicken Run." In other words, when we took off, and we didn't take any of the Cambodians, you know, who worked for us. The loss of life was far greater in Cambodia than in Vietnam. The American planning did not foresee taking out any Cambodians. Maybe because the Cambodians didn't want to come. Be that as it may, Cambodians were not taken out. It was a very neat operation completed within a couple of hours while life was normal in Phnom Penh. All right. Now in Vietnam we had a very different situation. First, Saigon was swollen with refugees. Secondly, we had the examples of Danang and Nha Trang where there was unbelievable chaos. Tremendous loss of life. Tremendous suffering. Also, American prestige was far more involved in Vietnam that in Cambodia. So, Ambassador Martin felt that: (a) we must take out a lot of Vietnamese; and (b) if we move prematurely, everything is going to collapse around our heads. Now taking out Vietnamese in large numbers was never the American plan. In fact, even a week before the final evacuation, the Federal Aviation Agency was fining American airlines for carrying undocumented Vietnamese. And our Air Attaché, Brigadier General Richard Baughn, who got himself kicked out of Vietnam for that reason, carried out people secretly, and as a result got fired. And the fact that we then brought out 80,000 or 90,000 Vietnamese—that was something that Ambassador Martin achieved through a chain of circumstances and accidents, but something that our military had never planned. Now, you asked me earlier, did the CIA have a plan for an evacuation. Of course we had a plan for evacuation. We printed up beautiful little laminated plastic cards which our people were going to get. The Vietnamese who were working with us, and this laminated card would get you on board some American aircraft or naval vessel, and they're going to take out some 800 people—and in fact, the final approved plan called for the evacuation of not more than 1,000 Vietnamese who could be brought into the United States under a parole and exclusion procedure. And this was approved by the Attorney General. Now, all of these things went by the wayside, because all the planning was based on the proposition that there would be some orderly exit—a negotiated exit.

Well, there was, in fact, an orderly evacuation going on, because as Military Region One and Military Region Two fell, a lot of people from those regions ended up in Saigon. And, clearly, nobody had any use for them. They couldn't give them any jobs, and they did have an orderly evacuation, but there were lots of troubles. First they used DC-9s with seats in them and they could carry very few people. And gradually there was a big buildup of personnel at Tan Son Nhut, and they had what was, in effect, a refugee colony in Tan Son Nhut. And then the other big problem was that it was possible to take a relatively small number of people out through military channels to the Philippines, and they could be accommodated in the American military installations in the Philippines; but the Philippines never wanted to get any large number of Vietnamese. And strictly speaking, our military had no authority to carry Vietnamese from point A, namely Saigon, to any point B. Because under international conventions, you know, international travelers had to have passports and visas, and so forth. And the military, with the best motives in the world, short-circuited all those provisions. Well, you could do that with a couple hundred people, but you couldn't do it as you were getting up in the thousands. And some of my most dramatic cable exchanges with Washington were over the fact that Washington was telling me to get the endangered species out, but I had no place to take them. Because Thailand refused us permission. Malaysia refused permission. Hong Kong refused permission. And that was the range of our planes. The ones that were available to Air America.

During the last couple of weeks of April, I had the impression that a lot of the cable traffic that was coming out of Washington was "for the record," so to speak. People wanted to put themselves on record without any realistic expectations that the instructions that they were sending were going to be implemented. It was one big "cover your ass operation." And so, I have testified to Congress about all this back in 1975. The problem was, you cannot move a large number of people unless you have some place to move them. And that was lacking. Because you could never get the agreements of the governments in the Philippines and Thailand, and these were the two likeliest places to take people in large numbers.

I think it was the preponderance of opinion that we would have a Danang-type situation if ships are being loaded in an area that we could not physically control. Now we didn't have enough—our Marines had no authority for any even police-type action. Their authority was limited to defending the Embassy. The Defense Attaché's office in Tan Son Nhut was in a relatively good position because they were surrounded by Vietnamese military installations, specifically the Joint General Staff compound, and the access to Tan Son Nhut was always controlled. And having an aircraft take off is less of a proposition than loading a big ship. So—yes, I would have subscribed to the Ambassador's position that it would be an uncontrollable situation unless we could have brought in ground troops to provide a perimeter around Newport. But let's face it, it was a terrible situation. But for every plan, you have got to have a concept. You have to have some kind of concept, and you make a plan on how you are going to implement it. But the idea that we are going to abandon South Vietnam to its fate was simply not within the policy ballpark. We couldn't say it. And I think that many people couldn't even bring themselves to think it. As other people might have told you, I was pushing the negotiated surrender theory. This would have permitted an orderly evacuation, but Kissinger was blowing hot and cold on it. One day he was for it, one day he was against it. In fact, the

American government could never organize itself to move specifically in any direction. We just sort of let what came up on us come up on us.

Of course, the CIA doesn't make policy. The CIA is supposed to collect intelligence on which, if all goes well, policy is based.

Well, I learned one lesson, and this is not only true about Vietnam. It is very difficult to act on intelligence which runs against your preconceived conceptions. Just as President George Bush couldn't bring himself to believe that the Berlin Wall would fall, or that the Soviet Union would collapse, then Kissinger couldn't bring himself to think in terms of giving up on Vietnam. They couldn't think in terms of fighting for it either. So, when we, in 1974—and I'll never forget the particular incident. It was a beautiful Sunday, and my wife and I decided to drive out to Bien Hoa, which was the headquarters of Military Region Three, and we had a particularly good intelligence collection effort going, and it was, as I say, a beautiful Sunday, the dry season was on us, and I got two bottles of sparkling burgundy, and we were going to have a nice lunch with my base chief in Bien Hoa. And when we got there he said, "It's really wonderful that you came, because I just got this intelligence report from our best source and it says that the North Vietnamese have changed their policy." And as you may have heard from other people, we had some particularly reliable sources on North Vietnamese intentions, and sure enough, this document read very similar to the document that the Politburo issued prior to the 1972 spring offensive. And, clearly, this 1974 document was a repeat. They were going to try it again. And we sent this to Washington, but by that time, the paralysis was arising from Watergate—so nobody could energize themselves to move. So that was a beautiful illustration that even the best intelligence isn't going to do you any good if you are unwilling to act or are unable to act.

The military regions sort of collapsed in numerical order. First, Military Region One, then Military Region Two, then Military Region Three. All right. When Military Regions One and Two collapsed, we were able to bring out our entire staffs from those regions. And those were evacuated with reasonable efficiency. Then the other Military Regions started to collapse. And things became more complicated. And Military Region Four—Can Tho—never actually collapsed, but people were anticipating the collapse. But their only means of transportation from Can Tho was first to Saigon. Now in the end, as you may have heard, on the last day, the Consul General there, Mr. Terry MacNamara, sort of established his own navy and came down the river, but that was after all the rules had ended. There were no more rules. Yes, individual officers tried to bring out people who worked for them and their families—and there again, we ran into the problem of the extended Vietnamese family. Our definition of family is different from a Vietnamese definition. So if we moved masses of people, and we had a lot of people who served in Vietnam, and now they suddenly remember that they lived there with a lady and the children, and now let's get her and the children—and in the last couple of days, certainly a good part of the CIA station's energies were spent in rounding up these long-forgotten relatives, and siblings, and what have you.

Everybody was doing the same thing. And the reason you had to do it that way was because you couldn't put an ad in the paper that said everybody that wants to leave for the United States report to Tan Son Nhut. And again I emphasize, and now it's a vow, you should have paid no regard, there was no law that would authorize us to take these people out. The law was ignored, but there was still no legal authority. And that's why we had to first take people to the Philippines, and then the Philippines said that you can't keep them there, and then we had to take them to Guam, and then the Navy said you can't keep them in Guam, because the typhoon season is coming, and those tents that we put up for 40,000 people won't stand up under those winds. So then we established these big camps where the Vietnamese were being held until the legal bureaucracy—the Justice Department and the Immigration Bureau—sort of found some modalities to cope with the situation.

At the very end, on the 30th of April, the numbers constantly kept changing, and you had two factors going. First, there was a great nervousness in Washington that there will be some incident. And second, the people in charge of the fleet naval operations felt that the pilots were flying beyond any reasonable level of endurance. And thirdly there was the consideration—and I think that Kissinger felt this particularly keenly—that maybe the North Vietnamese will lose patience and at daybreak they would storm the embassy and capture those of us still in it. And so—yes, at the end, a major flying helicopter Lady Ace 09 was given the order, "You will board the Ambassador on your aircraft, and that will be the last aircraft except for those to evacuate the Marines. And if the Ambassador doesn't follow you, you are ordered to physically carry him onto the aircraft." And that is when I left. It was about three or four o'clock in the morning, and for the last couple of hours all the remaining senior staff were in the Ambassador's office. There was no eating. There was no drinking. Everybody was quiet. There was nothing to be said. The Ambassador was still trying to argue with Kissinger about how many more flights there would be. Until we got this order. And we got it through the military communications network that Lady Ace 09 is supposed to take off with the Ambassador. And he must have accepted that this was a direct order from the President of the United States. And the Ambassador accepted that order, and then he told several of his senior staff that they would be going out, too. Certain people would be going out with him, and that happened to include me; and others would go with the

Deputy Chief of Mission, Mr. Wolfgang Lehmann. And the Ambassador's group ended up on the *Blue Ridge*, and Lehmann's group ended up on one of the landing ships. It was all very somber and very sad. The Ambassador's office was on the third floor. We took the elevator up to the sixth floor, and then there was a narrow little staircase that led out to the helicopter pad. And then we got into the helicopter, which was, I think, a CH-53, and off we went. It was traumatic and sad, but it was not dramatic in the sense of any hysterics or theatricals. By the way, in 1991 I went back to that rooftop in the Embassy. I went there as a consultant to British Broadcasting Corporation, and everything was exactly as we left it. The steel helmets of the Marines were still there. The sandbags were still there. The North Vietnamese hadn't done a thing to that rooftop. And I didn't want to have any problems with the Vietnamese, so I was identified as the former CIA station chief, and their reaction was, "We're so glad you came back." So returning to the Ambassador's departure. It was quiet, sad, but all these stories you might have heard about how the Ambassador and I were cursing each other and so forth; there was nothing like that. I don't remember anything closely resembling that. In fact, once we got on the *Blue Ridge*, the Ambassador and I had most of our meals together.

If ever there was a good man who was the wrong man at the wrong place at the wrong time, that was Ambassador Martin. Until he came to Vietnam, he had a very distinguished career. He was a colonel in the Air Force during the war, and then he made a switch, and he joined the State Department, but he joined the State Department at a relatively high level in the refugee relief administration program. So he didn't come up through the ranks. He sort of entered the State Department at the rank of ambassador. But then subsequently, he had some very lucrative postings after Paris where he was on this refugee program in the Marshall Plan. From there he went as Ambassador to Thailand, and from there, Ambassador to Rome. And from Rome he was posted to Vietnam. Now Ambassador Martin was a favorite of Nixon's for one very simple reason: not only was Martin a reliable and enthusiastic anti-communist, but after Nixon lost the California governorship in 1962, and he traveled to Thailand, most diplomatic posts didn't want to have anything to do with Nixon. I mean they figured that he was finished. Ambassador Martin didn't figure that Nixon was finished, and he invited him to stay at the residence, and he gave him the full treatment. And Nixon never forgot that. That there were times when everybody, sort of, was peeing on him, Martin stood by him, and treated him like a possible President of the United States. So when Ambassador Bunker's turn came to retire in '73, Martin is Ambassador in Rome, he seemed like a very logical choice. He was a southerner. He had had a couple of big posts. It was no problem that he would be confirmed as Ambassador, which with the Congress in 1973 you couldn't automatically assume that just anybody would be confirmed as Ambassador to Vietnam.

OK. President Thieu is coming to San Clemente in 1973, and some of us are invited to be present at this great event, including myself. And including Martin, the new Ambassador, who is not yet here. Martin got his marching orders from the Nixon, Kissinger, Halderman, Ehrlichman White House. And it was, carry the anti-communist fight to the North Vietnamese. And Martin sincerely and emotionally was for that. Even at the time, when shall we say, the applicability of that policy had passed. But nobody told him it had passed. His marching orders were never reversed, so whereas some people in the American Administration thought that we should be making some kind of a deal with the North Vietnamese, because it was never truly vocalized, but the attitude in Congress surely was that, "Let's bring this to an end. Let's stop the supplementals; let's stop the logistical support. The war is over."

Well, nobody told Martin that the war was over. And he counteracted any, however subtle, trend there may have been in South Vietnam toward normalizing relations with North Vietnam. And he actively sabotaged any possibility that this Provisional Revolutionary Government, that is, the Vietcong, would be given any kind of a policy role in Saigon. Now, of course, you know that the PRG was a sham. We always knew that. It was just a facade that the North Vietnamese put up for their own purposes to fool the credulous abroad. But, I happened to belong to the group that felt that going by the wartime example in France…Vichy France was better than occupied France. So I thought that we should go for some kind of a deal. Maybe it wouldn't have worked forever, but you know, on the other hand, maybe it would have. In Germany, it worked for a lot of years before it collapsed the other way—in the other direction.

So Martin was the wrong man in the wrong place. And he never could bring himself to adjust emotionally to the concept that the war was lost, and that everything that he stood for all these years is down the tubes. Then there was a particularly unfortunate incident that he got so personally engaged against Congress, and he not only lost credibility with Congress, but the cause suffered because of his constant arguments with Congress. He had a Congressional Delegation in February, I believe, of 1975, and Martin forced himself to go back to the United States on the same plane that the Congress went; they had their own plane, he wasn't invited; but he said that he had to go back because he had to have some major dental treatment. He went back, not only for the dental treatment, he also went back to argue for the supplement. Well, that battle was lost. He had the dental treatment, but, in fact, he was out of Vietnam from the end of February until the day that he came back with General Weyand, which I believe was the 30th of March, or thereabouts. So he was gone from Vietnam during a very crucial six weeks during which we had a sea change. And he never caught up with the fact emotionally, and even intellectually, I believe. He never caught up with the fact that the situation to which he came back to was not the situation which he knew so well when he left. That so much could have changed in six weeks. But, you know, we are talking about the collapse in Vietnam, and I mentioned the corruption, and I think the corruption was a problem. A problem, but not leading to collapse. We forget how quickly France collapsed in the spring of 1940. And that was a completely organized country with a wonderful infrastructure and no corruption and they had the biggest army in Europe, and yet when they got pushed where they didn't expect it, they collapsed.

Chapter 10

Leaving A Pregnant Lady

Richard Armitage, a former official in the State and Defense departments during the Reagan Administration, served four combat tours in Vietnam. As he assesses the collapse of Saigon, Armitage blames "gutless" senior American military personnel and "duplicitous" political leaders. Over the course of more than a decade, members of the joint chiefs of staff were more concerned about their positions than in offering fearless advice to policy-makers who "were crippled by duplicity," Armitage adds.[1]

By the spring of 1975, Armitage had returned to Vietnam as a special consultant to the Defense Department. He found the emphasis at the end of the war being placed on retrieving American assets instead of rescuing Vietnamese refugees. The image he uses to illustrate America's position is that we had become "a runaway dad."[2]

I had left military service after four combat tours in 1973, after the Paris cease fire agreement was signed. I then went to work in the Defense Attaché Office as the navy, marine, and later airborne advisor. I resigned that post. I came back to Washington in December 1974 screaming that Vietnam was going to hell in a hand basket. I screamed around the Pentagon but no one paid any attention, so I went home to San Diego.

I was home when Eric Von Marbod called me up and said, "Get to Washington." He said, "Bring your family because you aren't going to see them again for awhile." I took my wife to Washington and I met with Von Marbod. Eric said, "You're going to Vietnam tomorrow if you're willing. Here's the task." Officially, I was a consultant to the defense attaché. We cleared up the pay later.

Von Marbod, who I had gotten to know when he worked in the Defense Department's Vietnam office, came to Vietnam when I was stationed there earlier. I had taken him a couple of places, had gotten him shot at a few times, and he remembered it. In 1975, Von Marbod was the defense department's comptroller for Vietnam. He had responsibility for what we had bought South Vietnam. In 1975, he was intent to do what he could to deny those assets to the North Vietnamese. He was to get out as much as we could and destroy the rest.

As I mentioned, I left the DAO in December 1974 and returned to Washington. I could see it coming. I went back to Vietnam in March 1975, to Danang. There was no doubt that things were imploding. I wasn't very confident about the leadership in the embassy. That's why I had come back to Washington earlier and screamed. I didn't think I had gotten anybody's attention, but Von Marbod had heard.

The CIA station chief, Thomas Polgar, was the one who let down the home team. My understanding was that he listened to the Polish-Hungarian members of the ICCS. The unfortunate thing for us is that we could have gotten all the assets out; we had planned on having a couple more days to get this done. We were going by the intelligence. I have no question Tom Polgar was believing the intelligence he was putting out but he was using those people, the Poles and Hungarians, as his sources. They assured him that there would be more time. It was stupid. It prevented us from removing all the naval assets, small boats for instance, but we did have a lot of them destroyed.

I spoke Vietnamese. I was aware in December 1972, during the Christmas bombing, how close we had come to victory. That is a matter of record now. We had the sons-of-bitches on their asses and we let them go. I think Henry Kissinger lost his nerve and the president lost his nerve. Nixon was beginning to be weakened. Later, the Congress voted a cessation of all funds. It was over. It was over. You had a president who faced massive violation of the cease-fire and he couldn't intervene. And you had a Congress that said, "No more money." It was black and white.

While I served in country, during my military tours, I was opposed to massive numbers of American ground troops. "Why could we carry rifles better than the Vietnamese could?" But I believed in our effort to support the country. I resigned my commission after the Paris Peace Accords were signed because I found it very akin to getting a lady pregnant and leaving town. It's not a pretty image, but I thought we were a runaway dad.

On April 24, I flew into Saigon on the last Pan Am flight. The city was awash with refugees and was taking 122-mm. rockets at night. Refugees and rumors were the order of day in Saigon. Life had an eerie normalcy. It was very strange. On April 26, I went down to a base near Saigon that was under attack. I went in a jeep. There were endless lines of refugees in the highway walking toward Saigon from Vung Tau. They were full of provocateurs and spies, the enemy.

The admiral who went down there with me went into the base. There were wounded everywhere. One guy, a sapper, blew himself up while we stood there. We came under another attack. The refugees streamed by, unaware. It was surreal. The North Vietnamese were all around us. The South Vietnamese were fighting heroically. I used to be asked, "Do you trust them?" I always said, "I trust them 200% because I'm the guy with the radio. They know I'm the one who can get them out."

I had the benefit of four combat tours and I could speak the language. After my first tour, my wife will tell you, I came back so pumped up. I loved the culture. The second time I got frustrated. I wanted the South Vietnamese to go out and fight. By the third tour, I was balanced. There were some days you wanted to go fight and there were some days you would take a bye.

All of us wanted it over in a year because that was the length of our tour. The Vietnamese had a different time frame. The protest songs talked about a thousand years fighting against the French, the Chinese, a hated government. And, by 1975, they had spent twenty years fighting against each other.

On April 26, I went to see Eric and I said, "It's over." He agreed. I said, "We need to plan this evacuation." So I went down to navy headquarters and did it. The plan was, simply, to tell naval personnel that for reasons of safety they should come to the base. And then, when we gave the signal, we were to go the coast. The major ships would leave from Saigon. The smaller ones would make their way to the coast and be picked up by the larger boats. Unfortunately, our time frame and the time frame acknowledged by the communists were different.

On April 28, I went to Bin Hoa Air Force Base. We were bombed. Here was a deserted base, being bombed by the North Vietnamese. We were to get the equipment ready and destroy it. We operated forklifts. All of a sudden, some South Vietnamese showed up. The deal was, "If I get out, they would get out." So they started going to work for us. Then I got a call from Eric, "I'm sending a helicopter for you. Get out now." By this time we had thirty Vietnamese helping us. I told Eric, "I can't." So we continued working. All of a sudden a CIA proprietary airline, Bird Air, flying out of Thailand, landed, spun around on the tarmac, and we all jumped in it as the base was overrun.

We came back to Saigon and Eric was on the tarmac. We were being bombed. I said, "It looks like it's going to go." So we went down to navy headquarters and the next day we left.

I would like to think our government was happy with the refugees I got out. But I think they wanted the assets denied to the enemy. Of course, so did I. I didn't know any way to deny the assets and not accept the people.

Many Vietnamese were left behind because we lost those extra days. There was only so much space and so much time. I wish we had gotten them out.

Chapter 11

"Politics Is An Evil Thing"

As a computer expert, John Guffey sifted through electronic data and helped compile quarterly assessments which painted an alarming picture. (An example of his views is reflected in a memorandum that Duffey sent to his supervisor less than three weeks before the final evacuation of Saigon in 1975. A copy of this memorandum is included at the end of this chapter.) The truth, which Guffey attempted to tell, too often became twisted—"doctored"—into an inaccurate distortion of the steady decline of South Vietnam's military capabilities. It seemed almost that politicians—American and Vietnamese— wished that the hard facts could be ignored in hopes that a miracle might occur and the "game" could continue awhile longer. Guffey became cynical toward our policymakers and a Saigon government which he deemed to be corrupt and ineffective.

Guffey's relationship with Mai Dang, the Defense Attaché's administrative assistant, is especially interesting. Eventually, Mai and John would marry. But in the final days of the war, John's major concern was to insure that the two of them escaped what he remembers as "a very ugly time."[1]

We were lying like dogs. In the mornings, we would give briefings. The military and the ambassador would join the South Vietnamese for the briefings at 6:00 A.M. Then, all the Americans went across the hall to look at the real enemy situation. We knew that everything was getting worse. I loved the country and I loved the people. I came to almost hate us.

Their government, however, was so corrupt. Almost all the officer corps, practically to a man, were French lackeys. Practically all were from the north and they came south in 1954 when the country was partitioned. They voted with their feet. They were Catholics. The CIA dropped leaflets alerting them that "the Virgin has moved south." While 90% of the Vietnamese were Buddhists and only 10% were Catholics, the Catholics were the ruling class.

Ambassador Martin had good intentions but he was afraid of what would happen if we tried to jump ship. Even to the very last minute, he was afraid that the South Vietnamese would turn against us. I have the idea he was trying to look out for his own, but he fooled around way too long.

The DAO's legal officer [John Green] and I wrote letters to the deputy DAO, General Baughn. He was fired in early April because he was helping the Vietnamese get out early. He was doing this under the table. And when they found out about it, he was forcibly retired. He let his feelings be known and he was supposed to be one of the team. He wouldn't play the game.

The party line was "Vietnamization is working and it will work. All we have to do is furnish the means and they will do the rest of it." As you know, we piled tons of equipment in during the interim. And then it sat out there and rusted and rotted. Some ended up on the black market. It was terrible.

The Vietnamese have a different outlook than you and me. It is not bad to steal as long as you steal from someone who has more than you, or you perceive it that way. That's how you justify it. It is a societal thing. That is the way I saw it. I had twenty-two Vietnamese employees and I tried to stop their theft. My colonel told me "Don't play Don Quixote." Unbelievable! They view it as only fair because we were super rich and they were super poor. Mai made 29 cents an hour.

The money that they had went into gold and diamonds because it was the only way to protect yourself against 100% inflation. I had empathy for the Vietnamese people but I told them "You don't carry off the toilet paper." We placed a Yale lock on the toilet tissue.

Mai had had a suitcase by the door since December. All of the Vietnamese who worked there knew that we were leaving because the office had a mile long line of people mailing their stuff out. We knew in January. The communists had cut the country in half, and then there was the debacle up in Danang.

Even though we were not married at the time, I had Mai listed as my wife. Another lady was listed as my sister-in-law. And some kids were listed as my responsibility. The embassy didn't care as long as we paid the South Vietnamese a payoff. At the last minute, my "sister-in-law" decided not to leave. She was afraid that she would lose her severance pay. She was thinking about her security. I told her that if she didn't get out of there, there wouldn't be any severance pay. Anyway, I couldn't convince her.

Bill Estep, a civilian Air Force employee, had started getting people out early. Some of the evacuees were bar girls. You know, bar girls were not bad people. I would play cards with them and buy them $1.25 drinks. They were supporting fathers without hands—without feet.

When I would go out in the field, I was shocked. The Vietnamese military didn't know what to do with the stuff we gave them. Only four or five could speak English. The repair manuals made no sense at all after they were translated. Nothing worked anymore. They couldn't talk to one another on radios. They never could.

As I think back on the end, this whole thing was in retribution. Roosevelt promised Ho Chi Minh that Vietnam would be an independent country after World War II. Truman rescinded that immediately. He put the French right back in there. So, Ho fought the French who were getting our assistance. We divided the country and promised elections in six months. There was no way our boy [Diem] could win. Ho was a nationalist despite what else he was. Ho went to the communists because we weren't going to help him. So, there was only one other way to get it and that was through the Russians. Politics is an evil thing. And you can't be honest if you are a politician. And you have to lie if you want to win an election.

AOSCE-S Team 3   11 April 1975

MEMORANDUM THRU: LT. COL R.E. Shaw AOSCE-S

           TO: COL E.H. Graham AOSCE

Sir:

During my two month tenure in CE Division, Team 3, I have become
aware of serious deficiencies in RVNAF C&E capability. I have
witnessed widespread incompetentcy among so-called ARVN technicians. In observing technicians at the bench I noted:

    1. Keying transmitters without dujmy load or wattmeter

    2. Sending out inoperable equipment

    3. Connection of cabling to wrong place

    4. Usage of inoperable test equipment

    5. Operating 115V equipment on 90V power source without
step-up transformer.

    6. General inability to use testing equipment.

    7. Non-use of technical publications

    8. Lack of basic electronic theory and/or trouble-shooting

techniques.

I hardly believed my eyes when I saw the pile of equipment await:
repair at the Long Binh TMDE facility. Lack of tools, standards
and technical manuals was extant. Knowledge or application of
supply procedures was frequently absent.

I have read the monthly reports submitted by ECCOI and see formal
and on-the-job training given continuously but no references to
the shortfall mentioned above.

I was, for two years, responsible for writing portions and editing all chapters of the RVNAF Quarterly Assessment. In that
period I noted no references to this appalling state of C&E
within RVN. Where have we been?

AOSCE-S Team 3   11 Apr 75

We, DAO have obviously failed to bring these shortcomings to
the attention of higher US and RVNAF authority. Furthermore
no pressure has been brought to bear upon the lower echelons
of ARVN, at least not enough to alleviate the problems. We
are now emasculating our "technical assistance" and abandoning
our espoused goal of "self sufficiency" by wholesale RIF
and notice to leave country.

To be honest my faith in the RVN government and military is
minimal but I wonder if our contribution (not money) was less
than we should have provided. Are other aspects, VNN, VNAF,
etc, as shaky as CE?

I am not privy to the whys of the current situation but without
communications the RVN military cannot be expected to withstand
the coming onslaught. Without us (US) all is lost. Is this
the legacy we are to leave the Vietnamese people?

I ask that you reconsider Communications Electronics priority.
ARVN needs you more than ever in the current crisus. Your
influence, direction and technical assistance is more important
now than before.

                              JOHN H. GUFFEY
                              Maintenance Specialist
                              AOSCE-S Team 3

2

The South Vietnamese Helicopters Come in Waves

Chapter 12

Underground Railroad

During the dark days of slavery in this country, courageous individuals guided African-Americans along a pathway, an underground railroad. Similarly, an underground railroad ran in Saigon as the communists approached. One of the "conductors" on this freedom road was William Estep. He boldly made it possible for scores of Vietnamese to escape Saigon in the weeks which led up to the collapse.[1]

Today, Estep continues to try to communicate with Vietnamese who were not fortunate enough to catch a ride on the underground railroad. Estep, with the support of the Church of Christ, broadcasts a daily fifteen-minute radio program into the communist nation. His translator here in Oklahoma is a Vietnamese man well into his 80s who, a quarter century ago, rode on Bill Estep's underground railroad.[2]

The Vietnamese in our office were monitoring where the communists were coming down. They followed the advance on a big wall map. Some of our older employees kept saying, "Thieu will hold when they get to the flatlands" or "he will hold a little later." But things kept tumbling.

Two of the ladies worked for us there at the embassy. One of them worked for us in personnel for fifteen years and three months. The other one had worked for us for five or six years. You can imagine what would have happened if we had left those people there when the communists came in.

We were afraid that there would be no evacuation of Vietnamese. That's why we started getting them out as quickly as we could. We knew they were in danger. So, we started our own evacuation in the latter part of March.

When planes came in bearing supplies, we were getting people out on return flights. One of our group would use the mail trucks—you know, they had a canopy over the back—and he would haul a load of Vietnamese out to the planes. If anyone saw the trucks drive by, they would think we were just unloading mail.

Even people who had no papers on them, we just bundled them up and shipped them out. We would tell them, "Take one suitcase with you and that's all." Then they [State Department] clamped down on us. From what I heard, Kissinger sent a message which said, "You will stop that." The decision was made in Washington. We shut down for about two weeks and just sent out the furniture of the people who lived over there.

I left on April 25. It was chaotic. By that time, the evacuation had started full blown. Well, I came out on a C-130. I was the only American on board besides the crew. If I could have stayed a few more days, I could have helped a lot of others out. One of my friends, an American, was a helicopter pilot who had come over there to train the Vietnamese pilots. And when his contract was up, he stayed on as missionary. He and I were getting everybody we could out at the last. He left after I did. He thought he had stayed too long. He probably got out a couple of hundred there at the last.

Only one time did I feel in danger. I got my landlady out. And her two children. Her husband was a captain. Of course, he had to stay there and fight. And he and I were going out to dinner together—afraid someone would put two and two together—so I was to meet him down at a certain restaurant. And I was walking down the street on the opposite side. I went way too far. I ran into a group of Vietnamese. They were speaking Vietnamese. And they were giving me a tongue lashing. I was running off and leaving them. That was the only time that I was in danger.

After it was over, I was talking to Senator Bartlett. I told him I just wished there had been a wave of B-52s sent over to push the communists back. The Vietnamese themselves would use the C-130s and they would roll bombs off the back. That's a haphazard way of doing it. They would push crates that had two bombs in them. They would push them on the tailgate and drop them as they flew over the enemy.

You do what you can, but you can't do a whole lot. They had stopped us from getting people out. They had stopped the underground railroad. Someone wrote their friend in Saigon a postcard, of all things, telling him to go to a certain location and that Bill Estep can help you get out. Everyone at the post office read that thing. So when I came home that evening, Vietnamese were lined up on both sides of the corridor with their suitcases. I had to try to explain to them that it was over and I couldn't get anybody else out.

I've always thought that there was a lot of money being made on that war. The group of us that were trying to get the Vietnamese out there at the last had a pact among ourselves that we wouldn't take any money for it. We tried to live up to it. There is no doubt about it that there was a lot of money to be made on that evacuation, but I couldn't do that.

Chapter 13

The Fall Guy

Ann Hazard was the Defense Attaché Office's Chief Disbursing Officer. For twenty-six years, she had competently handled significant sums of money for American personnel stationed in Japan, Korea, Pakistan, Greece, and Iceland. She served two tours in South Vietnam (1964–1969, 1973–1975) and was quite familiar with the proper disbursement of funds. In the last days of April 1975, however, Hazard found herself entrusted with $11 million in cash which was to be used as severance pay and travel assistance for South Vietnamese allies.[1]

As the evacuation accelerated, three and one half million of these dollars could not be distributed. This sum of money was placed, on General Smith's orders, in burn barrels in preparation for incineration. As Hazard and the last remaining Americans exited Saigon, it appears that these barrels were not completely ignited. Satellite photos seem to reveal that the receptacles were not torched. While a subsequent investigation exonerated all American personnel, Hazard believes that she, as a civilian, became the scapegoat for the lost money.[2] The most significant portions of the investigation report can be found at the end of this chapter.

As the DAO staff was reduced, the concerns over jobs were foremost in everyone's mind. Where and when would the shoe fall? A member of another department who qualified for duty in my office on paper, but could not perform the actual duties, was eligible to "bump" a non-competitive employee who was my deputy and had been for many years. On paper the individual qualified, but by the employee's own admission, could not fulfill, or perform, the requirements of the position. Through all the turmoil, and knowing I was fighting civil service regulations, the controller was at my side and in agreement with me, as he knew I was concerned with the operation and welfare of the office, not in personalities.

During this time, additional money for the ARVN, proposed to Congress and promised, was turned down. The resentment was high among many Vietnamese officials and rumors of problems in the northern sector of South Vietnam became numerous. Then things began to happen with unbelievable speed. Provinces fell and the exodus began. The attitude expressed to me by many Vietnamese employees was that this collapse would bring the American GI back and, with his return, Saigon would be flourishing again. That is: black market, bars, bar girls, and good times. I think that to the very end they believed that the American military would return.

When the refugees began arriving in Saigon I was assigned the task to pay per diem to Vietnamese employees of the DAO and the U.S. Embassy. Prior to many of the DAO and embassy employees arriving in Saigon, they went to Danang, Nha Trang, Cam Ranh Bay, and so forth. With the arrival of the refugees in Cam Ranh Bay, a decision was made by the ambassador that I would be tasked with the duty of flying to Cam Ranh Bay, and seek out and pay the employees of the DAO and the embassy per diem. There were no U.S. military MPs, and so I was to take an ARVN chopper and proceed on the designated Sunday morning with millions of piasters and no U.S. military guard or civilian guard. I was well aware that the chances I was to take were very dangerous, as I knew the chaos that existed at Cam Ranh Bay. I don't know to this day if the decision for me to go came from the Deputy Chief of Mission (DCM) or the DAO Controller. I feared for my life, but no one with the exception of a U.S. Air Force major and an employee of the DAO civilian personnel office realized, or cared, about the danger of the undertaking. The danger to me, in my mind, was not the NVA or VC, but the South Vietnamese refugees who would have knowledge of the fact I was by myself and had millions in Vietnamese currency and no military guard. To be on the safe side, I wrote to a friend, who later proved to be my only friend, and truly believed me, and told her things were becoming hectic, and if anything happened to me, where my personal affects were, and so forth. I was frightened for my life, but I could not send any of my three remaining U.S. civilian employees as they all had small children. Saturday night, at approximately 2300 hours, I received a phone call from a DAO civilian employee of civilian personnel, and the U.S. Air Force major, telling me the DCM had cancelled the flight. No one will ever know how thankful I was to those two men, and in later months, the Air Force officer would again offer his assistance. Monday morning, the comptroller came into the office and asked me how things went—he had Sunday off while we were working seven days a week—it was then I told him the flight had been cancelled. He was angry, but the decision had been made by the DCM so he could say nothing.

Days passed and the fall of South Vietnam was a matter of weeks, but not expected until after the rainy season—so they thought. Many of us in daily contact with Vietnamese had doubts about the time left in the country.

By this time, the MACV movie theater was turned into a center where one could get married, baptized, divorced, passports-visas issued and, from reports, a circus that was as comical as the Ringling Brothers. Marriages were performed between U.S. males and Vietnamese girls that were never intended to happen, as many U.S. military personnel and civilians retired in Saigon never intending to leave. For them, life in South Vietnam was good and simple. Military retirees had commissary and PX privileges, and the black market on Tu Do and Nguyan Way Street, as well as the central market, flourished. The Commanding General encouraged Americans to come in from the cold and depart the country. In the meantime, many Americans were entering the country in an attempt to find former girlfriends, wives, children, and so forth, to take out of the country as the evacuation of South Vietnam continued to accelerate.

Daily, American members of my staff were further tasked with the assignment of paying Vietnam employees of the DAO and the embassy. This involved risks with cash, as the pay line had been relocated in the heart of downtown Saigon, and the only protection they had was Nung guards who had been previously wounded. The Vietnamese were becoming more and more hostile to us as they arrived from the Northern parts of the RVN. They had nothing and had gotten to Saigon in various ways as the cities to the north began to fall. One day, while I was conducting the pay line—we all took turns—a very irate Vietnamese female came into the pay line shouting at the top of her voice. I knew she was angry at Americans from the sound of her voice, but I didn't understand. I noticed my guard move closer to me and put his hand on his M-14. He had previously been with the Phoenix program and lost a leg. I asked him what was wrong with her, and he said she had worked for the American Counsel General in Nha Trang and had been asked by a member of the staff to remain behind and she would be taken care of by the Americans. (This is her story as the guard told it to me.) Somewhere, somehow, things became chaotic and she was left behind to find her own way out. Her husband was in the Vietnamese army; north or south, who knows; so she took her infant child and tried to get aboard one of the commercial vessels in the harbor. In the chaos, she dropped the child and it drowned. I didn't blame her for being angry, but her anger and hatred that she was shouting at me frightened me.

The other offices of the DAO were shipping records, documents, and so forth out of the country. But the DAO Controller would not permit me to do this. He did not have any knowledge of American civilian payment regulations, knowledge of the vital records concerning salaries and retirement, and so forth. On weekends, I was in constant contact with

CINCPAC concerning this matter, as he did not work, only to find out that he was having my calls monitored. Conditions became worse. The civilian payroll supervisor asked to be returned to the U.S. as she would have no part of the loss of records. It was only then that he finally asked me about the records. Then and only then, the records and the chief of civilian personnel pay were transferred to Thailand.

A decision was made to terminate all the Vietnamese civilian employees, and on a Saturday morning, when all the employees were off, my secretary was sent to find some of the employees to compute the pay. The first information I received from the Civilian Personnel Office was wrong and had to be returned, therefore delaying payment. The next information was in error but paid anyway as it was an underpayment that was later rectified. At that time, a decision was made by the ambassador to pay in U.S. currency. This was a violation of the rules of the Government of South Vietnam; however, the pay was computed and the payroll supervisor departed Vietnam on the last commercial flight prior to the crash of the C5A. Had she not departed on that flight she would have been on the flight that crashed.

One day, while I was out paying Vietnamese, my deputy called me and told me I was to return to the DAO immediately and report to the comptroller. On my way back I gave a friend a ride, which was to be the next-to-the-last time I ever saw her alive. The fall of Saigon, and events prior to and after the capitulation of the country, have left thoughts, anguish, and memories and scars that, over twenty years later, I have not been able to put behind me.

The crash of the C5A has never left me and my mental anguish with what I should have done continues to haunt me. As November 11, 1993 drew closer, I wondered if I had given a different answer to two of the victims, per chance they might have attended the memorial instead of being memorialized. I was the DAO Disbursing Officer at that time, and on two different occasions on that fateful day, I was approached by two of the victims to help them. I had been called to the headquarters and briefed and told to remain silent. One of the victims rode from the Brinks BOQ to DAO headquarters with me, as her department head had called her to report to his office. Upon my return, I was briefed to the fact the evacuation of DAO employees had begun, and I was to pay the employees thirty days advance per diem if they requested it. And the information that I was given was classified.

Later the lady that rode back to headquarters with me came into my office and said her supervisor advised her to come to me for assistance. I couldn't tell her what I knew. I could only ask her if she needed money and tell her where to go for briefing. She was on the C5 aircraft. Another lady came to my office accompanied by a marine major with an M-16 and begged me to help her—not with money, but to stay in Saigon. I told her I couldn't help her that way. She was also killed. From that day forward, I have lived with the guilt that if I had told the first lady what I knew, she could have, like others, just not reported to the briefing room and be alive today. Although I didn't stand much of a chance against a marine armed with an M-16, I always regretted telling the lady that if she didn't want to go, not to; per chance she would still be alive today. Most of the victims chose to get their money from their bank account, not draw per diem. I stood in the passageway as they left and many of them wished me luck getting out. Two hours later, they were dead.

As the evacuation of Saigon went on, conditions became more and more hectic. Finally, the only office that remained operational was the Disbursing Office, and we were so tired the embassy doctor gave my deputy and myself drugs to keep us on our feet. The people would come in the office demanding money, which I couldn't give, only to be called a slut, bitch and many other names; and our lives were threatened if they saw us outside the office. Conditions became so bad that an armed marine was posted outside the entrance to the office. On Saturday and Sunday prior to the fall, all was quiet. Monday, conditions became chaotic, and during the afternoon the Housing Officer told me I was to move into a BOQ closer to the base. I was berthed at the Brinks in downtown Saigon. As I was counting money, I told her that I would move at 5:00 P.M. that day. At 5:00 P.M., I asked my driver to take me to the Brinks to move, and as we left the air base, the air base was bombed. We went further into town and encountered a fire fight between the South Vietnamese Army and the South Vietnamese Air Force. I couldn't get through, so I returned to the base where the ARVN at the gate demanded my watch before he would allow me on the base. Luckily, some CIA officials came along and rescued me. Later that night, about 0200, civilian security guards took me downtown to get my clothes and said they would pick me up at 0400. They never returned, as the air base was on fire, marines killed, and so forth. When I couldn't return, I called the comptroller's office and told him that I would somehow get back and not to touch anything. He laughingly said marines were killed and hung up. A marine captain later came and got me, and by the time we got to the base the general had ordered the money destroyed and the comptroller had departed for the *USS Blue Ridge*. My deputy put the money in barrels, and a hold was put on burning, as the barrels were wired to the building, as was the satellite which provided communication with President Ford. We waited around until time to depart the country. I took a change of clothes out of my one small bag, put $9 million in negotiable instruments and blank treasury checks in the bag, and departed the country by a helicopter to a ship at sea.

The next morning the captain of the ship showed me pictures taken at 30,000 feet. The building had melted as had the satellite but the barrels were still there. Little did I realize at that time that my career was over.

We arrived in Subic Bay five days later. When I went into the replacement center, two DAO civilians were waiting for me and told me that they did not know what was going on, but signs were all over the place telling me to report to a certain Navy commander. I have long forgotten his name, but not the way that he treated my three civilian employees and myself. I reported to him and that was the beginning of a long journey; and I was treated like a criminal being investigated for stealing money, accused of embezzlement, and so forth. I was told to call Hawaii to be told by a U.S. Navy captain that my case would take a long time before "they" would be through with me. He would be relieved before they were through with me. I didn't know what was going on. I was being held in Subic Bay until further notice. Rooms in a hotel outside the gate at Subic Bay were found for us and we had to wait for a bus at the Officer's Club to get there. (Welcome home.) While waiting for a bus, I met a Special Forces Army captain from Saigon who had just come off the *USS Blue Ridge* where the DAO, the commanding general, the comptroller, the ambassador, and the DCM were aboard, and he told me what he had overheard about me, and asked what was going to be done. I remained in Subic Bay going through records and, in about three weeks, I was ordered back to Hawaii and to report to the Commanding General. I flew back and reported to the general. He informed me that he would have preferred to have a military in the position I had, and he had guessed I had performed my duties. (He was later to apologize for those words when he found out what really happened, but in no way can I forget or forgive those first words to me.)

During the months in Hawaii, I was ignored, berated, humiliated and insulted by members of the staff. These were people whom I had gone out of my way to help in Saigon. Only one, an Air Force lieutenant colonel, remembered how I had helped him. One Army colonel who was leaving on permanent change of station orders came over to say what I thought was goodbye, and his words were, "We sure have you where the hair is short, so you will be around for a while." A few days before that, he was asking me to do him favors. So many boards of officers were convened on me that I ceased to care and turned to booze. During this time, two employees of the DAO dared to be friendly with me, and I will never forget them.

I had tried to get the money out of Saigon prior to the fall, only to have the DAO controller cancel the flight, telling people that I had been relieved as the Finance Officer, which was not true. And when I tried to contact the general, his aide wouldn't let me speak to him. At that time, the aide was a lieutenant colonel. He retired as a brigadier general. For me, my career was over, thanks to him.

For many years I managed to put the guilt of two lives in the recesses of my mind as I struggled with my own problems related to the events of those fatal days. As Finance Officer, I was responsible for many things as the result of the capitulation of the country. Monies were lost, destroyed—both U.S. dollars and Vietnamese currency—both of which I was accountable for. I was evacuated by helicopter to the *USS Mount Vernon*. Upon arrival in Subic Bay, and many months thereafter, I was treated like a criminal by the U.S. military and their civilian counterparts. As the result of the investigation against me, I was never able to obtain another position of any responsibility within the Department of Defense. Applications for positions were returned to me marked "Most highly qualified, not selected." I was assigned to a position in the mid-West that was nonexistent, and any positions for which I qualified that came up within the organization, action was taken to change the series of the position, and select someone else. Although under Civil Service regulations I had priority, I was still ignored.

I struggled for a year until my health broke, and I retired with acute hypertension. I had lost contact with friends I formerly had. I was heartbroken to learn that some people thought I had not burned all the U.S. dollars, over $3 million for which I was accountable, but had stolen at least part of the money. The lease on my apartment, which I could no longer afford, expired, so I had to move. Again, I turned to booze and food. I did that in Hawaii, then I decided to leave the U.S. forever. I went to live in Paris where I traveled with the excuse that I was looking for work. But I well knew I could not work without a work permit, and I couldn't get a work permit without a job. In addition, I was not bilingual. I went to Russia with intentions of never returning. But after a few days there, I stayed with the tour and returned to the U.S. Time passed, and with the money I had left, I joined some friends in Mexico. And while spending a few days in Acapulco, I gave up. I observed the people I was with enjoying themselves in a world in which I could no longer cope. I returned to my cabana took twenty-one valium, washed them down with a bottle of champagne and a cup of scotch. When I didn't join the group again, some of the party came to my room but I had not even gone to sleep. I guess at that time, I had sunk as low as one can, and returned to Boston, Massachusetts after failing at suicide to struggle with my problems and get on with my life. The thing that helped me most was that I reluctantly attended a reunion with some former employees of the Officer-in-Charge of Construction, RVN, in Orlando, Florida, and there, for the first time, I told my story and confronted my problems. I had tried too hard to bury the past, I couldn't remember former colleagues. However, once the ice was broken I was able to talk, and I will be forever grateful.

.1 JUL. 1975

First Endorsement on Colonel Elmer H. Graham, USA, Investigation Report of 31 July 1975

FROM: Defense Attache, Vietnam

TO: Judge Advocate General, Navy Department, Washington, D.C. 20370

VIA: Commander in Chief, Pacific Command

SUBJECT: Investigation to inquire into the circumstances connected with possible losses/shortages of US Government funds which occurred at Saigon, Vietnam, on or about 29 April 1975

1. Readdressed and forwarded.

2. The findings of fact, opinions and recommendations of the basic report are approved.

3. The Defense Attache, Vietnam, emphasizes that the circumstances under which the individuals whose actions are under investigation were called upon to perform were uniquely perilous and severe. The losses of funds which occurred are considered to be remarkably small--individually and in sum--given that situation.

4. The Defense Attache takes great pride in the actions of all DAO personnel during the particularly trying closing days of the U.S. involvement in Vietnam. No group better served the interests of the United States than those individuals who settled outstanding accounts with the DAO local national employees who had served with such loyalty and dedication.

5. By copy of this letter, the Defense Attache requests, on behalf of the persons whose accountability is under investigation in the basic report, that the Secretary of the Navy grant relief for all subject losses and overages of funds.

H. D. SMITH
Major General, USA
Defense Attache

Copy to:
Secretary of the Navy (w/enclosures)
Navy Finance Center (w/enclosures)
Colonel Elmer H. Graham

31 July 1975

FROM: Col Elmer H. Graham, USA

TO : Defense Attache, Residual USDAO Saigon Office

SUBJECT: Investigation to inquire into the circumstances
         connected with possible losses/ shortages of US
         Government funds which occurred at Saigon,Vietnam,
         on or about 29 April 1975

Ref: (a) JAG Manual
       (b) NAVCOMP Manual

Encl: (1) Appointing order of the Defense Attache of 24 June 1975
       (2) Summary of enclosures (1) through (45)
       (3) Sworn statement of   of 1 July 1975
       (4) Sworn statement of   . of 17 July 1975
       (5) Sworn statement of   of 3 July 1975
       (42) Sworn statement of   of 10 July 1975
       (43) Sworn statement of   of 21 July 1975
       (44) DAO MSG DTG 152135Z Jul 75
       (45) Certified copies of Cash Receipt Certificates

Preliminary Statement

1. In accordance with references (a) and (b) and pursuant to
enclosure (1), COL Elmer H. Graham, USA, has conducted a formal
one officer investigation into the shortage/loss of $8,032.87
by the Defense Attache Office (DAO) disbursing officer (DO)
and shortages/losses of funds in the amount of $150,401.47 by
DAO Paying Agents.

2. The method used to conduct the investigation was to closely
question all personnel having knowledge of relevant actions who
were present in the Hawaii area. These persons were then assis-
ted in formulating sworn statements attesting to facts they knew.
Persons not residing in the area were sent a list of detailed
questions to be used by them in formulating sworn statements.
Statements thus obtained were sifted and facts were compared
and analyzed and findings of fact were produced. Statements
of opinion and recommendations were then formulated from the
facts.

3. Due to the complexity of the subject, the report of investigation is structured with the following features:

    (a) One preliminary statement is made which relates to
all accountable persons whose actions are under investigation.

    (b) Sections I through XVII are provided, one for each
accountable person, presenting separate Findings of Fact,
Opinions and Recommendations. Section I deals with the
accountability of the DAO Disbursing Officer,

The remaining sections deal with the various agents of the
disbursing officer -- paying agents, imprest fund cashier and
custodian of miscellaneous funds.

    (c) A concluding statement of opinion and recommendation
relating to the investigation as a whole is included below as
an aid to readers who do not require the detail contained in
the various sections.

Concluding Opinions

1. That a shortage in the accounts of the DAO Disbursing Officer, in the amount of 17,197.21 US$ and an overage in the amount of 5,339,387 VN$ (equivalent of 7,072.03 US$) may be treated as a shortage of 10,095.18 US$ and was the result of the abandonment of some 5,000.00 US$ in change during the evacuation of DAO Saigon and cumulative counting (cashier) errors made by exhausted personnel handling a very large volume of money.

2. That various losses in the accounts of paying agents were the result of a combination of (in minor degree) counting errors by disbursing personnel prior to turnover of funds to agents, and (in major degree) cumulative counting errors by paying agents who were inexperienced and required to count large quantities of new Treasury notes under conditions of high stress.*

3. That no violation of pertinent instructions and regulations occurred which were not justified by or understandable in the light of the deteriorating military situation in the Republic of Vietnam in April 1975.

* It is useful to hypothesize that counting errors occur in a random manner; however, it is to be expected that the magnitude of such errors would be biased towards overpayment. This is because underpayments would almost surely be brought to the attention of the paying agents for redress while overpayments would not necessarily be so reported.

4. That in almost every case, each accountable person behaved in such a way as to bring credit upon him/herself and the U. S. Government.

5. That subject personnel performed under very trying circumstances where many persons around them were in fear for their personal freedom and safety and during a time when regular functions of the U.S. Mission were at best abnormal.

6. That no theft or other criminal act was committed by the persons whose accountability is under investigation.

Concluding Recommendations

That the Defense Attache, Saigon, in behalf of all persons whose accountability has been investigated and is reported herein, request relief from the Secretary of the Navy for losses of funds entrusted to such personnel incident to their assignments as DAO disbursing officer and agents of the disbursing officer.

ELMER H. GRAHAM
Colonel, USA
Investigating Officer

Chapter 14

An Ad Hoc Plan

At the Army War College in Carlisle, Pennsylvania, Colonel Stuart Herrington teaches a generation unscathed by Southeast Asia about the war which still haunts him. As a military intelligence officer, fluent in Vietnamese and married to a native, Herrington was part of the commission which regularly traveled to Hanoi in 1974 and 1975 to discuss the missing-in-action issue.[1]

Sensing the end approaching, Herrington shipped his belongings back to the United States in early 1975. In late April, Herrington had a front row seat to watch the disintegration of our ally. He continues to be frustrated by members of Congress who wished to renege on our commitment to South Vietnam. He has spent a quarter of a century dissecting the micromanagement and political factors which hampered the last days of our ally. Herrington contends that the images of thousands of unruly South Vietnamese shoving themselves onto overcrowded helicopters are misleading. Rather, he stresses that one more hour of flights could have transported to safety the last 420 Asians we left behind in the embassy's parking lot.[2]

Here is what I believe happened, and I have really spent a lot of time trying to figure this out. I can tell you that in the White House, now that I have sat down with Kissinger and talked about it, that the word was constantly being passed that the walls of the embassy were not secured and that if we evacuated for another two weeks we would still have 2000 left. The picture that was arriving in the White House situation room on which the decision to call a halt was made was that it was out of control. Yet, it is clear that—and the Ambassador personally came down and so did Lehman and they walked in the parking lot and they knew that the situation was under control. We were getting the word into the embassy. I believe the embassy communications were up until midnight–1:00–2:00. The CIA communications were open until at least 2:00. There was a telephone there which, up until midnight, they could call out to the DAO. Just pick up the phone and call the Emergency Evacuation Center. What I think happened is credibility was lost during the day of the 29th. In other words, and maybe it is true that during the day the crowds were growing; and then the buses came back and deposited more; and there were a certain number of wall jumpers. Every time we turned around, and just when we thought we

were getting it under control, we would find another 200 people hiding in one
of these buildings; or there would be some guy who would arrive, you know
some American would arrive with his whole family, and there would be a big
struggle to get him in. So, for a long time during the day, the report of the
numbers just did stay up there. I think it is the man who cried wolf. What I
think happened is that there were so many reports. Choppers were coming in
and taking people out, but every time they asked, the same number of people
seemed to be there. They stopped believing anything they heard out of the
embassy. And I heard the statement made that, "Martin has lost it." "Martin is
too emotional." "Martin is trying to evacuate the whole city of Saigon through
one conduit, the U.S. Embassy." So I believe what happened was—those
numbers, the smaller numbers, were getting out and not believed, and were
filtered by the time they got to Washington to where Deputy Secretary of
Defense Clifford, on the phone to the JCS, was telling Kissinger and Ford,
"You have got to call a halt to this. The pilots are tired. Someone is going to
get killed and the North Vietnamese patience has run out. The situation and
morale is still a mess at the embassy. Martin has lost his objectivity." And that
is what Kissinger is being told. At no time did anyone say, "Finally, they've
got a handle on it. Now they are down to a thousand. Now they are down to
four hundred. If they get eight more birds it will be a clean sweep." That word
never got to the decision makers.

Dr. Kissinger said that there are those that say generals shouldn't run
squads. Or why was this in the White House? His answer was, "We had it by
default. No one wanted to touch it. The Pentagon didn't want to touch it. The
Pentagon position was, basically, if there was to be an evacuation they wanted
to pull the Americans out and leave. Period! The Ambassador wanted to take
out as many Vietnamese as possible. The President wanted to take out as many
Vietnamese as possible, and I wanted to take out as many Vietnamese as
possible. We were the only ones, the only ones who had that sentiment in
Washington—Ford and me. If Schlesinger was left to do it, Schlesinger was
going to do a Phnom Penh, Operation Eagle Pull. He was going to come in and
take out the Americans and go, and the President felt, and I felt, that was
unconscionable. We had to take out as many Vietnamese as possible. We had
let the Vietnamese down and we needed to not compound that by ignoring
those Vietnamese to whom we had a debt. So by default; meaning no one else
would execute it with any view to anything other than the quickest of
operations, rather than an all day, all night, flying way beyond what safety
regulations permit, in the face of sixteen North Vietnamese divisions; the
White House took control."

So what Kissinger says, and I accept this; at least on the fact that I have
seen Schlesinger on the screen state that he said, "Mr. President, we need to get

the Americans out." And, I had seen President Ford—I have got President Ford's book. Everywhere I go it is clear to me that the depiction of Kissinger was—that the only way to go was to prolong the evacuation. Oh, and Martin agreed. Martin wanted to prolong it to get out Vietnamese. He had made commitments. He was in Saigon. He had all of these Vietnamese in that embassy, and all the U.S. Information Service personnel. Kissinger negotiated the Paris agreement. Kissinger got the Nobel Peace Prize. The whole thing came crashing down. This is yours, Henry. This is your mess. You handle it. And his depiction of why it was being run out of the White House versus the Pentagon was that.

Now, you may ask the secondary questions. Why wasn't it being run right out of CINCPAC or Thailand? Well, I can only tell you that if you know the history of the Vietnam war, and of command and control, and the patterns of command and control that developed in the Vietnam war, you know that President Johnson scheduled the targets for the bombing. The concept, however flawed, of long lines of micromanagement from Washington, is grounded in the—you know, the whole history of the Vietnam war. So should we be surprised that in the last chapter, it was one of the major flaws in the execution of the war? I mean, central planning and decentralized execution is the concept that we try to teach when you teach command and control. This thing was centralized planning and centralized control of the executions, step by step. Kissinger was ordering how many more helicopters there would be. The only thing that I can tell you is that the Vietnam war was characterized by that flaw for the whole conduct of the war. The war itself was such a traumatic mess. So misexecuted that by the time you get to the collapse of Saigon, with all those Americans involved, the buck stopped where? I mean Kissinger says, "I didn't have a lot of advisors that night." Meaning, "This is yours. You signed the agreement." But, the specifics as to why in Washington—. The White House versus the Pentagon was very clear to me. Why it is in Washington and not decentralize the field bothers me. Because we did stupid things like that for the whole war. It would have been just as easy, in hindsight, for the President to have sent a message out to the field, or as the Commander-in-Chief, forced the Secretary of Defense to send a message out to the operating forces saying, "I want the evacuation to make maximum effort to bring Vietnamese out, consistent with the safety of Americans." And, that would have been a recipe for the commanders on the ground to have stopped that evacuation 12–24 hours sooner than they did. Guaranteed!

You think about it. If you are a commander, and you are commanding the helicopters, and you get guidance which says that I want you to take as many Vietnamese out as you can consistent with the safety of Americans, and you are flying helicopters in there, and Tan Son Nhut is being rocketed, and the

South Vietnamese are firing an occasional potshot out there, and there are sixteen North Vietnamese divisions armed with triple A, and you have one chopper go down in the water with what turns out to be mechanical failure, and the pilots are flying the limit of their endurance, and it is night and it is raining, and the landing zone is a postage stamp; those are an invitation for you to call a halt to it. If we would have done that, it would have ended 12 hours sooner. I am aware that the Marines were gutsy. Of course, the Marines had guys on the ground in that embassy. The Air Force didn't, they quit flying, as you know, off the *Midway*. They got to 18 hours or so, and stopped.

As a military man, in principle, I deplore the command and control of the whole war being in the White House. It just isn't the way we do things now. President Bush said, "We are not going to do that." But, as someone on the ground who personally wanted to get as many Vietnamese out as possible, that evacuation, by virtue of being run in the White House, was carried out approximately—at least 12 hours longer. There was great pressure during the day of the 29th to stop it at sundown and then consider resuming it in the morning. And these were the options considered, and the White House said to press on. So my own belief is that, however I deplored it was being run out of the White House, knowing what Schlesinger's desires were, had it been left to him, we wouldn't have gone as long as we did. We would have left more than 400 people in the embassy. We would have left 1500.

Martin was fearful that if he commenced a visible evacuation, that he would accelerate the fall of the country, thereby lose the country sooner, and thereby lose more people, possibly including Americans. So he was like a deer in the headlights; that is what it was. While he was like a deer in the headlights, privately General Smith's people were moving people out by the thousands; and Martin, in my opinion, was not a dumb man. Martin kinda knew what we were doing. General Smith explains in great detail in the C-Span symposium about the authority he felt he had from the Ambassador to evacuate, without calling it an evacuation. He said, "Mr. Ambassador, every single salary, every penny that is paid to keep this huge DAO open, is money that is out of the security assistance account. If you will permit me to draw down the DAO, drastically, all of those dollars which would be used to pay these people could be used for purchasing ammunition and security assistance." We had one account to help the South Vietnamese and our entire swimming pool was being paid for out of that account, as well as ammunition for their artillery. General Smith was very clever. He told the Ambassador, "I need to draw down because the money will be freed up to use to fight off the North Vietnamese." The Ambassador agreed. That was how Smith managed that. Under that umbrella guidance, we ran to daylight. We put people on that airlift that you wouldn't believe. They were legitimately frightened. Afraid that the embassy was going to be stormed. They had heard that Judge and McMahon had been killed.

Ten thousand people around the embassy is nonsense. Journalistic exaggeration. I once sat with a guy at *U.S. News and World Report* who swore there were 10,000 people around that embassy. I said, "You know, I don't think you know what 10,000 people look like." You were down in the street and surrounded and you were being buffeted and there was crying and wailing and weeping and gnashing of teeth, but if you would have been able to hover fifty feet above and look right and look left, you would have found that you were in a crowd of five hundred (200 were just watching). Then the Air America choppers were landing on the roof and were dropping people off. People were being brought into the embassy by Air America from all over Saigon. The CIA was going out and picking up people whom they promised to get out, and they were bringing them to the embassy with the idea that they could be brought out of the embassy in buses, and when the bus thing broke down, they kept bringing them here with the idea that we get them out with heavy lift. People were frightened. You could see these folks praying before their turn on the helicopter comes. You could see them sitting quietly on the roof. We would bring them out in groups of 100. If it was a big CH-53, we crammed and peeled ten off and put ninety on. If it was a little helicopter you could divide them into half and put fifty on. Eventually, we backed all of the black sedans around us, all pointing in, and ran the engines and turned the headlights on. Then the embassy engineer and I found a carousel projector and we put it up on the roof of the firehouse and when the choppers came in we just turned on the carousel. Big white square line. It had started to rain by dusk. We decided to put the choppers down up on that rooftop pad. The embassy engineers said that it wouldn't hold them. We said, well, we will find out, won't we? We did this because we needed to run two landing zones simultaneously to get these people out. So around dusk, the 46s started landing up there, and the 53s in the parking lot. One right after the other, and we fed the people in the stairwell by the hundreds. Eventually, we had to pull those people out of the stairwell. All night the CH-53s came.

I was home on Christmas leave in December 1974. During the time that I was home they attacked Phuoc Long Province, which was the province to the north of Saigon. They came out of Cambodia and they actually captured the whole province, including the province capital. The South Vietnamese did not have the wherewithal to eject them. All of the plans that we had said that we would bomb the you-know-what out of them in the event that they were definitely violating the cease fire act in a massive way. None of that happened. This is December 1974, and President Nixon resigned in August of 1974, and morale in the South Vietnamese armed forces is very, very low. All the cuts in military aid have been announced. Then Phuoc Long was seized and we did nothing about it. Nixon was gone. And Nixon made the commitments without the Congress signing up to help in case of a violation. Nixon said that we will give you the tools to do the job if the fighting continues, and if they violate the cease fire in a massive way, we are with you. We didn't give them the tools to do the job in that the will wasn't there from the Congress to continue authorizing aid. Congress felt that you could end the war by cutting off the weapons and help for the South Vietnamese, which was right. Strange way to end the war. When Phuoc Long happened, and nobody did anything about it, I knew from that event that we did not have the will or wherewithal to contest the North Vietnamese. The morale amongst all of my Vietnamese friends was defeatist. I concluded when I arrived back in Saigon, contacted my friends, and did sifting about, that the situation was hopeless. And so I quietly began to step out. Take steps. Contacting my counterparts and essentially setting up little codes. If you hear from me and I tell you about the party in my apartment in Saigon, it is time to get away. It was not fashionable and I didn't run around crowing. In fact, I brought the boxes in to mail them out just one at a time, and I was very discrete about it.

The problem was that the Congress had already passed the Church Amendment which said no military forces can be employed in, under, around, or near Southeast Asia or Indochina. And the injection or the reinsertion of American military power in a war fighting mode would have obviously been in violation, and it would have been hell to pay, no question about that in my mind. The problem was that you had a commitment in writing from Nixon to respond with full force, which was one of the things that Nixon used to influence Thieu to sign up. So you have the President who is responsible for the conduct of foreign policy making a commitment in writing on the one hand, and you have the Congress on the other hand saying "time out." Congress doesn't agree, and it is the Congress' role, constitutionally, to raise armies and navies and to go to war or not go to war. There is no question in my mind that the only way that President Ford could have avoided a constitutional crisis and to intervene in January 1975 with bombing, for example, would have been to have gone to the Congress and said, "Our credibility is at stake. We have lost 58,000 lives here. These people are our allies. This is a flagrant violation of the treaty. My predecessor made a commitment that if this happened, the bombing would resume, and I therefore request a resolution from the Congress to permit bombing." And do you know what would have happened? They would have laughed in his face. He would have never gotten it.

I go places and do things and I come back and read about it and I say, "If that was Panama, then where was I? If that was Saigon in March of 1975, then where was I?" The media frequently misses the mark. They frequently miss the mark. Was there looting and public disorder in Saigon in the last 24 hours? You are darn right. But was there at any time a threat to the evacuation aircraft? Did they ever shoot at evacuation aircraft? Did the North Vietnamese take any steps to keep us from getting out of the city? They did just what they told us in the beginning. They gave us time to leave. No question about it. Sometimes the media just go for sensational footage or media people are not trained observers. They get into a situation—but then, if a media person is not a trained person, then who is? But, the media reported 10,000 people around that embassy. I am here to tell you that they weren't there. I was there from roughly 9:30 in the morning on the 29th all the way through the end. And there were tense confrontations at the gate; poignant things, poor people holding up letters. That embassy had a crowd control problem at the gates. A couple hundred people pushing and screaming and shoving and young people climbing up on the walls and being screamed at by the Marines. And another crowd, the secondary crowd, standing along the far side of the street just basically gawking.

Amongst that group that we left behind were a significant number from the South Korean Embassy, including the military attachés from the South Korean Embassy, of whom one or two of them were South Korean intelligence officers. These guys, a couple of them were taken up to Hanoi and put in prison. My understanding was that at least one of them was beaten to death. General Summers knows more about that than I do. We left behind some of the staff of the South Korean Embassy. And, of course, those poor embassy employees, those firemen. By that time, we had gotten all of the Americans out of that crowd. The rest of them—now I realized that everybody says, "Well, the people in the embassy were Vietnamese to whom we owed an obligation." The truth of the matter is that all of the attempts to develop this in an orderly way—get the Vietnamese employees to whom we had an obligation—get them into the embassy so that the right Vietnamese were taken out—that was all good intentions, but it didn't work. When push came to shove, Vietnamese got into that embassy, over the walls or through friends, who no more had a greater claim to sanctuary in the United States than any other Vietnamese. And the Vietnamese who should have been in that embassy frequently couldn't make it to that embassy. But to characterize those left behind, I would only say that amongst them were embassy employees and their families, and some members of the South Korean Embassy; and there was a German priest down there, as I recall, that had helped us, who was one of the unlucky ones. The rest of them were just a hodgepodge of Vietnamese. I couldn't characterize who they were, but I do know of those who got out that day, it just depended if you were in the right place at the right time, then you got out.

I wrote *Peace With Honor*—first of all, I didn't even write the thing until 1980 because I was so angry by the time I went off the roof of the embassy. It was clearly not a time to write. It would have been an emotional hip shot. That is the problem with Frank Snepp. Frank Snepp writes too soon, apart from his other character flaws. But I finally put pen to paper. The first outline of the book was drafted in December 1976, but all I did was write an outline. *Peace With Honor* wasn't written until fall 1979 and spring 1980. Then it was rewritten in 1982, before it was published by Presidio. There was a certain mellowing even up to that point. The last chapter of *Peace With Honor* was an attempt to say, "Okay, there is the story, and now what does it all mean?" You notice that I tried to be balanced about it. That is the hard part. I tried to be balanced about it to Dr. Kissinger because I was quite angry over the Paris agreement. I felt that it was a sellout. It was a precipitously signed thing, but if you read carefully the story of the negotiations, and what was dumped on Kissinger; in hindsight, you have to hear him out. Where you can read him in his memoirs, this was a terrible thing to come in on your watch. Five hundred forty-three thousand Americans in Vietnam, and as Kissinger has said, the people that had put them there had all joined the peace movement. Then, all of a sudden he and the President were faced with extrication. Dealing with an adversary who held all of the cards and who didn't live by the same kind of rules of international conduct that we do (i.e., that treaties should be obeyed and executed). And the North Vietnamese signed the treaty, which was only a tactical gesture on their part, to achieve the goal of getting the Americans out. Once the Americans were out, they knew that they then could eventually have things their way. So yes, I feel that I have mellowed about it. It wasn't understandable to me in 1980 or 1975, and it remained a mystery for me for all of those years, but now that I have had a chance to find out what happened. I know that the culprit—. Where did the news get filtered out? Somewhere between the parking lot and the White House. Somebody filtered it out; decided not to report it, or decided that it was not credible, that we had a finite number. And I don't know where that was, but it was somewhere in the military chain of command.

This is just a tiny little molehill, the issue of 420 people. My view is that, during the period of that evacuation, when the dust settled, 130,000 people got out, and we pulled approximately 2,500 out of that embassy. General Smith got out of DAO another 3,000 or so. And there was no plan to pull anybody out of the embassy, other than a few off the roof, and then a few buses—a couple hundred people. We came up with an ad hoc plan, created right there on the spur of the moment. Then we executed it, and we exceeded any reasonable expectation—to include the flyers who flew down that terrible vertical pipeline into that little square parking lot. I focus on the 420 people because it was very painful for me to be there in the parking lot with them, meet with them, and promise them that we were not going to leave them. But in the broader perspective of the whole show, this is just one more tiny tragedy. It is not a big story.

HEADQUARTERS
U.S. DELEGATION, FOUR PARTY JOINT MILITARY TEAM
APO San Francisco 96393

FPJMT-NE   14 April 1975

MEMORNADUM FOR RECORD

SUBJECT: Saigon-Hanoi Liaison Flight of 11 April 1975

1. Flight: The flight was routine. Departure was at
0830 hours, with arrival in Hanoi at 1200 hours. At the
request of the RVN Delegation, departure on the return trip
was moved up thirty minutes in order to provide for an
earlier return to Saigon. RVNDEL's concern was the early
curfew in Saigon. Arrival in Saigon was at 1930 hours.

2. Significant Observations: Gia Lam Airport was quiet.
DRV airport personnel directed the C-130 to park approximately
200 meters from the main terminal. A bus was provided to take
all passengers to the reception room. A PRC AN-12 "Cub"
transport aircraft was parked near the end of the runway. A
30-man Peoples Army work detail had completed unloading its
cargo and were preparing to load the wooden crates onto trucks.
The city itself was crowded with military and civilians alike.
The center of town (near the Hoa Binh Hotel and Museum of
History) was bedecked with brightly-colored banners. The
theme of all was the "GIANT VICTORIES" in the South. Vertical
banners (hanging from utility poles) depicted crossed "PRG"-
DRV flags, and slogans celebrating the "Brotherhood" of the
Liberation Movement and the DRV. Other banners proclaimed
"Congratulations: Liberation of Hue - 26-3;" "Liberation of
Da Nang - 29-3;" "Hearty Congratulations to the soldiers and
the people of the South on their general uprising and gigantic
victories;" "1975 - the year of victory!" Outside the Hoa
Binh Hotel, laughing children reached out to touch the hand
of one USAF officer as be boarded the bus.

3. Significant Conversations: Upon arrival in the Gia Lam
Airport Reception Room, I immediately informed Major Huyen that
SPEC 7 Bell's wife and son had been killed in the crash of the
C5A in Saigon. I also informed our DRV hosts that Miss Barbara
Kavulia, a secretary in the USDEL, had also been killed. DRV
personnel were silent upon hearing this news. There were no
expressions of sympathy offered - just embarassed silence.
The silence was broken by Major Thinh, RVNDEL, who asked the

FPJMT-NE   14 April 1975
SUBJECT: Saigon-Hanoi Liaison Flight of 11 April 1975

DRV to arrange the day's itinerary to permit an early departure
because of the new curfew in Saigon. Although this request
took me by surprise, I supported Major Thinh, and suggested
that we could shorten the souvenier-buying time. I had already
agreed with the RVNDEL and the USAF crew that we would curtail
our purchases, informing the DRV that we had donated our
spending money to the refugee/orphan relief effort. When I
told Major Huyen this, silence again descended - this time for
almost ten minutes. Only when the bus had reached the Long
Bien Bridge did Major Huyen speak. "Our Foreign Ministry has
denounced the US scheme of refugee-orphan relief as a crime
similar to those committed during the Hitler era." I replied
"Major Huyen, I have always believed you to be an educated,
intelligent person. Therefore, I refuse to accept that you
really believe what you just said." The silence that followed
this exchange lasted until five minutes after lunch was served.

     At lunch a somber mood prevailed until one of the RVN
officers asked the DRV personnel when they planned to visit
Dalat. This remark seemed to unplug the dike, and several two-
way exchanges broke out simultaneously. The atmosphere was
vitriolic, sarcastic, and angry. The USDEL interpreter, Mr.
Ngo, has recorded large portions of his conversations with
DRV personnel in the attached report. His report accurately
depicts the mood of that unusual luncheon, and I concur with
his conclusions concerning the attitude of the DRV escort
personnel. While Mr. Ngo was sparring with his escorts at one
end of the table, the following conversation took place between
me and other DRV personnel.

     Mr. Quang (DRV Ministry of Public Security): We are in
the process of building a better system - a socialist system
superior to your political system in the United States - just
as the Soviet Union is superior to the U.S.

     CPT Herrington: Excuse me, Mr. Quang, but when was the
last time you were in the Soviet Union?

     Quang: I haven't been there yet.

     CPT Herrington: Oh? How about the U.S.?

     Quang: Not yet.

     CPT Herrington: Germany? France? England?

     Quang: (Shakes his head)

     CPT Herrington: You mean you've never been overseas?

     Quang: Not yet.

2

FPJMT-NE   14 April 1975
SUBJECT: Saigon-Hanoi Liaison Flight of 11 April 1975

CPT Herrington: Excuse me, Mr. Quang, but I don't see how
    you can compare the various political systems if all you
    know is what you've read in books. Let me make you an
    offer. You go to your Ministry of Foreign Affairs and
    request a passport and exit visa. I'll give you my parents'
    address, and when you arrive in the U.S., I will personally
    guide you. We can then go to Europe. I've been to West
    Berlin. We could visit East Berlin one day and West Berlin
    the next. Then we could go to the Soviet Union. When our
    travels are over, Mr. Quang, then perhaps you can lecture
    me on your view of comparative government - but, I'm sorry -
    not now.

(Silence)

    Oh, I forgot. They won't let you go, will they. That's
    too bad - but maybe some day your government will open its
    doors. If so, my invitation stands. I would be pleased to
    escort you - or you, Major Huyen.

MAJ Huyen: (Flushed and angry) I was on the first plane that
    landed in Saigon after the cease-fire! (Turns angrily on
    Mr. Ngo - who has first made a comment on Socialism) Mr. Ngo,
    you don't know anything about Socialism or Communism. The
    United States must stop its violations of the Paris Agree-
    ment. In particular you must implement Article 21.

CPT Herrington: I'm sorry, Major, but hearing you demand that
    my country implement the cease-fire at the very moment
    nineteen   North Vietnamese divisions are south of the 17th
    paralled - that is just funny - very funny.

MAJ Huyen: What about Article 4 (U.S. will cease its military
    involvement in VN) and Article 5 (Total withdrawal of troops,
    advisers)?

CPT Herrington: How can you talk about this and not mention
    Article 7? That's the article which says you are forbidden
    to infiltrate 19 divisions into the South.

Mr. Quang: (Speaking to Major Thinh, RVNDEL): It is clear
    that President Ford is throwing you away.

MAJ Thinh: You obviously did not yet hear President Ford's
    speech this morning.

MAJ Huyen (interested) : Oh! What did he say.

3

FPJMT-NE   14 April 1975
SUBJECT: Saigon Hanoi Liaison Flight of 11 April 1975

MAJ Thinh: He reaffirmed the U.S. commitment and asked for
     722 million dollars in immediate military aid.

MAJ Huyen: How will be get it? The US people are fed up with
     the U.S. intervention in Southeast Asia.

CPT Herrington: It's true that U.S. opinion was divided on
     military aid to the RVN. But, your current offensive and
     complete refusal to cooperate in the purely humanitarian
     refugee relief effort have united the U.S. people against
     you. A month or two ago, an appropriation of 300 million
     dollars was regarded as difficult to obtain - now, however,
     President Ford is taking advantage of the new mood in the
     States to obtain a more realistic aid appropriation.

MAJ Dien: (Euphoric) We are establishing a real democracy -
     Where the people live in true freedom.

CPT Herrington: I know. The first free elections have been
     held in Hue, Danang, and Nha Trang - and the people voted
     with their feet - just as the Russian Soldiers in 1917.

The meal ended as it began - in silence. While in the bus on
the way to Gia Lam, Major Huyen told me that he didn't think
there was any reason why Americans and Vietnamese cannot be
friends. "I have been an Americanologist for years, and I see
Absolutely no obstacle to good relations between our two
countries." Major Huyen stated that he admired and respected
me, and "Ithink I know what is in your heart." I expressed my
hope that the future would see peace return to Vietnam, but told
Major Huyen politely that based on our lunchtime conversation,
I seriously doubted that he really knew what was in my heart.

At Gia Lam Airfield, our departure was delayed because CPT To
and SGT Lan allegedly had a flat tire on their jeep. After ten
minutes, a phone call was received - and I was told that CPT To
and SGT Lan would remain in Hanoi. (Note: This means that
CPT To - Press Officer and Negotiations Assistant - and Major
Mai Nguyen - DRVDEL Secretary - are both in Hanoi - while COL
Tu and LTC Bao - Chief & Deputy - are in Saigon). I had the
impression that there was no flat tire - CPT To just wasn't
returning.

Finally, as the aircraft was about to start - a DRV customs
officer ran up to the door and thrust a small "gym bag" into
CPT Traylor's (USAF pilot) hands. The bag weighed about 12
pounds, and had a paper label reading "Send to Mr. Luong Manh."

FPJMT-NE   14 April 1975
SUBJECT: Saigon-Hanoi Liaison Flight of 11 April 1975

I took the bag, felt it - and instructed Mr. Ngo to run out
and return it to the owner - explaining that there was no one
named "Luong Manh" on board. Mr. Ngo complied - and the owner
took back the bag. There is no one named "Luong Manh" in any
of the FPJMT Delegations (RRV, DRV, "PRG"). Whatever the bag
contained - at a minimum it was contraband cargo - I was unwilling
to keep it on board. All official DRV cargo is loaded at one
time - and DRV cargo handlers are very sensitive about U.S.
personnel touching it.

4. Suggestions and Recommendations: As revealed by this report
and its attachment, U.S. Delegation Local National employees,
in the service of our government, continue to risk frequent
exposure to both "PRG" and DRV cadre. I strongly urge that
immediate steps be taken to insure priority consideration of
these people in the event that it becomes necessary to evacuate
the US.mission from the RVN.

                              Stuart A. Herrington
                              STUART A. HERRINGTON
                              CPT, USA
                              Negotiations Staff Officer

Chapter 15

Another Plan

As a nineteen-year-old graduate of the Vietnamese Naval Academy, Leon Nguyen participated in an earlier large-scale evacuation. In 1954, after the French debacle at Dien Bien Phu, Nguyen sailed into Haiphong harbor and guided anticommunist elements to safety in the south. Twenty-one years later, Nguyen was the Fleet Commander of the South Vietnamese Navy, and on that occasion he would oversee the evacuation of thousands of his compatriots as Saigon collapsed.[1]

Nguyen's command of the English language is impressive and is the result of three assignments at United States bases. His life today is a comfortable one because of his engineering degree from the University of North Carolina at Charlotte. His sharp analytical, planning, and organizational skills are tested daily—as they were tested in his homeland a quarter of a century ago.[2]

Let me start by saying I was very fortunate to witness the withdrawal of our troops from Central Vietnam. By that time, the spring of 1975, I was Fleet Commander and I had most of my ships out there. The night we evacuated Danang I was with the Commander of I Corps. We were in a bunker in Danang. The base received numerous rocket attacks from the communists. I was there with the Commanding General of the First Division. As the rockets exploded, the general said, "Let us withdraw, retreat, disband." There was panic there, real panic.

The general and I were flying in a helicopter and we were shot down, not exactly shot down, but we got a bullet in the gas tank. So the pilot said, "Let's make an emergency landing right there on the coast—on the beach." And just several feet away was Vietcong territory. But we were lucky and radioed another helicopter, and they picked us up. So I have witnessed from day one the withdrawal, the withdrawal of all Vietnamese troops from Nha Trang and Danang.

I went back to Saigon, my headquarters. The situation was not too clear. I got my staff together and asked, "What should we do?" We said, "Let's keep our men on ships and keep fighting." But in order to do that, we needed to provide some kind of safe haven for their families. That was the conclusion of my staff. So we loaded our ships with provisions, dry fish and rice. I sent men to get as much rice as possible. Then I passed the word out,

"Whoever wants his family with you in a safe place, fill out an application and send it to the commanding officer." There was lots of response. That was my plan. And that was two weeks before the fall of Saigon.

I was relieved of my command because this plan was considered by headquarters to be counterproductive. They said that this plan, having the families on board with my men, produced a false sense of alarm among the troops. So they relieved me of command as Fleet Commander. But the plans were ready. The plans were there.

When the final days came, we were able to execute my plan without me in command. By that time there were eighty-one ships in the command; landing craft, troop transports, patrol craft, destroyers, cutters. Everyone turned to me to lead them. I was able to get all of the ships that could move on their own power out.

A couple of small ships went on their own to Subic Bay. But the majority of the ships went together in a line. They came to me and said, "Show us. Forget about what headquarters has done to you." So I took the fleet again and we headed to Subic Bay. Nobody else at headquarters had the frequency of the Seventh Fleet. I was the only one.

We exited Saigon, went to Con Son Island, then to Subic Bay. I was able to contact the Seventh Fleet and alert them to our whereabouts. We got some fresh water. Our flagship was Number Five. I have tried to get some figures of how many people left with us. It was 22,000 or 23,000 people.

We went straight to Subic Bay and we turned our ships over to the U.S. Navy. We had an emotional ceremony as we lowered our flag. The Seventh Fleet assigned to each one of our ships one junior officer—a figurehead. We were instructed to disarm. We threw away our ammunition. Before we arrived in Philippine territorial waters, we conducted a ceremony. We lowered the South Vietnamese flag. We raised the American flag.

The Philippine government was scared. They didn't want to let us in. They were scared of the Vietnamese communist government—that there might be some retaliation later on. But we raised the American flag on our ships and saved them from the communists.[3]

My immediate family flew out on April 28. The DAO plan was to get the families of the senior officers in a safe place. They flew my family directly to Guam, all six of my children and my wife. The youngest child was ten months old.

I didn't know the country was about to fold until the DAO came and discussed the problem. He asked about my family and asked whether or not I wanted them evacuated. I said, "Yes." I wrote my former American boss, Admiral Mathews who was then working for a U.S. Congressman, "Take care of my children. I might not see them again."

My in-laws went out with me by ship, but my own parents decided to stay. Since I still had my grandmother living there, my father stayed behind. He suffered under the communist regime for six years. He was a branch manager of a bank. He was placed in a camp and then forced to train the new manager.

On the first flight out of Subic Bay to Guam, there were all the South Vietnamese admirals and generals and me. I wanted to find my family. By that time, early May, they were already safe here in America. Admiral Mathews had connections. When my wife arrived in Camp Pendleton, California, he was able to fly them to Mechanicsville, Maryland. I joined my wife and children there exactly one month after the collapse.

There seemed to be only one way for me to leave South Vietnam and that was by sea. We saw all sizes of boats. Some South Vietnamese helicopters flew out to our fleet. We had only one landing pad. Some pilots would fly low, go near the water, and just jump out. We were on our own.

Ambassador Martin should have been more visible. Before the evacuation, General Smith came to me. They assured me that they would get my family out; they honored that promise. They also promised that if that time came, they would send a helicopter for me. But on the last day, there was no helicopter for me. It was panic. As we were overrun by the communists, I headed out to sea with my fleet.

Chapter 16

Not A Teheran Situation

During our visit with Wolfgang Lehman, deputy chief of America's Saigon Embassy, we noticed that the former diplomat remained cool, calm, and unemotional about the events that swirled around him during the spring of 1975. From June 1973 to March 1974, Lehman had served as consul general in Can Tho. His final post was as Ambassador Graham Martin's deputy.[1]

In his condominium's study, photographs of various officials lined the wall. One of particular interest is not of a diplomat, but, rather, of Admiral Stansfield Turner, who served as Jimmy Carter's Central Intelligence Agency Director. In early 1975, however, Lehman was the dispassionate envoy, methodically preparing for whatever fate awaited South Vietnam. He argues, in our interview, that the communist offensive was "not as easy as they thought it would be." Clearly, nevertheless, the North Vietnamese sensed that time was on their side. Spiraling oil prices, withdrawal of American troops, a reduction in financial support for the Government of South Vietnamese by a skeptical U.S. Congress (see the message from the embassy to the Secretary of State at the end of the chapter) all boosted the communists—as did a December 1974 meeting between North Vietnamese officials and their allies in Moscow.[2]

Lehman stresses that, considering the chaotic circumstances occurring in South Vietnam during the spring of 1975, the evacuation was professionally handled. As he and Ambassador Martin, in the early hours of April 30 sent the State Department "the last message from Saigon," he "turned off the lights in the tunnel" and headed for a helicopter.

We began packing and sending out embassy files and records at the beginning of April or maybe it was even early March. This was the kind of thing that we could do quietly. Nobody would see that. Things could be packed up and shipped out. Our records were going all the way back to the United States. We also, for example, had the bubble that had to be gotten out. That's a rather large and unwieldy thing and, of course, that was a visible act. Most people really don't know when they see big pieces of plastic lying around in the courtyard, so that was sent out. Whatever documents that were not sent out at the time or taken out by us individually along in our briefcases toward the end were destroyed, including some during the night of April 29 to April 30. In any event, everything was either sent out or destroyed. Nothing fell into anybody's hands. This was not a Tehran situation. I get rather upset every once in a while when I still read stories about the situation in Tehran having the greatest intelligence loss since the evacuation of the embassy in Saigon. We didn't lose anything. Also, the same applies to the consulate generals. The consulates had either sent back or, in their cases, mostly destroyed, all their files and records. That's true for all four of them.

There was a research reactor in Da Lat, so-called Triga reactor, that had been part of the U.S. AID program many years before. After Tet 1968, there was some nervousness in certain circles in Washington about fuel elements of that reactor. I recall distinctly then, when I was director of the office of atomic energy, and then Paul Nitze in the State Department, being approached by the Atomic Energy Commission to get those fuel elements out at the time. Ambassador Bunker quite correctly just ignored that nonsense. In any event, we did want to get the fuel out in April of 1975. Again, it was one of those things where we wanted to act in time but not before time.

For about a week before we finally decided—and I did—to move those fuel elements, there were a couple of special C-130 aircraft standing by at Clarke Field in the Philippines with technicians and the equipment necessary to pull the fuel elements out of that small reactor. I finally permitted them to come in and go ahead with that. I believe it must have been around mid-April. Then we did preserve the proper forms in all of this as much as I asked the Vietnamese government to give me a formal letter requesting that we remove the fuel elements, and they did so. It was a slightly hectic operation. The NVA was beginning to approach the area. This was in the highlands, of course. It took all night, but it was done and properly done.

First of all, let's keep in mind that at this point we had been operating around the clock C-141 and C-130 flights from the airport since Monday, April 21. In the middle of that week and the latter part of that week a kind of lull set in on the battlefield. There wasn't much by way of North Vietnamese offensive action. But, they were beginning to approach Saigon. It was shortly after that a rather tough battle at Xuan Loc, where the ARVN had really distinguished themselves and fought very well, indeed. At that time there was, of course, some speculation as to the reason for that lull. There are two possibilities. One was that it reflected a political decision in Hanoi to have the whole business end in some form of an ostensible government of national reconciliation which they always said they had wanted. This would have been, of course, a complete farce—with the idea of negotiating with President Minh, who had replaced Thieu. He was, therefore, from their standpoint the ideal candidate with whom to negotiate this charade or farce.

The other possibility, of course, was that, having conducted extensive offensive operations, they simply had a logistical problem and needed to regroup and reorganize. There is still a third possibility that it was a combination of both of those things. In any event, the first option I mentioned, if it was ever considered, was dismissed. In retrospect, it is probably evident that the lull was due to a need to regroup, reorganize and look after their logistics.

On Thursday, I decided that the time had come for us to evacuate the last of the wives who were simply the wives of senior officers including my own, Hank Woodrow's wife, Nancy Bennett, the wife of the political counselor, and one other lady and two children who we still had. They were the children of the divorced consular officer, Peter Orr, whom we had to retain because we needed him in our operation. I also had Mrs. Martin on that list but her name was deleted by the ambassador. To do this we had the Army send in a U-21 from Thailand, because we didn't want to have the departure of the senior wives noted out where most of the evacuation was taking place. We also needed to maintain the fiction that they were simply going to Bangkok for an extended weekend. That was done on Friday, April 25.

The lull, as I mentioned, did continue through Sunday, April 27. Beginning on Monday morning, April 28, it became quite clear early on that the North Vietnamese were actively resuming their offensive operations. At about six o'clock in the late afternoon on Monday, April 28, a number of A-37 aircraft, obviously manned either by North Vietnamese or defecting South Vietnamese pilots, attacked the flight lines at Tan Son Nhut airport.

At the time that occurred, I had just left my office and gone out into the second courtyard of the embassy in the area where the swimming pool and the snack bar were located. I had gone there to straighten out the problem that was reported to me about having buses with evacuees leave from there to go to the airport. This was an area where we were assembling evacuees to bus them to the airport. I was told there was a problem of a delay and I had gone out to look after that just at the time that that air strike in Tan Son Nhut took place. Now, there have been some rather lurid accounts of that particular event. When the strike took place, it precipitated a certain amount of quite unnecessary rushing around and a bit of upset. I might note parenthetically here that, being a veteran of the Italian campaign of World War II; including the Casino Line, the Anzio Beachhead and quite a few other events; I can differentiate between the difference of unfriendly high explosives coming down in your immediate vicinity, in which case you would have a very strong, direct personal interest, and something that is happening a mile or two away. In that case you can afford to take a detached professional interest in what is going on. This strike at Tan Son Nhut, lurid descriptions in some books to the contrary, was in the latter category. It was quite a distance away. There was no immediate danger to the embassy or anybody in the embassy. This did not prevent our very solicitous, protective Marines from immediately surrounding the minister with weapons drawn to protect him. This was very touching but it was somewhat overdone.

On April 15, sometime earlier, we had activated an evacuee holding facility out at the DAO compound. The system was that anybody being evacuated by fixed-wing aircraft—which, as I mentioned, were operating around the clock beginning April 21—would come out there or be bused out there either from the embassy itself or from some other designated locations in town, notably staff housing areas. That was continuing at that late date, until the air strike on the flight line at Tan Son Nhut on Monday evening. The attack on the flight line in which at least one C-130 was destroyed in effect ended the fixed-wing airlift.

The air strike took place at six o'clock in the evening. After we had rather quickly assessed the situation and in the course of the next hour, a decision was made that it would be too risky to continue fixed-wing operations out of Tan Son Nhut because of the danger that we might lose an aircraft full of people. The people that were out at the DAO compound remained there. The people that were in the embassy at the time remained there for the time being. After we had made the decision to discontinue fixed-wing operations, the rest of the evening was taken up with reviewing the final plans for the increasing likelihood, but not yet a decision, that we would have to go to a helicopter evacuation—which is technically known as option four of "Frequent Wind"—the following day.

That went on throughout the early evening. Shortly after midnight—the night from Monday to Tuesday morning—the ambassador decided that he and I should return to our residences and try to get some rest in view of the likelihood that a lot of major and crucial decisions had to be made the next day. I got back to my house between one and two o'clock in the morning. I tried to get some sleep.

With regard to most of the staff, we had earlier worked out a shift system. Because we had designated certain elements of the mission to worry about various categories of potential evacuees—the defense attaché to worry about the Vietnamese military, the political section to worry about politicians, and other people to worry about relatives of Americans, etc. These things had gone on a shift basis somewhat earlier so that nobody would work more than about twelve hours or so. That was the attempt that was made. For the absolute senior staff, it was on a more irregular basis.

You got what rest whenever you could.

The helicopter evacuation plan called for some of the helicopters to land on the roof helipad and others—notably the rather heavy CA-53s that the roof pad could not support—land in the courtyard of the embassy where this famous, beautiful banyan tree was located. It always was obvious that, when push came to shove, the tree would have to come down. One of the problems here, however, was that the tree was not only large but it was also very visible from the street. The streets were getting increasingly crowded as panic was beginning to slowly develop in the city of Saigon. The removal of the tree would be a visible act that would undoubtedly spread like wild fire throughout the city.

As I was returning from the outer courtyard and surrounded by my solicitous Marines to go back to my office to assess the situation and try to find out just what had happened out at Tan Son Nhut, I was passing the tree. As I was passing the tree, one of our Seabees was vigorously but somewhat ineffectually chopping away at the tree with an axe in what was quite clearly a self-initiated attempt to clear the area for use as a helicopter landing zone. As I entered the embassy chancery building, I called the security officer to promptly have the Seabee cease and desist from the rather ineffectual and somewhat premature efforts, to bring in some power tools such as chain saws, etc., have them ready, but not to take any action regarding the tree until instructed and until the time was right. I then forgot about the tree and turned on to other things that we discussed in response to an earlier question. As a matter of fact, I'm not sure that Graham Martin ever knew anything about the tree.

I didn't really get any sleep. I got to bed between one and two and dozed off for a while. At about 4:15 A.M., I was roused from my dozing by a series of explosions out in the direction of the Tan Son Nhut airfield and the defense attaché compound. About ten minutes later, at about 4:30 A.M., the phone rang and the report—I don't recall now whether it was directly from the defense attaché or from an officer at the embassy chancery—was that there had been a rocket attack on the DAO compound and that two of the embassy Marine security guards out there had been killed.

That, of course, ended the rest period. I got up, showered, went down, and my major butler gave me some breakfast. I packed some extra underwear, an extra pair of socks and a couple of little things in my briefcase. I had a last conversation with my butler who had previously told me that he did not want to leave and wanted to remain. He was an elderly man. I made some final arrangements with him to get some money to him in addition to money he had already been given—that's dollars, not piasters. That money, incidentally, was delivered to him later by Bronson McKinley and Bob Martin. After having a little breakfast, I went back to the chancery.

Ambassador Martin arrived from his residence just a little bit later. We jointly began to review the situation, getting reports from General Smith out at Tan Son Nhut as to the details of the rocket attack which intermittently continued throughout the area. Other facilities were also being spotted, but it was the first time, at a little after four that morning, that an attack appeared to be targeted specifically on an American installation. The cause of the death of the two Marines was a direct hit on the sandbag emplacement in which they were. It was just one of those things.

Ambassador Martin decided to go out to Tan Son Nhut and review the situation personally with General Smith. While out there, he had a telephone conversation with General Scowcroft back here in Washington which, however, did not result as yet in a definite conclusion on whether or not we would continue fixed-wing airlift rather than go to option four of the evacuation plan. Ambassador Martin then returned to the embassy. Meanwhile, it became very clear that damage to runways at the airfield and other things made it quite impossible to continue a fixed-wing airlift. Ambassador Martin then got on the telephone again, this time from the chancery, with General Scowcroft. A decision to go to option four of Frequent Wind, the helicopter airlift, was made between 10:30 and 10:40 on Tuesday morning.

The initial moves by helicopter directly out to the fleet were by Air America helicopter. We were using Air America, our own helicopters, first in the morning to move people from the assembly areas either to the embassy or to the DAO holding facilities out at the airfield. Later on, we were using the Air America helicopters to move evacuees directly out to the fleet. The plan called for the Marine ground security force to arrive at the DAO compound at Tan Son Nhut—which had priority on the evacuation under our plan—one hour after the option four execute order was given. To illustrate that plans would go wrong, the ground security force arrived three hours later and not one hour later. Of course, the first helicopter evacuees, using fleet and Marine Corps helicopters, were on those same choppers that brought in the security force and then would lift evacuees back out.

This was between one and two in the afternoon. That delay cost us something at the end of the whole operation. I found out much later that the reason for that delay was that there had to be some cross-loading out at the fleet to carry the Marines that were supposed to come in to secure both the DAO compound and the embassy compound and were not the same ships as the helicopters were. They had to move people around.

By early or mid-afternoon, the embassy was surrounded by masses of people—mobs. The security situation became increasingly risky. It was only with some difficulty that we managed to get into the compound. Some people for whose evacuation we had really special responsibilities—for example, Trang Kon Gu, the leader of the Vietnamese Labor Federation, and his people; Mu Vien, the minister of the interior; Tran Van Lam, the former foreign minister who had signed the Paris agreement. Nonetheless, all this was accomplished, but the security situation was really getting touchy. I, therefore, telephoned General Carey, who was out at the DAO compound, and told him that we urgently needed about a platoon of Marines in the compound, in addition to our embassy guards, to maintain the security. These arrived about an hour later. The famous tree, incidentally, had been removed and gotten out of the way well ahead of time.

I was not in Ambassador Martin's office when he had the conversation with Washington which resulted in the decision to execute the helicopter lift, but several of the other senior staff people were. I was busy in my own office doing various other things on the telephone. After the decision was made, Hank Woodrow walked over into my office, told me the decision was made, and I went back to see Graham Martin to have it confirmed directly. I then walked out and told the security officer now to chop down that tree. The tree was chopped down long before anybody was ready to arrive by helicopter in the embassy courtyard. Timing was, indeed, quite adequate.

By the time we're talking about, all Americans still in the area were either at the DAO compound or in the embassy compound. A little bit earlier some of the last ones, including some journalists, had arrived at the compound and gotten through into the compound only with some difficulty to get through the crowds. I should be quite accurate here. All those who wanted to leave—there was one fellow, a contractor who turned out later on to somehow not get the word. It was his own fault. He was left behind. Then, of course, there were a couple of journalists who stayed on deliberately.

The priority was evacuation from the DAO compound at Tan Son Nhut. So most of the initial lift by helicopter went out of the DAO compound. That operation was completed by 2000, 8:00 in the evening on Tuesday. On its completion, General Smith and the few remaining DAO staff left a few minutes after eight that evening. That ended that phase of the operation.

Up until that time, we had relatively little lift out of the embassy compound. It is correct, of course, that that lift—which was really only beginning in the mid-afternoon out of the embassy compound—did involve the lighter helicopters, the CH-46s—from the roof. The heavy ones, the CH-53s, were from the courtyard where the famous banyan tree had previously been. We were putting as many as 70 people into a CH-53, which was overloading it somewhat. Since many of them were Vietnamese, they were rather small.

What all these poor people were desperately trying to do was to get into the compound with the hope that somehow they might be taken out. There was an occasional shot fired from outside the compound, but we could not really determine whether that was directed at an incoming helicopter or not. In any event, it did not in any way interfere with the operation. At this point, we did have enough Marines to secure both the inner and the outer embassy compound, although occasionally someone might have slipped in who shouldn't have. It did not affect anything.

In the course of the evening—and I can't remember exactly when it was, but I suspect it was around 8:30 or 9:00—the military suggested that we suspend further helicopter operations and resume them at first light the next morning. The ambassador and I vetoed that very promptly and insisted that we would have to continue the operation throughout the night. That insistence was based on both what the intelligence were still able to gather about the North Vietnamese—and there were some that were still available to us—and on a judgment that the situation around the embassy, even with the larger Marine detachment was becoming increasingly untenable.

At that point we may have had somewhere between 1,000 and 1,500 people in the compound, both American and Vietnamese, with a heavy preponderance of Vietnamese. During the night, therefore, the lift continued, although at times there would be long intervals which, in our view, were excessively long intervals between arriving helicopters from the fleet. I understand, and I think we understood then, that there were deep problems of refueling, fatigue of the crews, etc. But it was clear that the operation definitely had to continue and could not be stopped and resumed the next morning.

The pilots could not see their way in. The situation in the courtyard was dealt with by having embassy cars parked around the perimeter of the courtyard with the headlights on. That illuminated the courtyard situation, which was a tricky thing for the pilots. It was very tricky, because of walls and antennas and other mass nearby that they had to get over before they could clear the courtyard with their heavy loads.

One of the things that became a matter of some concern is that sometime around midnight or a little bit later it began to rain very lightly. Remember, we were now in April and at the beginning of the monsoon. It began to rain very lightly, and the mere fact of water on the hulls of the helicopters added to their weight. So we had one very critical moment where a pilot with a load full of people tried to lift out of the courtyard and could not get enough altitude. He had to put back down and they had to unload some people before he could get out. They did not want to get off. So that was a moment of great concern because, if we had an accident in the courtyard with a broken helicopter, that would have finished the lift out of the courtyard and we would have had to rely entirely on the smaller choppers coming in on the roof. As I said, we could put as many as seventy people in the CH-53s, and I think the maximum number in CH-46s might have been about forty.

There was no panic among any of the people. We had people waiting in the courtyard. We had people waiting in the stairwell of the chancery building to go up to the rooftop, but there was no panic. At one point, when we had reduced the number still waiting to a more manageable proportion, we abandoned the outer embassy courtyard—the area where the swimming pool, the snack bar and the administrative section were—and moved everybody into the inner courtyard which gave us also a smaller perimeter to protect against the crowd outside.

As to priorities, well, you know, your priorities as far as we were concerned—the first obligations, of course, to Americans. Certainly, the second was to any high-risk Vietnamese—to our employees. But, we did not have a priority question as such arise. The small group that in the end was left behind that I mentioned earlier, largely due to the fact that the entire lift operation began about two to three hours later than it should have, was a mix of Vietnamese and Koreans.

At about four o'clock in the morning, the ambassador and I went to the remaining communications setup, the last one. We sent our final message. The date-time group of that message was 291215 Zulu which, of course, is Greenwich time. The message said, "Plan to close mission about 0430, 30 April local time. This is the last message from Embassy Saigon."

DECLASSIFIED

 Department of State **TELEGRA**

SECRET

AN: D740221-0655

PAGE 01 SAIGON 10622 01 OF 02 130814Z

10
ACTION SS-30

INFO OCT-01 ISO-00 /031 W
--------------------- 051188
R 130440Z AUG 74 ZFF5
FM AMEMBASSY SAIGON
TO SECSTATE WASHDC 7710
INFO SECDEF WASHDC
CINCPAC HONOLULU HI
COMMUSSAG NKP THAI

S E C R E T SECTION 1 OF 2 SAIGON 10622

EXDIS

EO 11652: GDS
TAGS: MASS VS
SUBJECT: FY 75 DEFENSE ASSISTANCE TO VIETNAM
REF: A. SECDEF DTG 072210Z AUG 74
B. CINCPAC DTG 080611Z AUG 74

1. THE RECENT ACTION ON THE HOUSE FLOOR FURTHER REDUCING THE FY 75
MILITARY ASSISTANCE LEVEL FOR VIETNAM TO $700 MILLION IS DEEPLY
DISTRESSING. IT COULD HARDLY HAVE COME AT A MORE INOPPORTUNE TIME
FROM THE STANDPOINT OF ENCOURAGING THE NORTH VIETNAMESE TO CONTINUE
AND PRESS THEIR MILITARY OPERATIONS. WE HAVE MADE FULL USE OF THE
MUCH APPRECIATED PROMPT AND FORTHRIGHT PUBLIC REACTION BY THE
STATE DEPARTMENT'S SPOKESMAN AND SECDEF'S ANNOUNCED INTENTION
TO URGE THE SENATE TO RESTORE THE FULL AMOUNT REQUESTED IN THE
BUDGET IN ORDER TO REASSURE THE VIETNAMESE.

2. I HAVE REVIEWED THE ARITHMETIC WITH GENERAL MURRAY. IT IS
CLEAR THAT $700 MILLION APPROPRIATION WOULD AT BEST LEAVE ABOUT
$475 TO $500 MILLION TO THE RVNAF IN ACTUAL ASSESTS IF THE CURRENT
GROUND RULES UNDER WHICH VARIOUS UNPROGRAMMED AND UNEXPECTED
COSTS ARE CHARGED TO THE DAV PROGRAM ARE NOT MODIFIED IN A MAJOR
WAY. (IN ADDITION TO THESE ITEMS ENUMERATED BY CINCPAC IN
REF B WE NOW UNDERSTAND WE ARE TO BE CHARGED FOR DAMAGES INCURRED
TO AIRCRAFT BEFORE THEY LEAVE THE US AND THAT THE AIR FORCE
PAGE 02 SAIGON 10622 01 OF 02 130814Z

SECRET

DE ASSIFIED

SECRET

LOGISTICS COMMAND PLANS TO CHARGE TO DAY SALARIES OF PERSONNEL
ENGAGED 75 PERCENT OF THEIR TIME WITH VIETNAM PROGRAMS.) EVEN A
RESIDUE OF $475 TO $500 MILLION ASSUMES A DRASTIC CUT IN ADMIN-
ISTRATIVE COSTS INCLUDING PERSONNEL CUTS WHICH WE CAN HARDLY AFFORD
AND A REDUCTION OF OVER 50 PERCENT IN CONTRACTS INCLUDING CURTAIL-
MENT OF VITAL SERVICES SUCH AS AIRCRAFT MAINTENANCE AND COMMUNICATION
S
SUPPORT.-

3. THE REMAINING $475 OR $500 MILLION WOULD LEAVE NO FUNDS FOR
ANY INVESTMENT ITEMS (OTHER THAN THE 77 F-5ES WHICH WE AND THE
VIETNAMESE WERE TOLD WERE PAID FOR FROM PRIOR YEAR FUNDS) AND
ENTIRELY INADEQUATE FUNDING FOR OPERATIONAL SUPPORT. EVEN IF WE
HAD FULL FUNDING AMMUNITION STOCKS COULD NOT BE KEPT ANYWHERE
NEAR THE LEVEL WE ARE ENTITLED TO KEEP THEM AT UNDER THE PARIS
AGREEMENT. AT A $700 MILLION FUNDING LEVEL AMMUNITION STOCKS WILL
BE STEADILY DRAWN DOWN AT PRESENT LEVELS OF FIGHTING EVEN WITH
STRINGENT ECONOMIES WHICH OF COURSE INVOLVE ADDITIONAL CASUALTIES.
(SOME INTELLIGENCE INDICATORS NOW SUGGEST A GOOD POSSIBILITY OF A
MAJOR NORTH VIETNAMESE OFFENSIVE EFFORT IN EARLY 1975 WHICH WILL
BE JUST ABOUT THE TIME THAT THESE SHORTAGES WILL BECOME MOST SEVERE.)
THERE ARE SIMILAR DRASTIC EFFECTS ON POL REQUIREMENTS, MEDICAL
PROGRAMS, SUBSISTENCE, SPARE PARTS, AND COMMUNICATIONS, AIR SUPPORT
AND NAVAL OPERATIONS.

4. APART FROM THE PRACTICAL EFFECTS TOUCHED ON ABOVE THE WORST
DAMAGE OF A REDUCTION OF MILITARY ASSISTANCE IN THE ORDER OF
MAGNITUDE
SUGGESTED BY THE HOUSE VOTE WOULD BE POLITICAL AND PSYCHOLOGICAL.
WE ARE AT A CRUCIAL POINT IN THE LONG DRAWN OUT PROCESS OF DECISION
MAKING IN HANOI. IT IS EVIDENT THAT HANOI HAS BEEN DISAPPOINTED IN
ITS EXPECTATION THAT VERY QUICKLY AFTER THE WITHDRAWAL OF AMERICAN
FORCES ND MILITARY ADVISERS SOUTH VIETNAM WOULD FALL INTO ITS HANDS.
AFTER LL, IN HANOI'S VIEW IT WAS A COLONIALIST WAR. BUT THIS HAS
NOT HAPPENED. THERE HAS BEEN NO COLLAPSE AND HANOI HAS BEEN
TAKEN ABACK BY THAT FACT AS WELL AS THE PERSISTENT FAILURE FOR THE
CONSTANTLY PREDICTED "MASS UPRISINGS" TO OCCUR. NOR HAS THE POLIT-
ICAL ALTERNATIVE OFFERED ANY ADVANTAGE FROM HANOI'S VIEWPOINT.
RECOGNITION OF THEIR POLITICAL WEAKNESS IS FOR EXAMPLE THE REASON
FOR THEIR PERSISTENT REFUSAL TO DISCUSS A DEFINITE TIME SCHEDULE FOR
THE HOLDING OF ELECTIONS CALLED FOR BY THE PARIS AGREEMENT. IN THE

PAGE 03 SAIGON 10622 01 OF 02 130814Z

SECRET

DECLASSIFIED

DECLASSIFIED

LAST YEAR THEREFORE THE DECISION MAKERS IN HANOI HAVE BEEN IN A DILEMMA. FACED NOT ONLY WITH DISAPPOINTMENT OF THEIR HOPES IN THE SOUTH BUT ALSO WITH SERIOUS ECONOMIC PROBLEMS AT HOME AND LIMITATION ON THEIR ABILITY TO OBTAIN SUPPORT FROM THE PRC AND THE SOVIET UNION THEY HAVE OBVIOUSLY HAD PROBLEMS IN DECIDING WHAT TO DO NEXT. THEY STILL ARE IN A PREDICAMENT. THEIR RECENT ACTIONS ALL SUGGEST THAT THEY STILL CANNOT DECIDE WHICH WAY TO GO AND THERE IS CERTAINLY A GOOD POSSIBILITY OF DIFFERENCES OF OPINION AND CONTROVERSY WITHIN THE LEADERSHIP.

DECLASSIFIED

DECLASSIFIED

SECRET

PAGE 01 SAIGON 10622 02 OF 02 130705Z

12
ACTION SS-30

INFO OCT-01 ISO-00 /031 W
------------------------------050636
R 130440Z ZFF5
FM AMEMBASSY SAIGON
TO SECSTATE WASHDC 7711
INFO SECDEF WASHDC
CINCPAC HONOLULU HI
COMUSSAG NKP THAI
S E C R E T SECTION 2 OF 2 SAIGON 10622
EXDIS

5. FOR THE TIME BEING THEREFORE HANOI HAS APPARENTLY DECIDED TO
CONTINUE EMPHASIZNG A STRATEGY OF LIMITED INITIATIVES WHICH WILL
ENABLE THEM TO MAINTAIN AND STRENGTHEN THEIR POSITION IN THE SOUTH
WHILE CONTINUING TO DIVERT SOME OF THEIR RESOURCES TO DOMESTIC
DEVELOPMENT. THE BALANCE BETWEEN THE TWO PRIORITIES OF REUNIFICATION
AND RECONSTRUCTION, HOWEVER, REMAINS EXTREMELY DELICATE. ACCORDING
TO RECENT INTELLIGENCE REPORTING, SHOULD THE NORTH VIETNAMESE
CONCLUDE THAT THE US IS DISENGAGING POLITICALLY AND ECONOMICALLY
FROM THE SOUTH, THEY WOULD SUSPEND SERIOUS ECONOMIC PLANNING
AND HOLD THEIR RESOURCES IN RESERVE, TO USE MILITARILY AGAINST
SOUTH VIETNAM AT SOME OPPORTUNE MOMENT. SOME INTELLIGENCE SOURCES
INDICATE, IN FACT, THAT THE COMMUNISTS ARE ANTICIPATING A
"DECISIVE" POLITICAL OR MILITARY BREAKTHROUGH AS EARLY AS THE SPRING
OF 1975 WHEN THE SOUTH VIETNAMESE GOVERNMENT'S EQUIPMENT AND
MATERIAL SHORTAGES COULD BE MOST SEVERE IF THERE IS NO ADDITIONAL
US ASSISTANCE. HANOI'S LONG AND SHORT-TERM INTENTIONS THUS HINGE
CRITICALLY ON ITS CURRENT ESTIMATES OF THE EXTENT AND DURABILITY
OF US COMMITMENTS TO THE SOUTH VIETNAMESE. BY HANOI'S OWN CALCU-
LATIONS, A U.S. DECISION TO SHARPLY REDUCE MILITARY AID AND
ECONOMIC SUPPORT TO THE SOUTH VIETNAMESE GOVERNMENT WOULD MEAN
THAT THE COMMUNISTS COULD PURSUE THEIR OBJECTIVES IN THE SOUTH WITH
AS MUCH FORCE AS IS NECESSARY FOR PROMPT AND ABSOLUTE VICTORY.

6. ON THE OTHER HAND HANOI'S ONE SUCCESS---AT LEAST IN THEIR
EYES---HAS BEEN THEIR PROPAGANDA CAMPAIGN. THEY MUST CERTAINLY

SECRET

DECLASSIFIED

DECLASSIFIED

SECRET

PAGE 02 SAIGON 10622 02 OF 02 130705Z

CONGRATULATE THEMSELVES WHEN IT IS SAID IN APPARENT SERIOUSNESS IN
THE UNITED STATES THAT ASSISTANCE TO SOUTH VIETNAM IS BEING CUT IN
ORDER TO SERVE NOTICE ON THE SOUTH VIETNAMESE GOVERNMENT THAT IT
MUST NEGOTIATE WITH HANOI. SHARP AID REDUCTIONS TO FORCE THIEU TO
NEGOTIATE IS EXACTLY WHAT RADIO HANOI HAS BEEN URGING FOR MANY
MONTHS. IT ALSO IGNORES ALL THE FACTS INCLUDING THE FACT THAT SUCH
NEGOTIATIONS HAVE BEEN OFFERED REPEATEDLY BY THE GOVERNMENT OF
VIETNAM (MOST RECENTLY ON JULY 20, 1974) AND HAVE ALWAYS BEEN
REJECTED OUT OF HAND. AND, FINALLY IT IS SIGNIFICANT THAT A RENEWAL
OF NORTH VIETNAMESE MILITARY PRESSURE RAISING THE LEVEL OF VIOLENCE
IN SOUTH VIETNAM TO ITS HIGHEST INTENSITY SINCE THE CEASE-FIRE
COMES AT EXACTLY THE TIME THAT CONGRESSIONAL CONSIDERATION OF AID
TO VIETNAM REACHES THE DECISION STAGE AND AT A TIME PERCEIVED BY
HANOI TO BE ONE OF GREAT UNCERTAINTY IN THE UNITED STATES.

7. WE BELIEVE IT LIKELY THAT A REDUCTION IN
MILITARY ASSISTANCE TO THE RVN BY OVER 50 PERCENT OF THE ADMINIS-
TRATION'S REQUEST WILL TIP THE BALANCE IN HANOI IRREVOCABLY IN
FAVOR OF A DECISION FOR THE MILITARY OPTION. AT THE SAME TIME
THERE IS ABSOLUTELY NO DOUBT ABOUT THE FACT THAT THE SOUTH VIET-
NAMESE WILL NOT SIMPLY QUIT BUT WILL FIGHT. IRRESPECTIVE OF THE
OUTCOME THE RESULT WILL BE MORE WAR RATHER THAN LESS, MORE
SUFFERING RATHER THAN LESS, AND FURTHER POSTPONEMENT OF AN
ACCEPTABLE POLITICAL SOLUTION RATHER THAN THE REVERSE.
LEHMANN

SECRET

DECLASSIFIED

Chapter 17

Atop Two Walls

As a State Department official, Glenn Rounsevell trekked across South Vietnam's delta in IV Corps. When President Ford announced in late April that the war was "finished," Rounsevell was astonished.[1] Still on duty as a political officer, no one had told Rounsevell. Making his way to Saigon, he frantically stood atop the embassy's wall searching for the Vietnamese contacts whom he felt obligated to evacuate. Twenty years later, Rounsevell's young granddaughter commemorated this heroic effort with the touching poem included at the end of this chapter.

Twenty-five years after the end of the war, Rounsevell sees the conflict in a broader context. While he left South Vietnam under strained circumstances, he refuses to see the war as simply a defeat for America. Rather, he points to the dramatic collapse of the Soviet Union as evidence that, in a sense, the failure in Vietnam did not doom the United States' long battle against communism. While his frustrating hours on the embassy wall have left Rounsevell with regrets and a certain sense of "shame for our betrayal" of an ally, he can also see them as steps leading to the eventual 1989 collapse of the Berlin Wall.[2]

I was sent to Vietnam by the State Department as a consular/political officer and was assigned to the consulate in the Mekong delta city of Can Tho. The delta was otherwise known as IV Corps. There I remained for almost two and a half years until I was evacuated from Vietnam on April 29, 1975.

My duties took me to many delta provinces, mostly by airplane, since the roads were constantly closed by the Vietcong or because of fighting. The first day on the job, I was given a .45 caliber pistol and told that I should learn to use it since there was no telling when I might find myself in difficulty. I chose not to do so, but to carry instead, a few wads of piasters or dollars so that if I found myself in a canal, a ditch, or behind a tree, I could wave bunches of money instead of a pistol. I figured greenbacks were the better defense against an AK-47 automatic rifle. Anyway, there was a good chance that I might shoot myself in the foot and, as you probably know, a .45 caliber finds it hard to hit something at a distance. As it turned out, I never used either and ended up losing both of these so-called defensive weapons.

During the final days in the delta before finally having to go to Saigon, I spent ten days or so helping a South Vietnamese major keep a unit alive and operating and successfully directing U.S.-trained South Vietnamese combat chopper pilots to go after infiltrating Vietcong. It was at this time, April 24 to be exact, that I heard President Ford declare the war "finished." I was totally astonished since here I was in the middle of the delta—yet with no assurances from my government that they would come to get me out. From all that was still going on, I knew damn well that the war was not "finished."

But that's another story. I was ordered, two days before the fall, to go to Saigon. Since I had been in the delta longer than almost anyone else and thus had come to know many of the Vietnamese personnel there, I was elected to try to get some fifty such key people and their families through Saigon to safety in the U.S. This then became my final mission. Little did I know how little time was left. In any event, in Saigon, I carefully arranged for an aircraft to evacuate these important and endangered people, with their wives, children and close relatives. I scheduled them to leave the next day, April 29, 1975, from Saigon's Tan Son Nhut airport. Tragically, it would be the day of the fall.

There were many acts of American heroism during the evacuation, but overall, if we had planned the debacle, I doubt if it could have been much worse. I will be forever guilt-ridden and saddened by what happened in the chaos that followed.

I awoke in Saigon at roughly 4 A.M. on April 29th to the ominous roar and shaking of bombs. I rushed to the roof of my hotel and saw the sky lit with the glare of flares and flashes of exploding bombs not far away—Tan Son Nhut airport was under bombardment. I could not be sure of what damage was being done to the airfield, but the loss of the airport would mean the probable end to any hope that I would be able to evacuate my list of the endangered fifty that day. Nor did I comprehend at that moment that there were now just over 24 hours until the surrender. What was to be done to get them out? There were no known alternative plans for evacuation other than via choppers from various preselected sites in the city, and as it turned out, everyone in Saigon had learned about these sites including the signal for evacuation (White Christmas on the radio). The embassy had sent out the confidential plans to Vietnamese printers days earlier. You can guess what that meant.

Still hoping that there was time and that surely an alternate method could be found, I decided that I must find out if, and how close, the NVA was to Saigon. I put on a flak jacket, took my walkie-talkie and passport, commandeered a jeep and driver, laid down in it and made my way to the embassy. With an absolute curfew on, the streets were nearly deserted. Nevertheless, a small crowd had begun to gather at the embassy entrance.

It soon became clear that the embassy and Washington were dead wrong in their belief (i.e., that the North Vietnamese would negotiate for the sanctity of a portion of South Vietnam, including Saigon). Instead, the NVA was going for broke. Tan Son Nhut was shut down. The primary means of evacuation was therefore gone.

So my only hope was that, if I could still somehow make contact with those on my list, I would have to have them come to try for evacuation from the embassy. Since I had been posted to the consulate in Can Tho, neither myself nor my charges were included in the Saigon embassy evacuation plans. I had to shift for myself.

I therefore enlisted the aid of an embassy officer and asked her to begin to call the telephone numbers for those on my endangered list. She agreed. I went downstairs to leave the embassy grounds, thinking that I could also personally get to the homes of some of these people, only to now find a mob outside the embassy walls clamoring to be allowed inside. The streets were in chaos. Tension was mounting. As a consequence, that part of my plan was thwarted.

Nor was I ever able to get back to my hotel. It was shot up and taken over during the day. I lost everything, including several thousand dollars in personal and escape and evasion money. This was nothing compared to the loss suffered by those fleeing their homeland or those killed trying to do their duty.

I immediately recognized the first couple of my charges (former employees) outside the gates. They had comprehended what was happening and had correctly guessed that I would elect to go to the embassy in lieu of meeting to go to the airport as originally planned. They were relieved to find me. I had the guards get them through the embassy gate just before the order came to slam the gates closed. The crowd outside was beginning to panic.

Two or three of the others on my list then appeared in the crowd and I realized even more that it would be foolhardy to leave in search of the missing. My hope now was that the others too would realize that our rendezvous plans and expected airport departure had to be abandoned and would come to the embassy. I told my volunteer telephone assistant that I would now walk the perimeter on top of the embassy wall and would search for those in my group. By this time, she reported that the phones were malfunctioning and that she was able to reach only a few. She kept trying until she was forced to depart.

Many Americans and Vietnamese could not believe what they were witnessing. With increasing signs of impending disaster, the embassy lot was beginning to fill with people. Water and food was short, children were crying, it was beastly hot and humid, ashes and smoke from the incinerators blew everywhere, the elevators stopped functioning, small helicopters were taking people off the roof of the building, young marine guards, just flown in, were threatening people desperately clamoring at the walls. At one point, I was ordered to come down; told that I might be shot by someone in the crowd, but I couldn't because being visible to those outside was the only way that I could be recognized and then be able to physically pull my people up and over the wall into the compound. To top it all off, there were uniformed officers going through the crowds with bullhorns saying, "Don't worry, we are not going to leave you." Like the rest of us, little did they know; many were abandoned.

To make the situation more wrenching, I had to turn away from others who reached through the gates saying, "But American boss promise take me. Vietcong kill me." "Please sir, save my son. Save my daughter. You promise. You promise." "I from Hue. I work for American ten years Danang. I have letter. Look." "Please sir, why you no help me? Not to leave me!" And even worse, I remember green American passports being frantically shoved through the iron bars by a woman pleading that these American passports were for her children—American citizens. I could only turn shamefully away from countless equally tearful pleas, being overwhelmed trying to locate and manhandle my charges and their families over the wall. I knew that I shouldn't be diverted from my main task. I couldn't help everyone, but it haunts me to this day.

Nonetheless, at one point I was forced to stop and calm a frightened young marine who was about to open fire with his M-16 on a group of Vietnamese that, in the panic, were trying to force their way over a gate. I had to convince him that they were not the enemy and that they meant him no harm. The crowd backed off and he resumed his duties, content then to keep control by simply bashing with the butt of his weapon the fingers of those trying to scale the walls and gates. I figured this was the lesser of the two possible outcomes and I went about my business.

In the end, to my everlasting regret, I only succeeded in getting out seventeen on my list of fifty—. What happened to the others—those left behind? I learned that some went to the river and escaped by boat, some later fled as refugees from other parts of Vietnam to Thailand, Malaysia, the Philippines. Others, no doubt, spent years in communist re-education camps. I can only pray that those who were left will not believe that I had willingly deserted them.

It was late that night, only when it became totally hopeless, that finally, and with the heaviest of hearts, physically and mentally exhausted, and with total shame for our betrayal, I had to leave from the embassy roof after the madness of that final day and night.

Mistakenly, the government didn't believe what captured documents and field intelligence reports were telling them. These reports told us in the field that the NVA was going for broke, that there would be no negotiation for Saigon or any part of the south. Washington and the embassy kept saying to the contrary (i.e., that it had evidence that the North Vietnamese would negotiate and declare Saigon an open city).

My personal belief is that both Washington and the embassy were "set up" by clever disinformation from the Russians. I believe that Dobrynin, the Soviet ambassador to Washington, led Kissinger to believe that the North Vietnamese would negotiate while at the same time, the Hungarians in Saigon, Soviet stooges, who were in contact with the embassy, fed the same story to their American contact (i.e., that there would be negotiations—that there would be time yet before leaving).

Kissinger and others, of course, hoped that this would enable the South Vietnamese to have time to stiffen enough to force a settlement thus averting what would be a total defeat. With the feed from the Russian Ambassador at one end and the Hungarians at the other, it was made to seem that this double-sourced information matched and was therefore plausible. The truth was exactly the opposite, as the field documents had revealed days before, it led to the panic that followed when the NVA unexpectedly began to pound at the outskirts of Saigon.

I vividly remember standing in the embassy parking lot, talking to an embassy Reports Officer two days prior to the end, chastising her for the apparent refusal of the embassy to believe what the North Vietnamese themselves were saying. This Reports Officer said she agreed with me, but "the embassy has a special source and reason to believe otherwise." Washington's information, of course, was false.

This part of my snapshot is not the total picture, but was a significant misjudgment—one of our many major miscalculations made in Vietnam.

In spite of a lot of heroics by individuals, the risks taken by many, the sacrifices and good intentions, we did an awful job with the evacuation. As I said, we did not believe our own intelligence. We got snookered by the Soviets. We weren't prepared. If the North Vietnamese hadn't permitted the Americans to leave in the end, I might not be speaking to you today and instead, still trying to learn Vietnamese. The departure was ignominious. One South Vietnamese officer said later that the tracer bullets fired at the choppers leaving the embassy roof that last night were from disgruntled South Vietnamese troops, angry at the fleeing Americans.

I witnessed waiters, bar girls, dentists, maids and an assortment of friends of ranking government officers being sponsored and put on evacuation lists ahead of those on my endangered species list.

Our Ambassador Martin was a space cadet orbiting another planet when I observed him the final day. He had insisted that Saigon was a family post to the last and that evacuation would panic the populace. I believe that he had become a totally crushed man when on April 17 Congress finally refused to authorize another dime of aid to South Vietnam.

And upon the order to begin the evacuation, was the embassy ready to receive the choppers? No. The huge banyan tree that spread over the embassy parking lot still had not been removed on this, the morning of the evacuation! It seems the ambassador had refused to have it taken down even though the parking lot was the only place that large Hueys could land. The embassy roof could not take the weight nor the vibration of the big Hueys without collapsing. An engineering study had been made sometime before and it therefore recommended that the old tree be removed. The ambassador refused to the last and at a dawn meeting in the embassy the morning of the 29th, the CIA chief asked the embassy Administrative Officer if that tree had been removed. The answer, "No, Ambassador Martin won't permit it." To this the irate CIA chief reportedly replied, "I don't give a damn what the ambassador says, you go cut that tree down—. Now!"

Well, fine, but the tree happened to be one hell of a tropical banyan tree. Its huge old limbs covered most of the lot. It was at least six or seven feet thick, the kind that have vines that turn into roots and form part of a thickened trunk, and this tree obviously wasn't the type ready to give up without a struggle. Furthermore, according to my conversation with the engineer who participated in the aforementioned study, he had recommended that the embassy have on hand several large chain saws in case the tree had to go. The embassy had one. Guess what? It broke on the first pass. What to do? The evacuation had to start! Call on the marines! Tear the fire axes off the walls on each floor of the embassy and platoon chop that monster. The marines did so, chop, chop, chop, chop while the Hueys were impatiently waiting off shore. But that wasn't all. They then had to sweep up the chips and branches because the prop blast would injure anyone caught in the wash. More lost time.

Overall, the helicopter lift went on for over twenty hours, but the heavy lifts from the parking lot were delayed until afternoon waiting for our sweating marines to finish the job. This in turn put more flying hours way into that night. I have understood that not all of the pilots were accustomed to night flying, especially off carriers. Some were reported to be flying without night vision goggles. I have often wondered if that's why the two marine pilots (Captain Nystul and Lieutenant Shea) died in a crash at sea near my carrier, the *USS Hancock*, during the evacuation. This may have been the tragic end in the train of events stemming from the delayed removal of that banyan tree.

In short, I will let you draw your own conclusions as to how I think that the government handled the pullout.

With the marvelous advantage of hindsight, one thing that could have been done differently was to have taken more lessons from the successful campaign to thwart the communists in Malaysia. The U.S. appeared to have taken little to heart of what our British friends tried to tell us about techniques used on the Malay peninsula to finally quell the subversives waging basically the same kind of campaign.

Those who have read the McNamara book or are old enough to remember, will recall that the McNamara whiz kids' approach gave one the impression that they knew all the answers; that technology, massively applied, would overcome all opposition; that those poorly equipped, misguided peasants from North Vietnam would soon be overwhelmed simply through the addition of more sophisticated weaponry and more men.[3] The truth was that the use of the earlier, low-key techniques used successfully by the CIA early in Vietnam were more effective and successful. That is, go after the hearts and minds of the people. Such techniques became pushed aside in favor of the use of massive firepower. Massive firepower meant massive amounts of money and men, but it won few converts among the people we wanted to side with us.

The Brits, you will also recall, made the same kind of mistake with the colonists during and before the revolutionary war in this country. That is to say that many a settler in America was sympathetic to the Brits up and until the time British soldiers stole his animals or burned his barn. After that, the settler knew whose side he was on. In this respect, we unfortunately acted like King George's troops too often in Vietnam.

I have come to conclude that we did not have a clearly defined strategic interest in choosing to fight in Vietnam. It was a part of the world unknown, with names few Americans could even recognize, before we got involved. We fought a war with severe limits on targets and objectives, fearing Chinese or Russian intervention. Americans fought Hitler's Germany and Tojo's Japan with a clear understanding of their threat to us. There were virtually no limits in our effort to defeat either. Few Americans understood how North Vietnam equated to anything in WW II. And support at home withered.

Even when a clear victory was won during the 1968 Tet offensive, the government let the press convince people that it was a defeat. Still, in spite of the fact that we eventually lost the battle for Vietnam, as a learned Vietnamese scholar friend of mine points out, in a much larger and global sense, it can be argued that Vietnam made its contribution to our victory over communism and the bringing down of the Berlin Wall. That, too, is another subject.

To Grandpa Rounsevell, with love.

The Wall

The clinging ivy, tendrils wrenched,
Its grasp on the rampart forsakes—
A witness to withdrawal.
To uncalculated haste.
A reminder of the many who died for a mistake.
Lives engraved on a cold black wall
Traced softly by fingers,
Love's futile call.

—But etched deeper still
In heart sinews torn
Lies an anguish, a torment
By only some borne—

Those coffee eyes
Moon slivers when closed
—the groping hands.
—the frantic cries.
—the queries posed.

Lacerated promises.
Unintentional betrayal.
Again, that crying—
Drowned by helicopter blades and a siren's wail.

A phone call confirming safety,
The awaited anodyne.
But a fragment of the soul
A word of honor
Left behind.

K. Rodemann
Madrid. June 1995.

Climbing the Embassy Wall

Escaping to Freedom

Chapter 18

"A Fruitless, Terrible, and Tragic Fiasco"

One of the best journals kept by an American at the time of "Operation Frequent Wind" was compiled by Captain Joseph Gildea, a nautical engineer in the Navy Division of the Defense Attaché Office. Edited below are Gildea's impressions of South Vietnam's final two weeks and his evacuation from the Defense Attaché Office in Saigon.[1]

Tuesday, April 15, 1975

Yesterday was a day totally given to shipping my gear. Hot, long and disorganized, but it was worth the effort; that is, if the gear gets to Long Beach without being damaged too much.

The girls at the office were upset all day; for they did not know for sure where I was, as if the shipping of the household goods meant I was going. Tried to keep it from them, but you can't hide anything here.

Last evening had a couple visit me. The woman was one I had met at Slim Russel's. She was apparently from a well-to-do Vietnamese family, related through marriage to President Thieu. The man is the ex-husband of her cousin, who was also a friend of Slim's. She went to the U.S. right after Christmas and is still there.

Slim was sent home last week, so these two are looking for help. Today will send a telegram for them through MARS to the cousin asking that she somehow charter a plane to come to Saigon to take them all out. This man is a doctor and is obviously well-heeled. Even the rich ones are clutching. He told me he came from the north, spent four years in the Vietnamese (VN) Marines fighting the north, so he would be a target if they get here. Everybody is pleading for help.

During the night was awakened for the first time by a noise (over the sound of a running air conditioner). Thought the last clock had fallen or something. Looked out the front but could see nothing. It did shake the building. Today learned that an ammo dump at Ben Hoa had gone up at 0200. No details yet.

This morning made the rounds of the three offices to talk to the VGS people (Vietnamese working for the U.S.). Had done it last Thursday, before President Ford's talk. Couldn't give them much except explain the difficulties the requests will have in Congress.

Lots of questions like, "when they say U.S.-employed Vietnamese may be evacuated, how far into the relatives does that go?" Had to talk about the scope of the problem, for it could cover ¼ million people. Have to make them feel more realistic and see the problems are tremendous, and that the best solution would be for the South Vietnamese Army to stiffen and defend what is left of the south, so that the people would not have to leave their country.

The girls have such frightening stories about what is happening in Danang to the South Vietnamese. The ones who left the North in 1954 are singled out. They must gather up the decomposed bodies of the days of fighting and bury them. When one mass grave wasn't big enough, Co Sung says the soldiers made them take the bodies all out again, make the hole bigger, and bury all the bodies again. The girls are also saying that the north's soldiers are getting these same ex-northerners and cutting their big toes off, as a sign of traitors. Grisly. Don't know how much of these stories are true, but they certainly have the girls shook up.

Heard today that Brigadier General Baughn was relieved at the direction of the Ambassador. General Baughn was in charge of establishing an evacuation plan for Defense Attaché Office. We have gotten a lot of people out, Navy Division more than others. When five people go who have VN families and therefore passport problems, I'll be left with only three people in my whole group, out of forty-one just a few weeks ago. Expect that General Baughn complained about the slowness of the embassy in getting out their people. Wives and children are still here. So I understand that the Ambassador said that he didn't want him on his team. Hope to find out the story tomorrow.

Wednesday, April 16, 1975

Rumors are rampant. Co Sung has heard that Father McVeigh is putting together a list of people who would be evacuated by the Catholic Services Organization. Since Father is a friend of mine, Co Sung has been asking me to call and get her family on the list. Called, but Father was not in. He'll return the call later.

The girls say that President Thieu's wife has left the country. The article in the paper about the request to send Thieu's personal effects ($73 million in gold) has been denied in all the local papers.

Thursday, April 17, 1975

Received a call at 0400 this morning from Chuck Tevelson in San Diego. He had a man talk to me about me helping get a family of eight out of Vietnam. I told him all that I could do was to give their name and address to the embassy. There is still no word as to how, what, who, where, when, etc., the U.S. will do for a Vietnamese evacuation. It is going to be terrible if it does happen. Everybody is looking for a way out. Chuck tried to put through a call to Sheila, but she was on the phone. So I talked to Laverne Law. Gave her a message to pass along to Sheila.

This morning had an unusual situation come up. A girl who is a translator at the shipyard came for help. She said her sister was married to a U.S. man who went back to the States and has not been heard from. They had a daughter (guess about two or three years old). This girl's father (VN) works for AID, so they feel that his immediate family will get on an evacuation list. However, they feel that his granddaughter may not. She asked me if I could adopt the baby, and when it was out of Vietnam, they would take it right back, no problem. I showed her a picture of my children and said I really couldn't take the responsibility for a baby but I would let her know when the plan comes through, and that surely the baby would be allowed to leave with its mother. I really didn't know if the story of the U.S. father was true or not, but the way things are going, it could all be fabricated. Phony papers can be gotten cheaply, but the real ones are expensive and hard to get.

Captain Luan, my counterpart, spent some time with me this morning. He has nothing and is concerned about his family. He has an aunt who is in the U.S. with the Vietnamese Embassy. He would like to get his family to her.

Went home for lunch today. Heard a loud boom that shook the windows. Don't know what it was.

At 1800 yesterday had a meeting with the remaining Navy Division people. Will meet again at 1800 to set up responsibilities and actions for any last ditch stand. Doubt that it will be needed, but panic might take over.

Friday, April 18, 1975

Last night between 10:00 and 11:00 heard quite a bit of shelling. Don't know if it was outgoing or not. It sounded like a saluting battery in the distance, so expect that it was outgoing.

Co Na called this morning. She said while she slept last night, she saw me getting on a plane to leave. It is going to be tough on them when any more of us leave. They are depending on us to save them. The last people here in my group are Robbie Robertson, Joe Ustich and myself. We have another meeting tonight at 1800 with the Marines talking about how the last people here will secure the DAO. Made a list of my VN employees and put them in priority categories for possible evacuation.

Went to the Exchange today. Many Americans buying things to take home. Shelves are getting empty. I can imagine the feelings of the Vietnamese clerks who are seeing the place closing down, putting them out of a job and then leaving them.

As the girls left after work today, they all said, "Hope we see you on Monday!"

Saturday, April 19, 1975

Don't know whether I will be here to greet the girls on Monday. At an early meeting this morning at DAO, and also at 1900 last night, it appears that things are really ominous. The north is apparently massing for an all-out attack on Saigon. Will find out more this afternoon. Admiral Gaylor of CINCPAC is coming into the country today. He is in charge of the U.S. evacuation.

Went to the Commissary at noon today to get milk, ice cream, etc. I was one of about five customers in that whole big store. The shelves there are full, but I wonder what will happen to that.

Went home for lunch today. Ba Quan sadly informed me that she can no longer get me papaya for breakfast. It came from areas now lost. Had been having a slice of it almost every morning since Sheila was here.

Some of the ships are starting to get clobbered from shore guns. HQ 401 was damaged early in the week at Nam Cam. Several people were killed.

This morning HQ 503 was hit with a 130-mm. shell at Ca Na, near Pham Thiet, which fell last night. Afraid that they will soon take Vung Tau. That is where many of the displaced refugees are.

Told Robbie and Joe Ulstich today to be ready to go on a minute's notice. I'm ready. Carry passport, money orders, etc., with me at all times.

Monday, April 21, 1975

Really a quiet day yesterday. Although worked all day. Mostly trying to get the people with Vietnamese families all cleared up to go. They have paper problems, but I think that the embassy and DAO are finally going to cut the red tape.

The Vietnamese Navy (VNN) are really fortifying out front of headquarters. See two sets of antiaircraft guns recently placed there. And lots of 55-gallon drums filled with cement to form a big barricade.

Talked yesterday with Captain Kiem. He is resolved to stay with it and his family will stay with him. He says that if any of them go out of Vietnam, they would go to France, rather than the U.S. He wasn't outwardly resentful, but I'm sure there will be some that do show resentment about our backing out.

Almost first thing this morning, Mamasan said something about Mr. Ford and today she expects that I'll be explaining to them what is happening now that President Ford's deadline of 19 April for Congress to act has passed. Spent much of the day talking to the employees, trying to calm them.

In this push to get Americans out, rules are being relaxed and many are taking out girlfriends, riffraff, etc., just on their say-so that they will be responsible for them. Wonder how many will drop them immediately upon arriving in the States.

Our employees still haven't been told if, how, when, or anything substantial on how they will be taken care of if worse comes to worse. They are feeling that they are going to be forgotten when all the Americans have gone home. They say that the Vietnamese Navy and people will be down on them for making more money by working for the Americans, and the north will be against them for leaving the north in 1954 (in many cases), and then for having worked for the Americans. They are afraid, so you can see how they are watching my actions and worrying about my leaving.

Tomorrow morning, I'll go down to the shipyard to talk to the employees, for tomorrow, Joe Ulstich, the last American in the shipyard, is leaving. Will have problems, but will put the senior Vietnamese in charge of reporting to Robbie, who is now the only U.S. civilian in the Navy Division. I will have Robbie out in about three days, if things go as scheduled.

The news tonight of Thieu's resignation may slow things down on the military side for awhile, as they see if they are really going to talk together.

Spent quite a bit of time helping the doctor figure out ways he might get out if the worst happens. Plane, boat, etc. Latest is a message requesting that his ex-wife acknowledge that she is living in the U.S., so that he can get on a preferred waiting list for the evacuation of Northwest Orient Airlines employees, for whom he was a physician. Joe Ulstich is going to escort his two children tomorrow to Philadelphia, where their mother will meet them. So many sad stories, and only a few can be helped.

Approached many times today by people (the photographer who accompanied me on many trips, an engineer in the technical division, a translator in the ships division) with their particular story, concern for the safety of their families, and questions about evacuation plans.

Some of the people are really showing the effects of the strain. Co Diep said she listens to the U.S. radio news almost all night. At the 0400 news this morning, she said there were some words about the evacuation plan, which weren't repeated on the later hourly reports. They grasp at any straw they can, hoping that a means will be provided to allow them to escape. One of the secretaries supposedly somehow got on a plane and got out today. She must have had some American sign for her. This shakes the others up.

Tuesday, April 22, 1975

Got the children out to Tan Son Nhut this morning about 0930. Hard to see a father give up his daughter (9) and his son (7) to a stranger to give to another stranger to take them to the States. He knows it is for their good, but probably wonders if he'll ever see them again. They'll probably get out tonight.

The effort at the theatre and the gym today was a mess. Hundreds of them, mostly Vietnamese families, supposedly dependents of Americans processing out. I know many were fraudulent.

Gave an older American woman a lift from the gym to the theatre when she asked me where it was. She first came to Vietnam in 1954 with Dr. Tom Dooley, married a Vietnamese educator, had a family, and has been here ever since. He was a dean at the University at Hue, when they were chased out in Tet 1968. Living in the Saigon area since then, she decided it was time to get out, but he wouldn't go. She got her children out yesterday and has now convinced him to go. They're trying now.

Had a very sad visit from Mr. Wong, the man who had both his legs blown off as an Army officer and now walks on his remaining stumps. He came from the North in 1954, went to the Military Academy, spent a year in the U.S. for military training, was wounded, and has been working for the U.S. ever since. His request for help is included. So sad. But even if he got himself, his wife and his child out, where would they go? How would they live? Could he work? People aren't thinking ahead. They just want out to keep from being killed. Everybody looks at me as if I must save them. I wish I could, but it is going to take a big effort on the part of the U.S.

So many rumors. And they do so much harm.

Today word was started that the secretaries in the Personnel Office were all told to bring their bags to work, that they all would be taken out. Spread like wild-fire. Finally got to their boss and he said "Not so."

When I got home here, I found at my gate an ex-VN Navy lieutenant who works for supply. He is the naval officer who received the most, and the highest, decorations from the U.S. (Silver Star, etc.) for his actions in the war. I had met him before. Since he could not wait for Hank Hirschy who he wanted to see, I told him that I'd have Hank get in touch with him tomorrow.

Just got a call from Slim Russel in D.C. His friend, the mother of the two children, got on the line. Almost hysterical, she said all I had to do was get their family to Tan Son Nhut and put them on a plane. They have no direct connection in the U.S., so even if it were so that they were taking anyone, the U.S. employees would be the ones to go, if they wanted to. Most of them do.

After President Thieu's blast during his resignation, blaming the U.S. for everything, and all the U.S. words about just giving some token amount of money to insure the safe evacuation of U.S. people, I'm getting a little more concerned. Walking through the VNN Headquarters, with all those VN sailors carrying weapons, I felt for the first time today a little uneasy.

A letter from Nguyen Ha Wong, an engineer for the VNN, who lost both his legs while in the ARVN:

Dear Captain,

I was born in North Vietnam and came down to South Vietnam in 1954 because I could not live under the Communist yoke.

In 1956, I enlisted at the Dalat National Military Academy, and graduated as a Second Lieutenant. Then I was invited to go to the United States to get training at Fort Benning, Georgia and Fort Belvoir, Virginia.

After I finished the Infantry and Engineer course in your country, I went home and was assigned to the ARVN Engineer Department.

In 1964, I got wounded and have a 100 percent honorable disability.

I have worked for the Americans from 1968 until now. If the V.C. take South Vietnam, they will accuse me as a spy for the Americans. I will be shot.

I have cooperated with the Americans for a long time and it is sure that the Communists will kill me. So I ask you to make a favor to me and my family, allow us to emigrate to the United States.

Your consideration in this matter is greatly appreciated.

Respectfully yours,
Nguyen Ha Wong
AOSND-LTO

Wednesday, April 23, 1975

Another exhausting day. Trying to keep people's spirits up and convince the U.S.-employed VN that something will be done for them. Tempers are getting shorter. I can tell it in the way Co Na drives and the responses between the girls. In fact, today I got a little sharp with Co Sung, for she runs to me every time she hears a rumor or hears that someone has gone to the U.S. and why can't I help her.

I know that they are not getting enough sleep from worrying. And without enough work to keep them busy—we've destroyed practically all the records—all they do is talk and worry when I'm not there. I try to talk to all of them at one time, but if for some reason, I'm talking to just one, others move up to hear if I'm saying anything new or different.

While I was eating breakfast at 0700, the doorbell rang. It was Tam, the aunt of the two children who I understand got out last night with Joe Ustich. She said that a Navy Division employee had signed for her as her sponsor and could I take her at 0900 to his apartment. After going to work for about an hour (during which I talked to Captain Lich, the shipyard commander, about the fact that I sent the last U.S. civilian who had worked in the shipyard out of the country yesterday, and asked that I could leave the U.S.-employed VN in their offices 'till I knew what was to happen), I then picked her up at her house and took here there. He was at work, but she was to wait. Understand she was still there waiting after 1800 tonight. Guess he's having trouble with papers. I'll know more tomorrow. During the rest of the morning, went the rounds of the three offices where I have VNs. All upset, but just need some straight, factual statements, rather than rumors.

Two VNs from the shipyard had previously worked for U.S. Intelligence. They are to get special treatment. I saw the Intelligence Officer at DAO this afternoon and may have their problem solved. But that is only two of over 140.

While having lunch at home, the doctor, father of the two children, came by looking for help. I had received a phone call from Slim Russel in D.C. last night, telling us about that plane he wanted to rent from World Airways. He is going to have clearance problems even if he does get his plane. Told him I'd check that message at the DAO after lunch. Found when I got there that World Airways had pulled out of their office. Included that fact in a message to Slim today, telling him that the children were on the way.

While at the airport, a bearded American stopped me, because of my uniform, and asked me for help in getting some Vietnamese orphan boys out of the country to Boys' Town in Nebraska. He came in country two days ago commercially. We are trying desperately to get people out and others are allowed in. I had no help for him, but gave him Father McVeigh's address as a possible source for help.

After about two hours doing chores at DAO (with Captain Grigg, sending messages, talking with the Intelligence Officer, arranging space for me to move into the DAO compound this weekend, etc.), went back to the office. Found girls more distraught than ever. Some of their friends had gotten out illegally, etc.

Had the two intelligence people in to take information.

Commander Hung, a friend, came in to chat about his problems. He was going to send his family to the island of Phu Quoc, where there are already 75,000 refugees from Danang, Qui Nhon, and other places. I talked him out of that for now, 'till the U.S. spells out what will be done for the families of military people. I hope that will be defined quickly.

About 1715, received a call from the War College in Newport, Rhode Island. It was from a Captain Huong, who left here last July for a year-long course. He is very concerned about his family which is still here. I had previously talked to Captain Luan about them, so I was able to pass that on to him, and that I would see that they are taken care of if an evacuation by the U.S. is arranged.

Went to Anh Dao after work to pick up the carved tray. It was not finished, but spent about 45 minutes talking with Madame Anh Dao and her husband about their desire to leave to go to the U.S. They have relatives there. It is a shame that such a business of making such beautiful furniture will be lost. I'm sure they would have given me anything if I could have gotten them on a plane. Had to tell them that I could only keep them informed if there is an evacuation which included not only U.S. employees but also professional people who had dealt solely with Americans. They wanted my address to send the tray if I had to leave the country before it was finished. I resisted as I felt they wanted to send something else as a bribe or influence. If that starts, I'm in trouble.

Got home around 1900. While heating my dinner, the doctor came along again. Couldn't give him any encouragement, except to repeat what I had told Madame Anh Dao.

While reading the paper, I got a call from the girl Tam, who was still waiting at the place I left her at 0800. While talking, Dick Smith came in there. Maybe he got the papers out.

After a day like today, I expect to come out of this with some scars, if not literally, then at least some from remembering pleas which I could not respond to.

Saturday, April 26, 1975

What is happening is wrong, wrong and sickening. Almost all of the U.S. citizens are gone with their families. Now we are in the process of evacuating U.S. employees (VN) who want to go to the U.S. because of fear of reprisals for having worked for the Americans. This is going slowly, for the floodgates have been opened to all the dependents of all the officers in their services. When this started, I met with their CNO, Admiral Cang, about what his plans were for these families if the worst situation arose. He said if that occurs, he plans to move his people to Phu Quoc Island. In response to the "offer," which came from the Defense Attaché about families of senior "sensitive" types (intelligence, communications, etc.), he said he had put out the word to his people that he preferred that the families stay as long as possible, because morale would drop if the senior families go, and the lower families don't get a chance to.

Several like Ernestine, who were DAO employees, have already gone. He didn't object, but said he had no part in that. Since then, I know of at least one who didn't follow his recommendation and sent his family out. Also, in response to a question about some VNN officers who are presently in the U.S. for school, he said it was up to me about trying with the U.S. to reunite these families in the U.S. I'm working on this.

Now, back to the situation at Tan Son Nhut. There are officers of ARVN and VNAF all over the place with their families waiting and trying to get out. I expect the officers will go too, if given the chance. Everybody in this country wants to run away. The military should be expected to fight for their country to protect their families. With their families gone, all they'll think about will be how they can rejoin their family.

This country has lost all will to fight, if it ever had one. (I described the whole situation and effort, after a week here, to Rear Admiral Mills, as a house of cards, or a paper house. "Once it started to fall, it went fast!")

Sunday, April 27, 1975

The first group of VGS started their processing on the 24th. It included Co Sung and her mother (65 years old). I tried to talk her out of taking her mother. She'll not get far under these circumstances.

Had them meet out at my house, about eight people in all. At 1800, came out to Tan Son Nhut. They and I stayed in offices all night. Most of them slept on the floor. I was on a couch in Captain Grigg's office. On the morning of the 25th, took them over near the gym. They waited there 'till 1100 when they got on a flight to Guam.

Meanwhile the next group was already waiting. I spent till 0200 yesterday morning getting them on flight manifests. Everyone is working under pressure with very little sleep. The second group got out about 1800 yesterday. Yesterday morning met with the third group. (I tried to talk them out of it, but they are emotionally driven.) These people were taken to John Wear's office at 1300 yesterday. They stayed there all night and should make it out here to the airport this morning. They'll come in minibuses and cars.

This is like an exodus, with people carrying everything they own with them. So many sad stories, and so many people pleading with you to save their lives. It is tragic.

Day before yesterday, I visited with the family of Captain Huong, who is now at the U.S. War College. Trying to get his wife and four children out. Had a message from him asking for wife and children, but while at their house, all kinds of relatives appeared with bags packed. One older woman, an aunt I guess, pleaded with me, saying "Oh, please help me." I showed her the list of names for Captain Huong and had to force my way out. While in the car and leaving, she was at the window, begging, pleading and crying.

I guess that, over the years, they have seen U.S. people spend and waste so much material things, that they think that everything in the U.S. is nothing but a bed of roses. They won't believe it when you tell them about unemployment, cost of living, medical costs, housing cost, the problems of cold weather (which they have never known). They only have this mortal fear of the VC and the desire to run.

Yesterday, I got involved in a clandestine operation. I got word that there was an interest in VN doctors for the refugee camp. At 1600, I went to see Dr. Hoa, the father of the two children who are now stopped in Guam, that I could get only him out last night if he could be ready to go and would not tell anybody. They didn't find him until 1715. He said that since his wife and his children were out, he would go on those conditions. He said he would be at my house at 1900.

He said he hadn't called me earlier, for the girl Tam, his cousin-in-law, had told him not to. She said the CIA was watching me.

What a terrible panic! Even the mamasans and laborers want to get out of the country with their big families. They have no idea and won't listen to fact. They just want to run.

Back to yesterday's story. While waiting for the doctor, I noticed two small white cars across the street from my house, with several men in each. Thought sure I'd be in trouble. The doctor arrived shortly after 1900. I brought him in while waiting for the driver. (Co Na's car had problems, so we were to use another.) Just as we were going down the walk to the waiting car, the two white cars left.

We headed for Tan Son Nhut. About three blocks from the house, the right rear tire went thump, thump, blivit. Again thought I was in trouble. The driver and I changed that tire in record time with the doctor up in the back seat of the car while it was on the jack. We got him out to the airport without any further problem. He hoped to get to Guam, where he had word that his children still were.

Yesterday morning around 0600, I started the third group from the offices of the Director of Construction, Vietnam (DIRCON) to Tan Son

Nhut. Went by carryalls and cars with about fifty people. Worked with them all morning 'till I swooped down to get Mrs. Huong and her four children (two albino girls). Got them on their way.

2000, Monday, April 28, 1975

Well now I have had about everything. Was down here at the Tech Bureau near the shipyard, talking to the VN employees who wanted to be evacuated. Tried to talk them out of it. At 1830, a rocket went someplace close and firing started from all around. This building is right next to the big marine barracks. After about 40 minutes of bombing someplace in the distance, it stopped. (When it first started, I looked out the window and saw a C-130 and two small planes heading south. They were both VN planes. It may have been a coup d'etat or just the Air Force saying good-bye as a planeload of someone headed for the Phillipines.) Understand there was an attack on the palace and some bombs at Tan Son Nhut. Probably will know tomorrow what it was all about.

Anyway, there is a curfew now and everyone here is stuck for the night. Wouldn't go out anyway, for I expect everyone is jumpy. I have a curfew pass which permits going out after curfew. Used it one night last week transporting people after 2000, but not tonight. That one time, I was driving (for the first time in Saigon). Bill Grigg was with me. Going out Cong Ly toward Tan Son Nhut, I said that I didn't know what gear that old car was in. It wasn't Co Na's but another old one. The light on the gear indicator was gone. I looked down to try to see what gear it was in and ran right through a barricade which had been placed across a bridge as a traffic control. Its wooden frame with barbed wire flew up on the hood. I screeched on the brakes and it slid off the front of the car. We were lucky it wasn't a barricade of the cement-filled barrels that are used a lot around here. The only damage was a broken headlight. I casually drove around the smashed barricade and continued. Then we both started laughing like crazy.

Back to the curfew. I have two male civilians and Co Na caught here with me. We just had Chinese noodles and Coca-Cola for supper. We'll be sleeping on the chairs. It will be a long night.

Back to yesterday. Got the Huongs out about noon. Put the next group of DIRCON people out around 1400. Then had a cook-it-yourself filet mignon steak at the Command Mess. Got a relatively good night's sleep in Bill Grigg's trailer, on his extra cot.

This morning started early, getting a few more people who wanted to go. Co Diep brought a brother and a sister, and Co Tieu had a sister. They hesitated for a couple of days, but said they really felt they had to go. Picked them up at a corner near their house. A real tearjerker. Sad to see a father saying good-bye to his children. I'm going to have many sad memories of families broken up.

Last evening after seeing so many unfortunates going out who had no possible way to make a living for the gang they were taking out, Bill Grigg and I decided to do some good for those who would be able to care for themselves or had connections in the States. We felt bad for Tam, who had been trying for so long to get out. And I said I intended to arrange for the Anh Dao's and their two daughters. They are old to have a seven year old and one about seventeen.

0830, Tuesday, April 29, 1975

Spent the night at the Tech Bureau. Tan Son Nhut started getting hit hard at 0400. It went for at least two hours steady. I heard that two U.S. Marines were killed and that a U.S. C-130 was hit and burning. No shave yet, and after sleeping very little during the night, I am feeling dirty, sweaty, and not so hot.

I am now at the OPS Center at the VNN Headquarters. By the way, my pillow was a flak jacket. I also now have a helmet. I am with Rich Armitage. He's the Naval Academy graduate who was here for about three years as an officer and stayed on as a civilian. He speaks fluent Vietnamese, so I'm glad to be with him. We probably will start our trip out to DAO as soon as it is clear. There was a 24-hour curfew imposed, and I understand that the Tan Son Nhut gate is closed to everyone. I will feel better out where the helos probably are to pick us up. Last night felt more secure at the Navy area than at Tan Son Nhut.

1300, Tuesday, April 29, 1975

Sitting in the DAO theatre with a group of about 50, waiting for the helos to pick us up at a pad outside to go to a carrier off the coast. Really had a tear-filled departure from Co Na about two hours ago. She could have gotten out, but wanted to stay with her mother. Yesterday she decided to take her mother and go. But now? Never.

At about 0900, we left the Tech Bureau by jeep for the VNN Headquarters. The Navy base seemed secure but so armed.

Even with the curfew, I had to move toward Tan Son Nhut, so I got Co Na to come to headquarters and we started through town to pick up Joe Buggy at this home, then to DIRCON to pick up Dick Smith. That was our rendezvous point, and there were still people there, getting panicky and somewhat wild. Several I had talked to over the past week while trying to set up quotas to go. All were so very anxious.

Leaving DIRCON, we almost had to beat them off the car.

Going out Cong Ly and Cach Manh was really scary. So many young people in uniforms and all with weapons. Knowing that the Americans were getting more unpopular as the shelling continued, I was concerned. We couldn't get in the gate at Tan Son Nhut. We were stopped by a soldier about 16 years old and turned away at the point of a rifle. A mission warden car was nearby, but it couldn't get in either. We waited alongside the road, waiting for a convoy. Almost half an hour passed, with small arms fire all around. That must have been into the air. Many VN cars and people tried to get through the gate, but were turned away.

Am getting hungry, for all I've had since noon yesterday was the Chinese noodles and a Coke last evening. Also have only the clothes I'm wearing, and this is the second day for them. I left the bag I had packed for evacuation.

Am now under a table. A shell just hit close and shook the building. Guess it is clear for now, but I'll be glad to get aboard that carrier.

I left the gear in Captain Grigg's trailer, including the carved tray from Anh Dao, which I really wanted for Sheila. Under the conditions, guess its best left anyway. For my hide getting out of here will be enough.

Pete Bondi is in the group right ahead of me, and Bill Grigg and Hank Hirschy are ahead of him. So if we all make it as planned, I'll be the last active-duty naval officer who has served in South Vietnam. (Found that Commander Dick Ward is still in the evacuation center, so guess I'll be the last 0-6 and above naval officer in Vietnam.)

This is the end of an era, and the end of a fruitless, terrible, and tragic fiasco.

I am now aboard the *USS Vancouver*. Have a nice stateroom. My group was the third group of fifty to get aboard a CH-47 and head out to the carriers. The helicopters landed on a pad where the old tennis courts had been. The fences had been taken down to make the pad. We were all staged in the same building, and as soon as the ramp on the helo was down, we all ran out in line to get aboard.

It was a good operation. There was shelling going on in Tan Son Nhut all the while. The Marine security guards were all around the perimeter.

General Smith's house had been hit with a rocket during the night and was partially damaged. The two Marines killed were sentries at the corner where you turn down to the DAO entrance, where the mass of Hondas were usually parked. It was a direct hit with a rocket. I saw all the burned Hondas.

The CH-47 was loaded in less than five minutes and was away quickly. Was glad to see it climb fast, for the VC were all around Tan Son Nhut and they have surface-to-air missiles. It was around 1545 when we left on the twenty-minute flight. It was sure good to see the Navy ships with swarms of helos coming and going.

Caught some last glimpses of Vietnam as we were leaving. Huge smoke billows everywhere. And high over Vung Tau, could see literally hundreds of boats and craft streaming out of the harbor seaward.

When we deplaned, we went through a bag inspection. I had only a briefcase. When some of the ship's officers saw me, they asked if I wanted to see the C.O. Said I needed only a shave, a shower, and a bed. The Mess Treasurer took me directly to a stateroom and had a steward buy me a razor, shave cream, toothpaste and a toothbrush, soap and three sets of skivvies. It felt so good. Then went to wardroom in trousers and a T-shirt to get some chow. Later made it up to the bridge to meet the Commanding Officer, Captain Frank Suzan. When asked what he could do for me, said the only thing I needed was a set of khakis. He gave me a set.

Spent most of the evening talking with DAO officers and people and some ship's officers. Too keyed up for sleep, but it will catch up.

No other paper, so writing on back of some requests for help given in the last few days. Helped some, others didn't have time. How will I ever face any of those officers who asked for help in evacuating their families when time ran out? Will always wonder about and be haunted by those who were close to me and who I should have helped, like Captain Luan and Commander Hung. Both could have gotten out if I hadn't been helping DAO employees. There were just not enough U.S. citizens when we cut back to four officers and one civilian (Robbie).

Wednesday, April 30, 1975

The message I sent yesterday should be home by now. Went to bed at 0100. Didn't sleep much. Up at 0600 to go topside. Just starting to get light. Many small VN boats all over the place. Several abandoned ones were burning. All the VN will be transferee to one of two of the MSTS ships, the *Pioneer Commander* and the *Pioneer Contender*. They'll be taken to Guam.

We were here all day for that wrapup. Expect it will be a few hours before we head out for Subic.

Today was just watching. Understand the VN helos which came out bringing their own people were taken aboard some ships and then, since their props don't fold as the Navy's do for space, they were pushed over the side.

Have wondered all day what might be happening in Saigon to the people. It is rumored that there is a cease-fire. If so, that is good, but I still hate to think of the treatment some friends and their families will get.

After lunch, got four hours good, solid sleep. Feel much more alive.

The start of my twelfth month on this tour. How I wish this last month never happened. The *Vancouver* is still at anchor, being the receiving point for helos carrying VN, who will then be carried by the ship's LCMs to the MSTS ships.

Saw one helo unload about twenty-five young VN men, all ARVN. It really makes me sick to think of them getting out and all the wives and children of friends who asked that I help are still there. I wonder what the results of this morning's unconditional surrender will be. I am afraid for the Luans, the Hungs, the Vans, the Quyens and the DAO employees. The reprisals will be brutal. And I'll never know.

How that will haunt me.

2130, Thursday, May 1, 1975

Maybe the Navy officers and their families will be okay. At about 1800, many ships started steaming out of Vung Tau. At least four LSTs, one DER, about five WHECs, PCE, PGM, YOGs, etc. And all looked like they were loaded with people. They came in our general vicinity, and the *U.S.S. Vega* is going to give them food. If the Navy base was blocked off to keep the masses from swarming in from Saigon, the families did make it. Sure will be interested in how many and who made it out. I don't know what will happen to the ships. Maybe they'll make it to Subic, where they'd be turned over to the U.S. The people will go to Guam, I guess.

Will sleep better tonight.

Chapter 19

Mary's Place

A textbook example of ethnic assimilation is on display six days a week in upstate South Carolina, ten thousand miles and more than a generation removed from Saigon, 1975. A restaurant located near Interstate 77 is called "Mary's Place." The menu features barbecue, fried chicken, cheeseburgers, and a wide assortment of vegetables such as okra, green beans, and corn. The booths are always packed at the lunch hour as truck drivers and local business people savor the food and listen to country music. "Mary's Place" is one of the most prosperous restaurants in York County.

Presiding over the establishment, serving as hostess and chief cook, is Mary Vu. She and her helicopter pilot husband fled Vietnam on May 1, 1975. Within two years she had become so Americanized that she christened a new daughter "Amy" in honor of President Jimmy Carter's child. And, as her husband and two daughters tapped into the economic growth of neighboring "new south" city Charlotte, North Carolina, Mary opened "Mary's Place" "because I like to eat."[1]

We were the first Vietnamese family in Rock Hill. My oldest daughter was sixteen months old when we came. We had a couple that sponsored us. They have both passed away. We loved them dearly. They were very special to us. They did not have any children of their own, so we used to call them "Mother" and "Father." They were parents to us because we did not have any family here. They were very special to us. They lived here in Rock Hill, right there on Cherry Road. He just passed away about four or five months ago. She passed away four years ago. We miss them very much.

In Vietnam, I was a housewife. I went to school until I got married. My husband was in the Air Force. We got married in 1972. He came over here in 1973 for training. He went back to South Vietnam in 1974. About nine months later, we came here.

We left May 1, because where my husband was stationed is about 100 miles from Saigon in Can Tho, south of Saigon down in the delta. He was stationed there about nine months before we came.

We really are from Vin Wan, about fifteen miles from Saigon. We left to go to Can Tho about a year before the war took over. It was still peaceful until the 30th of April. A week before we got out, I heard on the radio that it was real bad coming from Saigon. I told my husband I wanted to go home. I wanted to go to my family. He told me he didn't want me to go because he felt, due to the situation, he wanted us together. It's a good thing I didn't go.

When we heard on the radio that President [Big] Minh had resigned on April 30, my husband decided to leave. So we took off in a helicopter, because my husband was a helicopter pilot.

We flew farther down to Con Son, a little island. We stayed overnight. So we see what's going on. Down there, nobody knows yet. They ask us why we came down there. I was honest, and told them because the Vietcong were coming. They told us they hadn't heard anything. But down there, they didn't like the communists because of their religion [Buddhist]. They didn't like them at all. So we left about 4 o'clock in the morning. My husband and some of those guys were looking for the American ships, but they couldn't find them. We were so scared. There were thirty-eight children and adults in the helicopter. We stood up in the helicopter. We flew out and found a Vietnamese Navy ship. They landed down. We missed just a little tiny bit, landing in the ocean. I think God looked out for us. I mean, gee! I really believe that very strongly. We went to Subic Bay in the Philippines. A whole week I stayed in that ship. I was crying because I didn't know where I was. I asked my husband, " Why did we come here?" My family didn't know where we were. I didn't see any houses; I just saw water. If something happened, they might throw me in the water. I was crying. We didn't have any food to eat, no water. I was so seasick. I didn't have any other family members make it out at that time.

It took a week from Vietnam to the Philippines. Then we changed ships to go to the American ship. Then we went to Guam where we stayed two or three weeks. We left Guam and went to Pennsylvania to a camp there. My husband knew how to speak English. When I left, I didn't have anything. I left everything behind. I didn't have any shoes. My husband went to the Red Cross, where they had a warehouse, and got me and my daughter some shoes. I mean, I would cry. I didn't know how my family was doing. Who had died? Who was living? It was a terrible feeling.

I will always remember the helo flight. It was maybe built to carry twelve people. And they threw the gas barrels and everything off to make room. We stood up, just jammed in there. It was very frightening. I was young, and in Vietnam, my family was very strong Catholics. I was very young then, but after I left Vietnam I was in all this mess—.

Two years after the flight, I heard about my family back in Vietnam. I had a friend who was Chinese. His brother owned Kit Chen's Kitchen

Restaurant, and I worked for him there. My husband wrote letters for him to send from Hong Kong to Vietnam, but they didn't get them. The communists had changed the addresses, and some of them had moved. So I couldn't get in touch. We had a Catholic missionary in Missouri, and my brother-in-law, who used to be a missionary, stayed in touch with them. One day my brother's brother in Missouri called. I talked to one of the priests in Rock Hill, and asked if he knew that priest. He said yes and gave me the phone number. So I called him and asked for that address. So he gave me the address. So I finally sent a letter home. I got the first letter, and my mother-in-law and my aunt had died. She didn't know where we were. My husband was an only child. It was hard. We sent a letter home, but they sent it back to us. They returned it because they didn't have that address. I cried and I told my husband, "I think that's it," because we were never going to get in touch with my family again. I cried for days and days. But finally I found out. We sponsored one of my older sisters, and I went home six years ago.

Oh, I cried when the pilot said we had touched down in Vietnam. I looked down there and I started crying. I was shaking because I was so nervous. I didn't know what it would be like now. I was crying because it had been sixteen years since I had seen my family. I was crying and one of the communist men said, "I know this must be the first time you have come home." And I said, "Yes." It looked beautiful. You know, you live here for sixteen years and you go home to your own homeland; it's just so beautiful. That's what makes you more upset. I was really thankful. It was a war country, and there was nothing we could do. Before 1975 it wasn't like that. We lived comfortably. When I went home six years ago, no, it's not like it was. Not half.

The communist officials were nice, but at the airport, when you come in they think you are bringing money home. That's the way the communists are. I guess they don't make a whole lot of money, and they want some. I gave them some. I don't mind because I thank God I got to come over here. I have freedom, and I can work and make some money. I shared with them. So I went home with some money to help my family. I didn't bring any money back here. I left everything I had over there. I came here with no money. I help the poor, the church, and my family. My family, thank God, they live fairly comfortably. They have jobs, but it's a lot of people—a lot of children.

We live very comfortably. There are a lot of Vietnamese now because people like it here because it's peaceful. A lot of people move from California and Louisiana because of the children. That's why they move

here. We love it here. My husband feels very comfortable here. The only
thing is he didn't have any family. His parents have both passed away. He
wouldn't have anybody in Vietnam or here. He feels he made the right
decision to come here. We both made the right decision to come here. We
love it here.

We have worked very hard for what we have. When we came to Rock
Hill, we had four cents. So I think we've been very lucky. Of course, you
have to believe in God to have the strength to make it to where we are now.
That's what I tell my children. You have to thank God for everything on the
table first, before you eat.

I have two girls. They are both in college. My oldest girl will
graduate in December from the university. She studies nursing. My
youngest is studying business at the University of South Carolina, also.
They do very well in school and we are very proud of them.

My husband works at IBM. He is a supervisor. We have another
business, too. We are partners in an electric printing business. They design
and manufacture boxes. It's over on Workman Street. He works seven days
a week. He works at IBM on Saturdays, Sundays, and Mondays. He works
over there and here.

We were the first Vietnamese here. When we went to church and
Father Joseph saw us and asked about it. They sponsored the Minh
family—Minh's grandmothers and uncles.

My husband learned English in Vietnam. He had to have it before he
came here to train. They had to take a test. He studied real hard and he
speaks English very well.

We are working very hard, but we don't mind. We are helping our
family in Vietnam. Helping the children go to school. We are happy every
minute.

We call my husband "Van." His real name is Ngoc, but when we
came to America my adoptive parents gave us American names. My name is
really Gua in Vietnamese, but they called me "Mary." My daughter's name
is Lam, but we call her "Lanni." My youngest daughter is "Amy," because
when she was born in 1977, Jimmy Carter was president and his daughter
was Amy. Momma—we call my American mother "Momma"—she wanted
us to give her an American name.

We have been American citizens since 1983. I do all the cooking.
People ask why I cook American style if I'm Vietnamese. I just learned
because I like to eat.

Chapter 20

Self-Preservation

As the chief of Saigon's Military Sealift Command (MSC) office, Donald Berney saw first hand the key role played by ships and boats in evacuating tens of thousands of Vietnamese. (See the specific numbers listed by vessel in the summary at conclusion of this chapter.) While he does not minimize the importance of aircraft, Berney stresses the ability of vessels such as the Green Wave *and the* Pioneer Contender *to load large groups of people and transport them to safety in Guam, the Philippines, or to the American fleet waiting in international waters. Sometimes, the ships provided by the Military Sealift Command became floating villages where conditions became chaotic. Still, the command zealously coordinated its part of the evacuation using a separate communications network to guide the evacuees to safety.[1]*

As it got down toward the end, we had five ships in port—in Saigon—in Newport, actually. We had been engaged in—basically refugee lifts from the northern part of Vietnam to wherever we could dump them off. Some of them were in the Saigon area. I think they moved some of them out to Con Son Island—and—oh, I don't remember the destinations of all of them, but this was a pretty hideous operation. One of our ships, the *Pioneer Contender*, I think it was—I think we ended up with something like 26,000 people on this freighter and, needless to say, when they came into port, they were not in very good shape. There were a lot of bodies—a lot of debris—excrement—they had to be cleaned. Anyhow, at that point we had five ships in port that were in the process of being cleaned up, and set up for whatever other work needed to be done, and I personally had very little confidence in the planning that was taking place at Tan Son Nhut and in Washington for the evacuation. It was basically airlift, and, of course, I have a certain bias myself, being a seafaring type, but I was convinced at that time that probably the most viable method of getting people in large numbers out of the country would be by sealift—at least as a backup for the airlift. I participated in a number of conferences out at the embassy, and all I heard was airlift—airlift—airlift. To really oversimplify things, all it would take would be one Vietcong at the end of the runway with one of those SA-7s, surface-to-air type things to stop the airlift.

The North Vietnamese let us walk away from the place. And, of course, that was to their advantage, too, but it was pretty sticky. Anyhow, as

I said, I had five ships in port. So along comes a message from the Joint Chiefs of Staff, addressed to me for action. And it directed me to sail the ships that I had in port based on—I think it was the DIA estimates of—this city was basically surrounded by long-range artillery. And what they were concerned about, of course, was that if we didn't get the damned ships out of there—if they started out down the river, they were liable to get shot up, and given the political situation at that time, this was totally unacceptable in Washington. So anyhow, I was directed to sail the ships. I protested to Admiral Hugh Benton, who was more or less in on my planning for sealift evacuation. There was a selfish motive there too, by the way, because I had—I was responsible for my employees, and people I had worked with— Vietnamese. And I was also responsible, of course, for our American employees—which at that point, I think we had six. So I got in touch with Admiral Benton, and—I'm not sure that I have the exact chronological sequence here, but the basic facts are correct. In any event, he apparently contacted, on a personal basis, somebody at the Joint Chiefs, and the order was modified so that we had two ships in port, and I sailed three. So I had the *Green Wave* and one other ship—the *Green Wave* was owned by Central Gulf Lines, which is an outfit in New Orleans, and was time chartered to the Military Sealift Command. And, as this thing came down, I was determined that I was going to take care of the people that I felt that I was responsible for. So, I guess, on the 21st or thereabouts—I was at the seaman's club, the United Service Seamen's Club, USS Club, which was at Newport, and the captain—the master of the *Green Wave* happened to be there—and he was pointed out to me. I hadn't met him previously—he hadn't been in my office—so I walked over and introduced myself, and I asked him if he would be interested in taking some refugees out that night, because I'd again received another directive—I had to sail the ships by a certain time to have them out of Vietnamese waters by—again, a certain time—and I can't recall now what the rationale was for the times, but in any event—so he very enthusiastically agreed. So this was, I don't know, around 12:30–1:00 o'clock in the afternoon, I guess, so we started trying to organize a sealift at that point.

Let me point out that what I was doing was commandeering a ship chartered to the U.S. Navy for a per diem of about $12,000 or $15,000 a day. I was contravening the laws of Vietnam. I was taking Vietnamese people out, obviously, without permission of their government. I was going to send them to the Philippines. And I was probably violating their laws, and, certainly, quite a few of the laws of the United States, to say nothing of the regulations of the U.S. Navy. You know, at that point, I didn't know what the hell was going to happen, and I figured, you know, whatever came down was going to come down. You know, the people were the most important thing.

So, I called Admiral Benton and I told him, basically, what I was doing, and my impression is that he was very unhappy to hear about this. But he didn't deny it or anything like that. I think he just didn't want to, officially, know about it. Because it, basically, put him in the position of being a collaborator. However, the message that came out was this one. The subject is "Sealift of refugees. Unclassified." First paragraph, "Classified" is now, of course, declass, "Possibility substantial outflow of South Vietnamese refugees via water craft to offshore U.S. ships in near future. Need guidance earliest on policy for taking refugees aboard ships, to include any numerical limit. Indications 12 MSC ships available with estimated total capacity of 58,000. Para two. Unclass. Related item: Approximately 1,000 refugees aboard MSC ship *SS Greenwave* on route Subic with Ambassador Martin's approval. ETA Subic Bay 270800Z April '75." Now this received Ambassador Martin's approval—evidently that's what happened—I don't know this—because, obviously, I didn't hear this, and nobody's ever told me, but I think that it is a fair assumption. Apparently what happened was that Admiral Benton went to Ambassador Martin and secured his approval for this thing. That's what I mean when I say that he saved my butt. Because, of course, Martin had plenty of problems of his own at that time, and might not even have thought of it, but he could have hung me as high as, you know, whatever, for this little caper I was involved in.

I'm pleased to say this—I got all of my people out with the exception of two who elected on their own to stay. They were women. One was the matron of my little guard force—security force—and the other was a secretary, and she subsequently—as I understand it—escaped. She changed her mind apparently and escaped, and wound up someplace in Europe. And I saw some correspondence from her. But anyhow, that's the story of the *Greenwave*.

The part that MSC played in this whole thing has never been a matter of record and I really deplore this. We handled the major part of the evacuation. Those ships sat out there and we scooped the people up as they came aboard. We were fully supported by the fleet, and—gloriously, I must say. Part of the problem was that a lot of these clowns that were coming out—Vietnamese Army, ARVN types—were armed and were in a pretty lousy mood, too, you might say—so we had had previous trouble—at least one of our ships, and I think possibly two—were basically taken over by ARVN people. Not at this incident, but previously when we were bringing people down from Cam Ranh and from Danang, and so forth. And so, of course, the masters of these ships were very reluctant to just take any inflow. Anyhow, to make a long story short, the fleet provided marine security groups, which included medics, and they screened these refugees as they came aboard our ships, and they also provided medical or surgical assistance where required. And this was fairly frequent, too. They also provisioned our ships.

On May 1 and May 2, we were very gradually moving out to get away from the outflow of refugees. Anyhow, as I said, we were supported very efficiently by the fleet, but it was the MSC ships that carried these people to Subic and to Guam. And, of course, they were the same ships that brought these thousands and thousands of people down from the northern parts of South Vietnam that fell to the communists.

One of the things that happened—as I said, there was one exception that I am aware of, where basically they diverted the ship—they commandeered the ship, and I think they were—I think that we routed them to Con Son island, if I remember correctly. And they wanted to come into Saigon, or someplace in that vicinity. Well, of course, the Vietnamese government didn't want these refugees coming into the city. You know, there was already an incipient panic, and all we needed was a bunch of frightened people floating through the population there. So, anyhow, they basically commandeered the ship.

On most of the ships there were some pretty competent people among the Vietnamese, and they let the Vietnamese organize themselves. Food preparation and medical, and, you know there were some doctors in the groups—and so forth. So it was a sort of a self-governing society. These were the better ones. Some of them, of course, were—it was just chaos—I mean, you know, people dying all over the place.

Well, you hear all kinds of stories. I don't know. One of the things that I got from an eyewitness—it was one of our contract employees—Alaska Barge and Transport (AB&T)—who was on his way down from—I think it was Qui Nhon—or some place up there—he boarded the ship, and was riding it down. And these refugees, ARVN types mostly—these were the guys that were coming down from the highlands that had been run out by the communists—as they boarded the ship, they apparently set up some kind of a screening process, and they were concerned, and I'm sure properly, about North Vietnamese or Vietcong infiltrators. And as they came over the side they would screen them—and if—one of the criteria, as I understand it, was that if they happened to have a pistol—a K-54—the Chinese model—or the Chinese model of the Russian weapon. Anyhow, if they had something like that or lacked ID, they marched them over to the other side of the ship, shot them, and threw the bodies over the side.

And this guy came totally unglued. This guy—our contractor employee—and by the time he got back to Saigon, the guy was a basket case. We had to ship him out. But that's another story.

There was another incident that I heard, probably second or third hand, but I have every reason to believe it's true, apparently they caught somebody—I don't know whether—there were women who were murdered, for example, for jewelry and gold that they had secreted in their rectum or vagina—and it may have been an incident like that—or he may have been identified as a collaborator—communist collaborator, or something like that—anyhow, on one of our ships there, they took him down to one of the refrigerated compartments, and—they have ring bolts in the deck—and they tied him down, and they took a hand grenade, pulled the pin and stuck it under him. We know about that because there was a hell of a mess to clean up.

I left on the 26th. I was ordered to depart by Admiral Benton, and also by the CINCPAC Fleet Rep in Saigon. And I left with him, incidentally, on a helicopter on the 26th. But, anyhow, I was told to go out to the *Blue Ridge* and set up our command post out there. At least that was the plan, which meant splitting our organization so this fellow Bill Ryder I mentioned earlier, stayed in Saigon—we flipped a coin to see who would go, and he lost or I won, or whatever you want to call it. Frankly, I was delighted, because I was scared silly. Well, anyhow, he did stay there and he organized the—or he continued running the ships from that point. He was the operations officer, and, basically, he was more familiar with what was going on than I was, and he was liaisoning with Admiral Benton who would call for a ship to go here or there, or something like that.

Admiral Benton had a big, big hand in running this whole thing. As far as I know, he never got any kind of public credit for it. Bill, as I said, ran things until we got the signal for the official evacuation, and at that point they contacted me—us, there were three of us by then—out on the *Blue Ridge*—we'd been sitting on our hands, basically, up to that point—just monitoring the message traffic, and one thing and another—and—he shut down the operation in Saigon. And we had under contract a bunch of tugs that were operated by Alaska Barge and Transport—and barges also—which included some specialized barges that we'd been using to haul ammunition up to Phnom Penh. And, of course, Cambodia had fallen by that time. And they were just sitting idle. And so these were staged in—at that time, I think most of them were in Newport—and they brought them up to the waterfront in Saigon, and loaded people—. But Bill was in touch, apparently, with some of the CIA people who had the same frequency we did in these little walkie-talkies—the Motorola jobs.

Anyhow, these people were diverted to the waterfront and we loaded them on the barges, along with a hell of a lot of Vietnamese—with help, by the way, from the Vietnamese National Police. That was very interesting, because we thought that we would run into problems with them. But they exercised crowd control while we loaded these people. Anyhow, Bill completed destruction of any files we had, packed up such weapons as we had—which we had no business having—. We had shotguns—I think we had a couple of submachine guns, and so forth—I don't know—It's a good thing we didn't get into a fire fight because you know who is going to lose. But, anyhow, he destroyed whatever communications equipment; the telephones and that sort of thing so that they couldn't be used; and packed up our radio equipment, and loaded it on the tugs and headed downriver, and then eventually joined us out in the fleet.

One of the more tragic vignettes that I remember was related to me by Bill Ryder. While they were loading these barges down on the water-front— many of the barges that we had had been set up to carry ammunition, and they had sandbag walls all around the perimeters—there was no longer ammunition on them—but they had these sandbag walls—and, parenthetically, in one case, people trying to scramble over on the wall—one of the walls collapsed, and I think there were several people injured or killed, but the part that sticks in my memory—there was a great deal of jostling and pushing and shoving that went on—and there was an old woman holding a baby, and she was on the perimeter of the barge—and it was only about, I think, three feet wide, or something like that—and she got shoved off, and she and the baby went down like a rock in the water of the river. And his comment was that, you know, nobody even looked.

Well, everybody's trying to save themselves, you know, and—ah— self-preservation becomes pretty damned important. One of the things that I discovered was that your whole damned system of priorities and—ah—order of importance of various things shifts rather dramatically in a situation like that. Things that you thought important one day are almost totally irrelevant the next day.

I don't know when I became persuaded that it was all over—I was in the business of preparing for contingencies at that point. If this happened, this is what we're going to do. I tried to cover—you know, the things that I felt that we were responsible for—evacuating people.

The first damned thing that happens when there is any kind of crisis is that communications implodes—it breaks down. We had—MSC had our own net. It was a single sideband net on 8130 kilocycles, I think that it was. Or kilohertz, I guess they call it now. And we had inherited this from AB&T, who had set it up originally for their communications countrywide. This had been a very, very large operation. So when the whole thing shrank down after the peace treaties and so forth, we soon discovered we needed some way of talking to our outposts, which were Vung Tau, Cam Ranh, Nha Trang, Qui Nhon, Danang, and so on. You know, we had people at all of these places. And, so, we took over the AB&T equipment. A lot of it was in the surplus down there in Saigon, and we were able to retrieve this. We were able to put first call on it.

So, OK. We had this net setup. Which over a period of time we refined, and put up some good antennas. We were able to hire a Vietnamese who was really an electronic hotshot, and so we had a real fine setup going. Then, when the evacuation started, and when things started crumbling, everybody lost their goddamned communication. The only thing that was really working throughout the country was our net. Everybody was using it. We had to continually go on the air—I mean the fleet was using it for public affairs stuff—for transmission of news, and all kinds of stuff. And we had to repeatedly—continually—go on the air and tell these people to get off of the net. That it was an operational net and—you know—there were lives and materiel dependent upon this thing.

Well, anyway, for a long time there we had the only functioning net—the only functioning communications within the country. And we had another setup, too, that had been set up originally for our convoys—our ammo convoys—which were running up to Phnom Penh—I never did figure out who paid for this—but Motorola was in country—they had their own technicians there, and so on and so forth—and they set up this net. These were these—it was like the cellular phone thing that we have now—and we had repeaters up and down country, and we could talk to our tugs, for example, all the way up the Mekong River into Phnom Penh. Down to Vung Tau, and so on and so forth—with these little hand-held things. You know, I could stand out on my balcony and talk to the captain of a tug that was up at Phnom Penh. It was really a great setup. And that became very useful, too. This saved the butts of those people who got stranded in Saigon during the evacuation when we took them, basically, in buses down from their building—down to the water front and loaded them on barges and got them out.

MSC REFUGEE LIFT
March 28 through May 15, 1975

Ship	Refugees
PIONEER CONTENDER	34,200
USNS MILLER	23,000
Tugs & Barges	6,800
PIONEER COMMANDER	22,000
TRANSCOLORADO	11,800
AMERICAN CHALLENGER	23,500
USNS GREENVILLE VICTORY	10,000
GREEN PORT	15,000
LST BOO HEUNG PIONEER	7,200
GREEN WAVE	5,200
USNS KIMBRO	8,200
GREEN FOREST	8,000
AMERICAN RACER	3,900
VIRA 8	150*
PIONEER CONTRACTOR	100
	179,050
	- 3,500**
NET TOTAL	175,550

*VIRA 8 - destination unknown

**Minus 3,500 refugees transferred from tugs and barges to TRANSCOLORADO.

Note: These numbers include refugees transported from the northern parts of South Vietnam south to Vung Tau, Phu Quoc Island, and other destinations inside the country; as well as those who left South Vietnam in its last days before the nation's capitulation on 30 April, 1975.

Chapter 21

Giving Away A Country

As the Military Sealift Command Saigon Operations Officer, William Ryder emphasizes the overlooked effort of numerous seamen to evacuate South Vietnam by water. In this interview, Ryder aims criticism at politicians and the media, who he argues, were "clueless" about the real situation in Southeast Asia. He is especially critical of the Washington policymakers who were more concerned about wrapping up the evacuation quickly instead of carefully rescuing all Vietnamese who wished to leave.[1]

Ryder, with a few contract workers who refused to flee, continued his efforts to ferry evacuees to safety beyond the April 30 surrender of President Minh's government. He does not consider himself to be a hero, but his dedication seems to be "heroic" in a war in which, as Ryder contends, the American politicians "gave away a country."

There were a lot of things that went on—you know—for example, the Ambassador's refusal to meet with CINCPAC and the rest us in mid-April to discuss possible evacuation plans. We had drawn up three of them. There were a lot of people who put a lot of effort into those things knowing we were losing the war—and I still believe that the ambassador probably never realized until the end that we lost the war. To me, either he did not because of his—he had a deep personal involvement—and there's no question of his love for the Vietnamese and his concern. I have never questioned that. Maybe that just made it impossible for him to realize that what we were doing was tucking our tails between our legs and running. The other scenario is that he may have been sold a bill of goods by his superiors that should we start evacuating that that would create panic.

They got fourteen or fifteen hundred people out of the embassy by helo—I had more than that on the first ship—one American flagship plus one Vietnamese ship—and the American flagship, of course, was sent out despite the ambassador's direct orders not to do it, because we had some people we had to get out. And there are several things that they don't mention. They don't mention the Consul General in Can Tho [Terry McNamara] whose helos were cancelled, and then he came out in a couple of Mike boats we had positioned up there just for a "what-in-case" scenario. I picked Terry up off the destroyer he ran into, sort of accidentally, that they had positioned there to land the helos on which he never got sent to him.

And he, literally, in a fog, almost just, like, ran into them. I picked him up—
I guess it was on May 1—and took him over to the flagship. But we spent
the night aboard the *Boo Heung Pioneer*, which was a chartered Korean flag
and former U.S. Navy ship. And Terry and I had a chance to talk that night
and he was not a happy camper.

He felt like his country and his boss just wrote him off. And as I say—
he was not a happy camper—and he and I got into an argument because—
you know, a Consul General is a big wheel, and I was a GS-12, and—since
the ship worked for me—the charter ship—the captain insisted on giving me
his cabin. And I wanted the Consul General to take it, and he wouldn't do it.
He said this is your damned ship—but he was quite a character.

But the other thing that I've never heard mentioned was that there
were two U.S. type CIA agents who had twelve busloads of Vietnamese CIA
agents that they had collected around the countryside, and they were either
told, or couldn't get to Tan Son Nhut, so they got to the Mike-Mike piers in
Saigon, and I picked them up on the barge I was taking downriver with me,
and we all went down together. Those guys were in the tug with me, and
these people were on the barge with a bunch of other folks. Four or five
bargeloads of evacuees. We got them out. That was due to those two agents.
And I saw them in the refugee camp at Camp Pendleton.

The water evacuation was as successful as we could make it with the
assets we had, and had we not been prevented from bringing ships upriver,
and had we not been forced to sail several ships downriver empty—with no
people aboard—then it would have been even more successful. The north—
and everyone knew it—the North Vietnamese had no interest in stopping us.
They had no interest in keeping South Vietnamese who wanted to leave the
country because the more of them that left, the less problems they were
going to have.

And, you know, President Ford stopped the air evacuation out of the
embassy from the White House in Washington, for Christ's sake. You know,
the people on the ground knew that they could continue it and take all of
those people out of there. They [the Administration] never asked. That's the
way that the whole damned war was run, which is why we lost it.

I'm obviously very, very prejudiced. I think that starting with
Kennedy we lied to the American people about why we were there. I think
had somebody—starting with Kennedy, and following through with Nixon,
and Ford, and Johnson, and everybody—stood up and said, "Hey, this is
over real estate. We don't want the damned communists taking over South
Vietnam because it is strategically important. It's not a democracy. That
ain't why we're there." I think that they would have gotten support. And
then gone in and gotten hold of—as President Bush did in Southwest Asia—
called up the military and said, "Hey guys, go capture South Vietnam." And

make it secure. Probably in six months time it would have happened. Well, I don't know.

But anyway—well there are several things—there's no mention of the numbers that we took out. I don't know—I guess that it was 30–35 thousand people out altogether. And there were people left who helped us so much—for example, a good friend of mine. He's Vietnamese. He was a businessman—did business with us—I called him several times and tried to get him to get up to Newport and come downriver with me—he wanted to save his fishing boats and so forth. He spent seven years in a Vietnamese prison. And finally got out.

I have no respect whatsoever for any of the American media people who were there. There was a case in—let's see—it would have been—early April—I guess—as the Khmer Rouge were capturing both sides of the river. One of my jobs was running river convoys up to Phnom Penh, and where they were capturing both sides of the river, and they were saving money and ammunition, and saving ammunition specifically by just tying peoples' hands and feet together and throwing them into the river. And, you know, there were lots and lots of bodies. I mentioned that to some of the American media people hanging around the Hotel Majestic bar, and their comment was that their viewers and readers were not interested in that sort of thing. If it had been South Vietnamese doing it, they would have been up there in droves.

A lot of things that went on were just pretty disgusting, and, you know, many of the government agencies made no attempt whatsoever to help their people. We did. The one thing that Don—Don Berney set it up, and I was in a position to carry it out toward the end. All of our people and their families who wanted to get out of Vietnam got out of Vietnam. And I'm proud of that. I'm very proud of that.

We had been told that we could not use the *Greenwave* for refugees. We put, I don't know, 800 or 1000 people aboard it, and suggested that the master might want to hold a stowaway search once he got down outside the three mile limit. Which he did. And he did report that he'd found, I don't know, 850 or 900 stowaways. Hugh Benton—in order to keep—I guess to keep my ass out of jail—eventually got the ambassador to agree that he had agreed. Which was absolutely not true but there was a message sent to that effect. That was an absolute fallacy. That was directly against orders. The other thing that has never been mentioned is that the only way that I stayed at Newport was because there were five contract employees of AB&T, who stayed once the contract was cancelled. Which it was, and their employer told them to get their butts out, and provided airplane tickets—this was early on. They had a meeting at the Seamen's Club, and I can remember that meeting—at lunch the day that the Seamen's Club closed because of the situation, and they unanimously decided that they were going to stay as long as Ryder stayed. Otherwise, I could not have stayed. They made it possible. They did get an award from MSC. But I was not left alone. They never got public recognition for that. Now, these were people who had no business being there, except that they cared. And as I say, there was no way that I could have stayed had they not stayed. Because, they, very honestly—they were better known to the Vietnamese Port Commander and his people, because they worked up there, and some of them had been in the country for years, had Vietnamese wives and families. They were better known to some Vietnamese than I was. The fact that they were still there kept us out of a lot of trouble. And that's never been recognized publicly, you know. And these people to me were much more—I don't like the word hero—much more worthy of recognition than I was. I was doing what I considered to be my job, and I was still being paid. They weren't. I don't give a damn if my name is ever mentioned anywhere, but I would like to see the true story of what happened there told. I would like to see the people who really did the job recognized.

You know, I can remember our tug ran out of fuel. We were—I guess that we had five tugs and barges. The barges all had sandbag walls—because we had used them to take ammo up to Phnom Penh—they were big 2000 ton barges—and the particular one I was in was the *Touchi Maru*, the crew had left and our acting engineer was an automobile mechanic, and, I believe, a Filipino—nobody had told him about the tanks—in a tug, generally, you physically pump the fuel up to a tank that's up over the wheelhouse, or up over the engine level, and it flows down by gravity—well, nobody had told him about that, so we ran out of fuel. And we were aground against the— I guess it was the east bank of the river, and we were taking an occasional B-40, and they were not serious—you know, some small arms—and eventually it all got figured out and we got underway again. And you know, the skipper of that particular tug happened to be Australian—all of my people running the Mekong were third country nationals and Vietnamese. No Americans were supposed to go up there. I called out to the flagship and asked them if there was any chance—I said that I'm aware that you can't fire on the North Vietnamese, and so forth—is there any chance of just getting a couple of aircraft to come in over the river real low, just to get these guys to put their damned heads down so that they don't get serious and decide that they really do want to blow us out of the water. And the admiral got back to Washington immediately, and came back on the air personally and said, "Bill, the State Department says that we cannot intrude on Vietnamese airspace. Now ain't that a shit?" And, you know, that's the way things were.

Well, they blew it big time. I think of the people who chickened out. Not the military. I hate to say this. I really don't think that the people in the

State Department had the feeling that we had—with the exception—the ambassador had the feeling. And maybe that was his problem. But the rest of them didn't give a damn.

We were still in the river on the 30th, which was, of course, when they surrendered. But we had been talking to these two CIA guys, with their buses, which is why we stopped at downtown Saigon at the Mike-Mike piers, and it was a Chinese fireboat drill getting out. One of my damned barges got stuck across the two piers and blocked in a South Vietnamese patrol boat, which pissed them off mightily. And my operations guy was piloting the *Boo Heung Pioneer*, the Korean LST, down. And those guys—they'd wanted to leave earlier, and I just explained to the captain that would be difficult when they started firing at his wheelhouse, so he stayed until we told him he could go.

There were a lot of things going on. They started rocketing much more. And we had been able to see them across the river for quite some period of time. And, you know, that's the other thing that pissed me off. There were videos taken from up on our roof with all kinds of credits given to the American television people—none of whom were there. The crew that came up and took those videos were South Vietnamese. There were no Americans anywhere nearby, except us. And, you know—those people are so phony. But we decided—I decided—and all of this was in conjunction with my AB&T folks—that we just simply couldn't stay any longer if we really had any interest in surviving.

It took us awhile to get down the river. Between running out of fuel and stopping at the Mike-Mike pier, and—you know—there are scenes there that I still—still don't want to think about, you know. We literally had to threaten to shoot women and children to stop people from getting on the barge after we figured we had all of the people we could actually carry.

You know, who the hell am I to play God!

You know, it was OK for the State Department and the President to play God, but they didn't have to look into the faces of those people.

What we were doing on May 1—we were out of the river. And we were doing several things. One, I was picking up the Consul General, as I said, and his folks, and took them over to the flagship. We took people off of fishing boats and distributed them around. This is all with the charter tugs we had who were still working for us. They were still under hire.

We made a conscious decision to let one of the tugs go back to Saigon because the Vietnamese crew on it had decided that's what they wanted to do. They decided that because their families were there and all, and there had been an unofficial agreement with them that if they would help us get that tug out with its barge that we would let them go back. The only way that they had to go back was to take the tug, and that belonged to AB&T. That happened to be an American flag company. With my acquiescence—my full acquiescence. There was never a doubt in my mind that those people had the right to do that.

I think that altogether—remember now, a lot of people left on their own by fishing boats and so forth, altogether we got 130,000 people out. And we spent a lot of time—as a matter of fact—with our supertugs—we had two very large, very high horsepower Japanese tugs—as we got the people off of those fishing boats just running them over and sinking them. Which, in retrospect, I wish we hadn't done, because I think they would have been valuable to the people who didn't escape. You know, they could have used them to help themselves subsist, perhaps. At the time it seemed like the thing to do.

Then there were the South Vietnamese helo pilots who flew out to the fleet. Immediately after landing, the helicopters were pushed over the side. There was no choice. Otherwise, there would have been absolutely no place to land, and, you know, there is another story there, and I don't think that there is any documentation on it.

There was a Vietnamese Air Force captain who, when he watched this awhile, figured out it would save a lot of time if he just jumped in the choppers, took them out a little bit—dumped them—jumping in the water first—and then got taken back aboard the flagship to do it again. He did that with I don't know how many choppers. And, you know, he saved a lot of time, and probably thereby a lot of lives. And, again, that's not been written up. The publicity has all been on those who flew out with their aircraft.

I think President Ford didn't have a clue. He was getting horrible advice. The State Department was making sure that he didn't get any information from the people on the scene who would have told him—and were trying to tell him, "That—hey, we can get the rest of these people out. We're not—you know, we're not risking—we're not grossly risking lives." Of course, we were risking lives. Any clown with a weapon could have shot down a helo. They're the easiest thing in the world to shoot down. And anybody who had really wanted to could have stopped me. But they didn't want to. And we knew that. And I think Henry Kissinger—I think he was— he's always been very concerned with how Kissinger looks.

But I think—you know—maybe had Nixon burned the tapes, the whole thing would have been different. He would have gotten support for us, and we would have stayed there—that whole war—we held convoys of ammunition in Vung Tau to go up the river to Phnom Penh, waiting for the Congress to expressly approve that particular amount of money to pay for it. And, of course, we lost Cambodia before we lost Vietnam. You know, they said, well the Cambodians won't fight. Well, the Cambodian Navy lost thirty percent of its personnel killed the first three months of 1975. Not wounded—killed. And the Army—no—they didn't fight, and if I were them, I wouldn't have either, because they weren't being supported. But the Navy sure as hell did. They—and I can remember the commodore, with tears in his eyes, at a meeting up in Phnom Penh, begging his Army counterparts to join the war and help him save his country. And they didn't. People properly led, Vietnamese, Cambodians—they paid for it.

I can find nothing that happened that I can take pride in, except for some minor accomplishments, like—like getting some people out that really needed to be gotten out. You know, like those twelve busloads of CIA agents—the relatives of the people who worked for us—the relatives of the people who worked for the port commander and for the pilots and the ship's agents, and so forth. But, you know, that's—that's so minor—you know—it's really so minor—we gave a—we essentially gave away a country. And they are still suffering for it. You know—they say that they didn't kill a lot of people. No, they didn't. But they put a hell of a lot of people in jail for a hell of a long time.

You know—I've got a framed copy of a drawing that a North Vietnamese made of my friend, declaring him public enemy number one. Riding a bomb, dropping American money on the populace, because he happened to be a capitalist.

Chapter 22

Last Woman Out

Sally Vinyard, a civilian employee of the Defense Department and reportedly the last American woman to be evacuated during "Operation Frequent Wind," spent seventy-two months in Vietnam on two separate tours beginning in 1967. As Director of Housing she played a key role in providing shelter for Americans and South Vietnamese as the population around the embassy compound swelled in April 1975. She recalls, "You really felt uneasy all the time." One of the most traumatic events for Vinyard was the tragic crash of the "Operation Babylift" C-5A plane. Still haunted by the horror of these deaths, Vinyard vividly remembers hearing about the crash.[1]

I was sitting at my desk going over the manifest, and this woman from the management office came running over screaming, "My God, Sally, they've killed all our women."

I got a call from Command Center. "Sally, we need all the sheets and pillowcases that you can get for body bags." The pillowcases were for the babies. I think there were over 300 babies on that C-5A, and there were over 200 killed. Thirty-four of the escort women killed were my personal friends.

I went around Saigon and stripped beds and took the sheets to the hospital. Then I had to stay there and get housing for the crew that didn't die. They were bringing in the babies and running with the babies, and it was the worst—the worst. Everybody was in shock. It was a nightmare.

That is when I began to understand that the evacuation had started. The rumor was that the crash was from sabotage and that there would be a major attack on Saigon. There was chaos everywhere after that.

That Saturday there was a memorial service. I had thirty-four friends on that plane. We went to the memorial service in the theatre, there were so few women left. You'd meet another female in the hallway, and you'd put your arm around her and just cry. At the memorial service, they didn't mention the women. They mentioned the orphans. I felt for years that those women were just forgotten. I guess I mentioned it in other interviews. Finally somebody in Colorado contacted me, and when we had the Vietnam Women's Memorial, we had a very special candlelight service for all those women. We took their names and a flower to the wall for them. Fresno City College has their names engraved.

Anybody who was out and about knew that the end was near. They [ARVN] kept saying they were going to hold. Like when Danang fell, "Well, they'll hold at Nha Trang." Of course, nothing held. Here they are right outside. They were right on our perimeter, cutting holes in fence. I saw a brand new Mercedes Benz slammed up against the fence to block a hole. That's what you did at the last. I mean, a Mercedes! We'd all love to have one of those, and some wealthy Vietnamese came in and left his vehicle there. I knew a lot of these wealthy Vietnamese because they were the landlords. We had property leased from them, and we got to know them pretty well.

It was something that nobody could ever imagine. In your wildest dreams, you wouldn't think of these things happening. In a way, I felt that I have had a lot of experiences in my lifetime. I was the one who brought the people in during the Tet of 1968. Back in the 60s, I helped them devise an emergency plan. We were always afraid we were going to be bombed, and had everyone assigned in emergency shelters. I was always good at things like that. I felt like my whole life had prepared me for that, because you were dealing with one crisis every minute, it seemed like. You just use your best judgment.

The doctor came down one day and brought me this whole big box of medicine. He said, "Now, I want to tell you what to do. If they're hot, you give them this." He started going through all this.

I said, "Now I have to play doctor, too?"

He said, "Well, you're already playing God, so you might as well play doctor."

In one way or another we did, but not in ways you ever would want to. But who else was there to do it? So you did it.

We formed a team to do the evacuation. There was a lieutenant colonel and some civilians. Out of that team, there weren't too many who were there at the very end. They left ahead of time for whatever reason. It was like any kind of threat, like the Tet of 1968. Some of the people; who prior to this period of time you didn't have a tremendous amount of respect for; they weren't too smart, or they weren't too ambitious, or whatever; and yet, they came sailing through when the chips were down. Other people who you had looked up to, people you expected a lot from, turned tail and ran. They just disappeared and looked after their own hides.

I'll tell you something. I felt like we were vacuuming up the whole country. When we started, I never went to bed the last ten days. I stayed right at my post. The first night they called me at my quarters. It was on a

Sunday. They asked if I could come out because there were some people they couldn't get out.

I said, "How many people?"

He said, "About two to three hundred."

I put up 1,000 people that night, and I never went back to my quarters after that. I think that was the 20th of April. It was a Sunday. I do remember that. From then on, it seemed like every person I ever knew would call. I was getting calls before I left my quarters, and calls all night long from the United States, saying, "Please save so and so." To be truthful, I had to just turn off my feelings in order to just operate. In order to just function. You had to turn off your feelings.

When we were getting so many people and that first little bit of chaos, I got everything all organized to keep people in their own separate groups, which was important. Then you had all these different people coming at you at once. Ten thousand requests for whatever. Finally, I said, "Okay! We're going to have to have a shepherd for all of these little flocks." My father was a minister, and we used to hear all about the shepherds with their flocks, and we used to have sheep when I was little. I said, "We're going to have a shepherd for each flock, and the shepherd will come to me with the requests because I can't deal with a hundred people at a time. I can only deal with one person at a time." They picked that up and called them the Shepherds. They'd have one person as the spokesperson of the group. They'd bring these different groups in, sometimes by the bus-load. We had all the orphans there at that time. There was a lot of trauma. I had nightmares for years. Still do sometimes.

I was in charge of the staging area of the center at Ton Son Nhut. At first, the military were quiet about getting people out. About the 20th of April, the numbers increased; the word was out, and I never went back to my quarters.

The exodus had started. For the next ten days I never slept more than a few minutes at a time. We worked around the clock. The first day we put up over 1,000 people.

My job was getting them organized into planeloads, and handling problems. One day we had 7,000 people to get out and, thank God, our team had gotten very efficient by then. We scrounged rice from the commissary and fed them canned beans and Cokes. Somehow, we found powdered milk for the little babies.

If somebody had told me I would have to do it, I would have said, "Impossible!" I have to have my eight hours of sleep. But I did become disoriented. The building would seem to move around, face a different direction.

One time a busload of orphans was brought in. Forty tiny babies. I had six bottles between my fingers. Because they had been on the bus so long and were so dehydrated, they couldn't hold the bottles. They looked like newborns, they were so small. The skin just hung on them. For the little two year olds, I sat them down, opened a jar of food and took just one spoon and poked from mouth to mouth.

That's all I could do to help. It just broke my heart. Finally, they got clearance to get them out. I know there's a lot of controversy about taking them out, but I think anything done for these children is a big improvement for them. To be fed and have a place to sleep is a lot more important than keeping the culture "straight."

The North Vietnamese shelled the runway at the end of April. I was the only American left at the evacuation holding the center then. They couldn't bring the planes in anymore and people were scared. I was so tired and hot I could hardly move.

That day I thought, "What the hell's the difference. We're all going to die here anyway." Then I thought, "No, I can't let up on being organized with them. If I do they're going to know the jig is up." So I kept on being disciplined.

Suddenly, the building next to where we were processing took a direct hit from a rocket. When that thing hit I felt like somebody had taken a huge pipe wrench and hit me in the stomach. We didn't have any warning. Usually I am really calm, but when it hit I really felt filled with terror.

I had no sense. I don't think I did anything, but I really thought I was going to die right there. I said to myself, "If I'm going to die, I might as well die doing my job." So I got out there in front where they could see me. Up above, this old fluorescent light was swinging wildly from the concussion.

I kept the Vietnamese down for two hours. They were all right as long as they could look up and see me standing there. They thought they were safe with me.

I got one call from the Command Center during that time. They said, "Sally, you're going to have to move these people, because there's a fuel truck parked right behind the building and we're afraid it will blow up and burn everything." I was stunned. "You just get down here and move that truck. There is no way that I can move all these refugees without panic." So they moved it.

After the rocket attacks, they started moving people out in helicopters. That day was six months long. A Vietnamese colonel, hysterical, ran in waving a gun in my face, demanding to know where the pickup point was. Something came over me and I just took charge of him and demanded that he sit down behind my desk. And he did. He was scared and he did just what I said.

Finally, we got out on the helicopters, and we were fired on as we left. I went to Guam and helped with processing there. When I got home to the States, I realized that no one wanted to hear about it. It was too embarrassing, or too painful, one or the other.

Operation Frequent Wind

Chapter 23

Not Normal

As part of the research for this book we requested and received declassification of a study prepared in 1976 at the Air War College. The authors of the study were three lieutenant colonels: John Hilgenberg, Arthur Laehr, and Thomas Tobin. In the foreword, these officers write, "the authors believe history will substantiate the evacuation of Vietnam as another of America's successful accomplishments." Buried in the monograph, however, is the observation "the evacuation of Saigon and Vietnam will be recorded as one of the most humiliating political/foreign policy defeats in American history." The authors reconcile these statements by stressing that the operation was "a monumental success" when judged "from the standpoint of individual performance and of aerospace power—."[1] The extent of the airlift's success was documented in the DAO Final Assessment *and has been excerpted for inclusion at the end of this chapter.*

For our book, we interviewed two of the colonels, John Hilgenberg and Arthur Laehr. The latter officer was the project officer for the "Final Assessment" regarding the evacuation. Throughout the month of April, Laehr worked as the airlift coordinator and assistant team chief in the Evacuation Control Center. The following comments are his views of the collapse of South Vietnam.[2]

I arrived in Vietnam in March of 1974. We had intelligence briefings every morning. The thing that hit me right between the eyes was that they basically did not have any exports in that country. It didn't take me long to realize that even if we did win this thing, we own it, and we will have to support it. The country was just not self-sufficient at all. That was my first indication of the problem. I never had that indication until I went over there.

Our intelligence briefings were pretty routine, but there were sixteen North Vietnamese divisions, with maybe 200,000 troops poised in the DMZ almost from the moment the Paris Peace Accords were signed. They just sat there. And when Congress cut funds, they just came south. They just kept coming.

Our whole thing was, "How long?" We started meeting because we did not know how we were going to get out of there. We decided that we weren't going to be able to get out of there unless they came to get us. So, when we found out the helicopters were going to come, it was big relief because we did not know what we were going to do until that decision was made.

General Homer Smith was an absolute gentleman. To give you an example, when I would bring a report to him, General Smith would read it, spin around, put a piece of paper in the typewriter and then say, "Do you have a few minutes?" "Just sit there," he would say. "How do you like this?" He could write extremely well. He was extremely diplomatic and polite. I had to make him move numerous times in the Command Center. I was embarrassed, but things were hectic and I needed a decision. It was two or three in the morning and he was always polite.

We quit going downtown about a month before the evacuation. We had some bad incidents where they were not too friendly downtown. And we were afraid one of us would get hurt or not make it back. I had an incident where I went down for dinner in a DAO taxi. I ate and the DAO taxi pulled over to pick me up. I opened the door and a guy on a bicycle came wheeling over and hit the taxi—came flying into the back seat with me. I thought we had killed him. I was trying to help him. A crowd started to gather. They were screaming and I could tell I was in trouble. I looked back and my DAO taxi driver had left. I saw anther DAO taxi coming down the street and I just ran in front of him. He screeched his brakes, and I said, "Get me out of here!" That was the last time I went downtown.

A lot of Vietnamese Army and service personnel stuck right to it until the very end. Others did not. The South Vietnamese Marines held on until the end and fought gallantly. A marine came to me and said, "If you will take our families out, we will fight to the end." So I requested two C-130s to come pick them up. All of the dependents rushed aboard while the marines kept everyone else off. And the Vietnamese Marines kept their word.

All reports had to be cleared with the ambassador before leaving the country. We would meet with the ambassador. He would tell us what to correct and what to chop. We would go back and revamp it and then send it out. He was easy to work with. The only thing I observed was that he wanted to be responsible for everything. Towards the end, we would tell him that the communists were bombing the runway and it was time to evacuate. He could not seem to bring himself to accept that the thing was over. The president ordered him out of there.

I worked in the Command Center. We had direct communications with the White House. We spoke directly to Secretary of State Kissinger. It was a weird feeling to talk with those people. It was my job to decide who went and when, and on what airplane. Mine was a bookkeeping problem. Communications went very well. Colonel McCurdy came in early and analyzed the communications and told us we were vulnerable. He told us the communists were going to cut our communications. We'd be sitting there without communications. So, he got permission to send in a satellite communicator. He brought it into the Defense Attaché compound and set it up in a protected area. He saved us. The lines in fact were cut. He saved a lot of lives. Colonel McCurdy rebuilt the command post down at the embassy, too.

Colonel John Hilgenberg and I worked the "underground railroad," worked extra hours to get people out through various spots in downtown Saigon that we kept secret. What we would do was assemble people we needed to get out of there, put them on a bus, get them to the DAO and place them in a separate ramp where Air America would fly them out without anyone really being aware of it.

Near the end, a Vietnamese Air Force colonel who I knew well asked if I could help get him and his family out. I told him I could help with his family. As we got nearer the last day, he said he wanted me to get his family out and that he would get himself out the best way he could. So we put them on the "underground railroad." On the last day, the colonel hopped on a Vietnamese fighter, stuffed himself in the cockpit, and he and the pilot flew to Thailand. He made his way by boat to Hawaii to join his family.

Once the Sixteenth Division came south, the whole climate changed. We had a lot of our civilian employees come out and live in the compound. The night the rockets hit and killed the two marines we were scared so bad. Then we realized that if rockets hit our trailer there was nothing we could do about it. So we calmed down and had a beer.

The South Vietnamese, in many cases, panicked. They didn't know if they were going to get out. There were threats made: "Take us or we will hold you hostage." You got small arms from all over the place— indiscriminate firing. You didn't know whether or not they were shooting at you. There were Vietnamese paratroopers who became rowdy and we made deals with them that if they would stop we would get them out. There were all kinds of deals made. We had the entire staff of the Vietnamese Air Force come into the building at the end—armed to the hilt. General Smith gave the order to Lieutenant Colonel Dick Mitchell to tell the Vietnamese that if they didn't give up their weapons, they would be shot. Mitchell looked at Smith and asked, "Just me?" But the Vietnamese knew General Smith. They laid down their weapons.

There was a lull on top of the embassy. The weather was not good at the end—low clouds, low ceiling, thunderstorms. There was confusion about timing and acronyms. For example, "L-Hour" means one thing to marines and something else to the air force. There were screwups, but we worked around them. It was a massive effort by everybody. It was an effort that I had never seen before. "Operation Frequent Wind" could happen anywhere—in Bosnia or Haiti. It was a massive evacuation of personnel. You have to have one air boss. We had such a bottleneck over there until a three star from CINCPAC came in and cut everything down to a one-page directive. You can't use normal rules and regulations because it wasn't a normal situation. I was on the last chopper out of the Defense Attaché Office. I was told to shut the Command Center down. We had lost power. We had emergency power. I was escorted out to one of the helicopter pick-up zones. It was late at night—pitch dark. I was just led to where I was going to go. I was put on the back of the chopper and I didn't know where I was going. On the way out, some guy said, "You want a swig?" His canteen was full of bourbon. As I flew away I was almost sure they were taking us someplace on land. And when we set down, I was shocked to see that I was on the *Midway*. I was on the ship when the Vietnamese family landed in the small plane. They wanted him to land in the water, but he was determined to land on the deck. He almost went off the flight deck; he had never landed on an aircraft carrier before, but he made it. And a big cheer went up.

AIRLIFT STATISTICS 1-30 APRIL

Day	Type of Aircraft	Daily Evacuees			Cumulative Evacuees		
		US	Others	Total	US	Others	Total
1	C-141	--------------Data Not Available--------------					
2	C-141	--------------Data Not Available--------------					
3	C-141	--------------Data Not Available--------------					
4	C-141	--------------Data Not Available--------------					
5	C-141	--------------Data Not Available--------------					
6	C-141	258	–	258	258	–	258
7	C-141	246	–	504	504	–	504
8	C-141	81	–	585	585	–	585
9	C-141	141	372	513	726	372	1,098
10	C-141	138	666	804	864	1,038	1,902
11	C-141	194	647	841	1,058	1,685	2,743
12	C-141	84	100	184	1,142	1,785	2,927
13	C-141	143	52	195	1,285	1,837	3,122
14	C-141	94	50	144	1,379	1,887	3,266
15	C-141	86	348	434	1,465	2,235	3,700
16	C-141	86	61	147	1,551	2,296	3,847
17	C-141	74	106	180	1,625	2,402	4,027
18	C-141	612	374	986	2,237	2,776	5,013
19	C-141	300	UNK	300	2,537	2,776	5,313
20	C-141	147	43	190	2,684	2,819	5,503
21	C-141/C-130	249	334	583	2,933	3,153	6,086
22	C-141/C-130	550	2,781	3,331	3,483	5,934	9,417
23	C-141/C-130	488	3,824	4,312	3,971	9,758	13,729
24	C-141/C-130	190	5,574	5,764	4,161	15,332	19,493
25	C-141/C-130	501	4,354	4,855	4,662	19,686	24,348
26	C-141/C-130	381	6,376	6,757	5,043	26,062	31,105
27	C-141/C-130	219	7,359	7,578	5,262	33,421	38,683
28	C-130	128	6,109	6,237	5,390	39,530	44,920
29	C-130/Helo)	1,373*	5,595	6,968	6,763	45,125	51,888
30	Helo)						

* Includes 855 Marines of the 9th Marine Amphibious Brigade.

Note: These statistics are from the *DAO Final Assessment* submitted to Commander, U.S. Support Activities Group, Nakhon Phanom, RTAFB, Thailand and dated 15 June, 1975.

Chapter 24

"Please Move Your Helicopters"

Major Bung Ly's courageous flight to the USS Midway *on April 30 has been featured on The Learning Channel. With his wife and five children he flew in his small Cessna from Con Son Island toward the carrier. He had heard on the radio that President Minh had surrendered and all South Vietnamese forces were ordered by him to lay down their weapons.*

Ly, however, was willing to trust his piloting skills which he had refined in Texas during earlier training sessions. Thus, he aimed toward the Midway *where he would drop a note to the crew requesting "Please move the helicopters." Dramatically, he smoothly landed as shown in the photographs that follow, and the crew of the* Midway *cheered his bold flight to freedom.*[1]

We really worked hard to stop the North Vietnamese, and for not a second did we believe we would move out of the country, or that we had lost the war. We were really short on supplies. We didn't have enough ammunition or enough fuel. We didn't even have enough bombs to do anything.

At the last minute we were told we must leave. All the families of the Air Force pilots had to move out of the base, move out of the country, and stay out. We didn't have the opportunity to fight harder. They tried to move all the families out. I didn't believe that. At the last minute, they say, "You have to go! Your family has to go." Then, April 28th, I believe, they bombed us. They bombed and tried to destroy everything. The night of the 28th, they bombed all night long until the morning of the 29th. The men in the squadron were there and ready to fight and take the mission. Early in the morning, I called everyone, but nobody was in control.

A friend of mine said, "Why are you still here?" I said, "I have to take the order." He said, "Nobody's around. Take care of yourself."

My wife and family were already on Con Son Island. I said, "What can I do now?" I just wanted to help, and I took off to see my family. Just to get away from the artillery, get away from the base. I said I was going to see my family. I'd be back if they needed me. So I flew out to the island on April 29th. I stayed overnight, and early on the 30th, we had a little radio, and I heard them say it was all over. You have to drop the gun and give up. South Vietnam is no more. Now I have to take care of my family. I decided I would bring my family on the little airplane I had. So, there I went.

The airplane was equipped with a radio, but it wasn't equipped with a headset and earphone. We just flew by vision, and I could not communicate. They didn't hear me, and I couldn't hear them. I tried to fly real low. I tried to do my best to drop the note down there and kept dropping, and kept dropping.

Every time I passed the *Midway* and tried to drop a note, they sent a red flare up. That means "No, No!" But I wasn't meaning to land. I was trying to tell them what I wanted to do. So I dropped the note, it hit the deck and flew off again. They sent up a helicopter to try to follow me just in case I had to ditch it in the water. That's what I thought. I believe that's what they meant. But I didn't do it. I couldn't do that with the family. An airplane with the wheels down will flip easily. So I tried to drop the note. I dropped one after the other from the window. The last one, I saw a lot of airmen running to grab the note. Then they ran back in. Then they started moving the airplanes because I told them, "Please rescue me. Please move the helicopters."

So I saw them move the helicopters, and I said, "Okay! I'll do it." When they moved the airplanes, I said, "Humm, I've never landed on a carrier before." The family and I were nervous and everything. So I came flying down for a first pass. I had to measure how strong the wind was, how the carrier was moving, and how fast. I came in once, and thought I'd do it on the second one. The second time I came in, I just shut off the whole engine. That way I could keep it short and stay on there. I believe I was back on about one third of the deck.

On April 30th, about two o'clock in the afternoon, my brother took his helicopter, and asked my family to go with him. His helicopter could land anywhere. But we didn't go with him. My family could have gone with him, but I had a few families from my squadron with me at that time. I tried to take care of them before I left. I tried to send them out. We had a lot of airplanes there, because at the last minute, everyone was trying to land on the island to just get away from the gunfire at first. There were a lot of C-130s, C-47s—the transportation airplanes. They tried to move about 2,000 people off that island. Most of them were Air Force families. I tried to help the squadron families without husbands to go first, then I would go. That's why I took that plane. Most of them went to Thailand. We were the last family and last airplane to leave that island. But I knew I couldn't make it to Thailand. It was too far.

This is what we suspected. In Cambodia, it took the Khmer Rougue three months to get into the capital. So we thought in order for the North Vietnamese to get into our capital would take at least three years. If we had enough ammunition and supplies, they could not get in. It took me by surprise. We didn't believe it a bit. No way they could move in. But, the farther we move, the farther we move, it was like, "Don't fight. Don't fight. Just don't fight." It was an order from somewhere. We don't know. We didn't believe it.

My brother's family got out the same way as my family. On the morning of the 29th, he flew his helicopter without me knowing. He landed on the same island that I would later be on. On the 29th, we lost contact with each other. The night of the 29th, we saw each other in the same place. Then early on the 30th, we stayed together until he decided to get his family out. He asked my family to go with him. That type of helicopter is supposed to take ten, but it can take twenty-five. They didn't care. As long as they could take off, they would go.

We met up together in Guam. We didn't know where they were, and they didn't know about us. "Where's my brother? Where's my brother's family?" We went through the same thing. He landed on the *Midway*. I landed on the *Midway*. We didn't know. We transferred to another carrier. We didn't know. We transferred to Subic Bay. We didn't know. We ended up seeing each other in Guam. By that time we knew we were both alive.

"Please Move Your Helicopters"

Chapter 25

Out On A Limb

Marine General Richard Carey had seen the war evolve—or mutate—from his initial assignment in 1963, to a return tour in 1967, just in time for the following year's Tet Offensive, and then back again after the signing of the Paris Peace Accords. As he observes, "So I had seen the beginning and its high point and its low point, and to me it was an extremely traumatic experience."[1]

Carey levels his fire at politicians and the embassy staff. The latter group seemed unable to make decisions and Carey, as commanding general of the 9th Marine Amphibious Brigade, notified Ambassador Martin that it was time for the evacuation to commence. Compounding the problem was meddling from politicians unfamiliar with conditions around the embassy. In his assessment, Carey judges the operation to have been a success—all things considered. His message is a clear one: let soldiers do their jobs.[2]

Politicians, for some reason or another, I think, feel that military men want to kill everybody. That is not true. That is not true at all. Military men really are trying to carry it off with as few casualties as possible on all sides. The politicians have just simply got to keep their noses out of it.

Probably, the best example of a case where the politicians stepped aside and let the military run it; and I think it probably resulted in an operation such as ours, and subsequent operations and prior operations; that when we got the Desert Storm thing they kept their noses out of it and you saw the results. You saw a highly successful, low casualty operation carried off in a matter of hours; and military men can do that if you just leave us alone.

You have so many examples where the politicians get in and try to run it. The Iranian prisoner operation where they tried to get the Americans out in 1980. You had almost direct control by the White House. You saw how screwed up it was. Micromanaging everything. You simply can't have that. You have just got to step out of it because the pros are on the front and they know what is happening and they are not going to go out and devastate everybody. Military are not trained to kill everything in sight. That is not the object of military operations, you know.

In the evacuation of Saigon, we had plans for just about anything to happen and we were confident that we were going to do it. We were going to do it very professionally and there wasn't any real concern. The only concern that I had on my part was how many planes we would potentially lose with noncombatants in them. People that were just trying to get out; the question was, "How many of them would we lose?" That was my major concern. I felt that we had enough plans and we had enough force and, obviously, I had a great confidence in my troops, so I knew we would pull it off. I wasn't concerned that we wouldn't get the job done. Not at all, and not at anytime did I feel that way.

At Tan Son Nhut, things were deteriorating significantly. From the morning when they had the rocket attack and they had the C-130s that were hit. Things went to hell in a hand basket, really. I think if it had good solid thought process, we could have gotten a lot more people out on the C-130s. And, it would have been a much more orderly process. I think, and part of the problem, also, was the fact that the ambassador wouldn't step aside. When I got in and called him, I said that I'm here and I have got the baton and he said, "No, I am staying." Well, that is what screwed a lot of it up down at the embassy.

That is a big part of why I haven't said much up to now, because I didn't want to get into a big donnybrook with him and have a big lawsuit going. If he had just stepped aside and let us handle it, we would have gotten the job done much more orderly, and much more precise, and much quicker. Frankly, I was very happy when we got them out because it was very simple after that. All they did was to screw things up. And, they are not familiar with how the military works; and the thing that you will find also is that many politicians do not have a lot of faith in the military. They don't think the military is, frankly, very smart and of course we think the same thing of them. You have got that kind of conflict going on all the time.

There has to be a plan, and I thought we had it. I thought we had in the plans that as soon as I arrived on the scene, I was in charge. That is the way it was supposed to be. Had that happened, we would have been out there about 8:00 or 9:00 o'clock at night, frankly. But, the way it turned out, where the ambassador and all his cohorts would not step out of the picture and wanted to try and micromanage the thing. And also, we did have a lot of feedback coming back from Washington, too. I had a communications organization set up in the DAO compound, and I was talking to everybody and his brother. Washington's feedback really detracted from my part of the operation. Trying to answer their questions. It was needless, and there comes a time when the military gets in there and they start the operation and they are told what their mission is—leave them alone. When you let the military do their jobs, they get it done well because they plan well. They have a very positive set objective that they are going to accomplish and they will get it done.

We were constantly developing and changing plans, depending upon the military situation, to take care of fulfilling our mission, and had we known that one factor—had I known that it was going to be a totally, not a totally, but a permissive environment where the North Vietnamese would not involve themselves with us, we would have had a lot different job, and it would have been much less difficult for us. I sent Al Gray out, the Regimental Commander, on one mission, one whole day to do reconnaissance to develop escape routes for us to get out. We had to do that and we had that plan and we had an alternate plan, and if we had gotten into a big problem at the embassy, we had an alternate plan to go to the soccer stadium. And we wouldn't have had to do all that if we had known that the Vietnamese were not really going to prevent us from doing the mission.

I felt like we were just kind of out on a limb. We were given a mission, and told to do it, with very little real information, and things had to be done quasi-secretly by us in order to get ourselves prepared to do it. I am certain that Henry Kissinger probably talked to the guys in the Alamo. That is the planning group that was inside the DAO that was doing secret planning on how they were going to get all of these folks out. They developed plans to move them from the rooftops and into the DAO compound and everything else. They had been working on these plans for quite sometime, and had to do a lot of it in secret from the ambassador. The ambassador did not want that kind of stuff going on. He didn't want the word to get out.

I think that his objective, that he held to until the very last, was, in my opinion, that he thought that Washington would change their minds, and that he would be able to stay. If you would have seen him when he came out, he was a mental wreck. He really was.

At about ten o'clock on April 29, I left; and the reason that I left is because my helicopters had stopped. My helicopters had stopped and I couldn't find out from the Airborne Battlefield Command (ABC) what had happened to my helicopters. So, I got on one of the last big aircraft going out with the Hotel Company of Marines, who were being evacuated from the DAO compound, and went back to the ships with the intention of going back to the *Blue Ridge* to find out what had happened to my helicopters. I wound up having to land on the *Midway* because they were putting aircraft in where they had the least congestion. Okay? Okay! So I landed on the *Midway*. Now I had problems. My helicopter was still in the DAO compound. I had left it for Colonel Gray to get out, and so I had trouble getting back over to the *Blue Ridge*. It took me about an hour and a half to get a helicopter to get back over there. So, when I got back over there, I found out that Admiral Whitmire had stopped my helicopters because the Air Force had said, "We are stopping; we have had too much flying for today. We are at our fatigue level—beyond safety limits and we are not going to fly anymore." So he keyed on that and stopped the helicopters, all of them. So I said, "Get my helicopters back in the air." And I put all of the Marines back in the air. So, once we got that going—it is now probably, by the time we got that all sorted out, about one o'clock in the morning. And now the White House is getting concerned about cutting this thing off because for some reason they had to cut it off. Now, to me it was because of the agreement that Kissinger had made and we were not privy to. We are not privy to this, and there again comes in that factor. Locked all this up for whatever reason in his own mind, or in his small circle of confidence, and so the White House came through and asked us how many more helicopters we had to have to complete the evacuation. That is when we called back into the embassy and said to give us a positive number, what is your total count?

They gave us a count and we sorted it out to the number of sorties and went back to the White House. And the White House said to limit it to that number of sorties. So we limited it to that. Now you have to look at the individual coordination of the HDCs (helicopter direction centers) coordinating this number of helicopters to get in there. In sorting it out, it is a matter of communications. You are going to find that we didn't actually get the word that there were still people on the rooftop until about 6:30 in the morning. All the helicopters, or what we thought were all the helicopters, had now been back, were back. We had another helicopter, and we still had some people on the rooftop. So we had to put another helicopter. We had to pull out another helicopter and coordinate that. As I said, about 6:30 we found out we still had those people [eleven marines]. So, by the time we ordered a helicopter, got it ready, got it from the ship back into the embassy and evacuated, it was approaching 8:00 in the morning. They weren't left there intentionally for any reason. It was a matter of communications, and you have to remember that communications was extremely difficult, because we had to go from the ship to the Airborne Battlefield Command and Control Center (ABCCC), down to the embassy; and that is the way it had been set up by higher headquarters. Again, people imposing their procedures on the operational command.

You know that we got ourselves into a war, if you will, and there were good reasons, initially, for going into it. For political reasons, we were not able to conclude it properly, so what we had to do was we had to do our best. It eventually came down to the fact that you had a small group of people trying to get us out of the situation with honor. We had to pull the operation off as well as we possibly could, to be as professional as we possibly could, with as few casualties as we possibly could, to maybe arrive at some false sense of success, including the miserable chaotic political decisions.

Chapter 26

0759, April 30

As a marine security guard, Sergeant Terry Bennington found himself very much isolated in the early hours of April 30. He was one of the squad of marines who, in the confusion of "Operation Frequent Wind," were left behind at the embassy. Twenty-five years later the emotion of those last few hours is still evident in Bennington's account of his role in the evacuation and the two hour wait for the last chopper out of Saigon.[1]

My job was to provide protection for Americans, classified material, and American property. That's what my job was, until the North Vietnamese Army decided to move down from the north to the south. Jim Kean was my CO back then. He was a captain. He assigned me to the rooftop evacuation site. I was the squad leader. During the evacuation, there were other duties he would assign to me as things would come up. But, primarily my job was to run the rooftop evacuation site.

From where I was, I had a pretty good view all the way around. In order to really understand it, you have to go back several weeks before April 30th. I think the event really started when that South Vietnamese pilot defected from the south, took the aircraft and on his way north, decided to visit the palace. I remember that distinctly because I had gotten off the post that morning, and for some reason, it rings true in my mind that between 0700 and 0800 in the morning, or around that time frame, is when he came into the palace.

The reason I remember that is because on that day I didn't feel like riding the guard vehicle back to the Marine house. I decided I was going to walk. I came out of the back gate of the American Embassy on that street Hong Tap Tu. The Marine House was on that street. It was only about six or seven blocks from the Marine House to the American Embassy. In between there was the palace. I was walking on the side of the street where the palace was, but when you get to the palace walls, you have to cross over to the other side because that's where they have all their outposts and all that. They had ARVNs in there. They had sandbagged positions and everything. Their job was to provide security for the palace wall.

I remember coming down the street, and just as I got to the palace wall, I remember an aircraft silently coming over. His engines weren't fired up, he was floating in. I can remember looking up at him, because it was kind of weird. All the ARVNs were pointing up in the air. People started getting on the ground and hitting the deck because the ARVNs opened fire with their small arms. This pilot must have kicked in the engines because I remember he dropped a bomb. You could hear it come down. But the first bomb he dropped, I don't believe it exploded. He took off, and I guess everybody figured that a big shoot 'em up was going on, but it lasted about thirty seconds. I figured that was the end of it, so I got up off the ground and started walking back to the Marine House. Unfortunately, he didn't leave. He came back and dropped the second bomb. The second one went off. At the same time that aircraft was dropping its load, every ARVN in Saigon, and there were quite a few of them, was shooting at that thing. Police officers, everybody, they were shooting all over the place. They did have antiaircraft positions in the side of the wall that opened up. So there was quite a bit of shooting going on. Of course, everybody was on the ground. I was pretty much across the street from the Marine House.

When they started shooting, the Vietnamese guards locked the gates. I went running across the street, beating on that gate, and that ARVN stuck his face in the little peephole there and "No can open." I took my .45 out and stuck it in there and told him to open it. He opened up and I slipped in there. That's really when the proverbial shit started to hit the fan.

As the intelligence reports came in, we knew that things were getting bad, because the population of the South Vietnamese Army was picking up in Saigon. They were mostly deserters. We knew the army was falling apart as it was coming down. We also saw on the news about the civilians getting on the road and coming down, too. The population in Saigon seemed to triple in days.

Most of those folks who had deserted the year before were already in Saigon. But, the North Vietnamese Army was pretty slick. Before they started anything up north, they had already infiltrated Saigon. They had sappers all over the place. As a matter of fact, one of the sappers was one of our taxi drivers. I remember him throwing a satchel charge when I was looking out over the embassy. But, that's the event when everybody realizes that this shit is going down.

Well—Ambassador Martin—you have to understand a little bit about that man. He was a strong-willed person. He had so much will, he refused a presidential order. I'll get into that, because I was the one who received the order and took it down to him. But he was a very strong-willed man. He dearly loved the Vietnamese people. He really did. He lost his son in Vietnam. You have to understand the power. If you were around the man, he just emanated power. He was like the Rock of Gibraltar. He didn't budge.

He was not a guy you could push. The President of the United States couldn't push him around. This was one strong-willed son of a bitch. He was strong willed, but a good man. Don't get me wrong. He may have been strong willed, but he had a heart of gold. I think the reason there was so much stumbling, was he honestly believed there was a political solution. He believed that to the end. He believed that they could fix it. I don't think he ever believed until he got on the helicopter, that the President of the United States would not land a landing force. I believe he really thought the President of the United States would bring troops in to repel the North Vietnamese attack.

The mood in Saigon, as it starts to build, starts in the normal populace. They were very afraid. You can sense the fear of the people. The way you sense it, they may still come to work, they may still try to resume a normal life, but that's all everybody talked about. You knew that the tension brought immense pressure. They were very concerned about their relatives who did not live in Saigon. They were very fearful that the North Vietnamese would kill them. They believed that if the North Vietnamese Army got to Saigon, they would kill everybody. They firmly believed that. In actuality, it wasn't a bad belief because the North Vietnamese Army did kill a few of them there.

It started out slowly and the momentum built. We had these women that would come in and do the laundry for us. All of a sudden, they started bringing their kids because they were afraid to leave them at the house. Then we started noticing they were staying at night. They wouldn't go home. We also noticed that on the streets of Saigon, more and more people were sleeping on the streets. The population started to expand very rapidly. We also noticed that a lot of the ARVN outposts were no longer manned. We assumed what was going on. The ARVNs were probably deserting, also.

The curfew pretty much went out the window. People were on the streets twenty-four hours a day. Before, that didn't happen. When they said curfew, those people weren't messing around. When there was curfew, there was nobody on the street, unless you were in a white embassy vehicle or something. They didn't play games with the curfew, but I noticed they got very lax on the curfew. But with all those people on the street, there's really not much you can do about it.

Around the palace, the fortifications started to get larger. They started to pull in tanks, more antiaircraft, more troops. That was basically right across the street from the Marine House, so we got to see a lot of that activity. We also noticed that at nighttime, you could see a lot of explosions of Korean rockets up north. Bien Hoa was maybe twenty-five miles from

Saigon. You could sit there at night and watch the firefights. You could see the rockets going off, the artillery when it hit. When that started happening, that's when the people in Saigon knew that the North Vietnamese Army was not that far away. They had all the news coming in from the civilian populace. The South Vietnamese were running from the north to the south, and everyone was headed to Saigon. They were getting all the stories of all the atrocities that were going on. I remember them telling us that the South Vietnamese Army was not only running, but they were leaving their vehicles, their tanks, and their weapons. The North Vietnamese were using them. Rumors started to fly that they were killing everyone up north. A heavy panic set in. But instead of the people hanging around the palace, they all started hanging around the American Embassy.

We got hit, and I wish I could remember this evening [April 28], because it started in the evening. I would say 1700 or 1800 hours tops. We were all, for some reason, down at the CRF (Combined Recreational Facility). They had a swimming pool and a restaurant there. I don't know how many aircraft hit Saigon that night, but it seemed like a lot. There were aircraft in the air. There were antiaircraft going off. The sappers hit a fuel dump and it went off. It was big time.

I think around the same time Ambassador Martin had left the embassy. He was at his quarters. If you came out the back gate by the CRA compound, his house was down about five blocks on the right. He was in his quarters. He wasn't even in the American Embassy. I remember the security officer told Captain Kean to get the Deputy Chief of Mission (DCM) inside the American Embassy. The DCM was over at the restaurant at the CRF. Kean told me and another guy to go over there and get him. So we double timed across the American Embassy compound, and ran over to the CRF compound. He's hiding underneath a table. We told him, "You have to come with us, because the ambassador is not in the compound or in the embassy. They want you there now." He hesitated. He didn't want to go. We didn't really give him much of a choice. We kind of reached under the table, got him on his feet, and started shoving him. When we got him rolling, he rock and rolled pretty good. We got him across the compound and into the embassy.

Shortly thereafter, the air attack—I don't know how long it lasted— came to an end. That was when Captain Kean made the decision that we would pull all the marines into the embassy compound. We always had marines on duty twenty-four hours a day. Our detachment was probably forty marines. That was all. He decided, at that time, to close up the Marine House and get all the marines inside the American Embassy compound. At the same time, they tried to pack up all of our equipment, clothes, and all that, and ship it out, too. Some of it we did get. Some of it we never saw again.

We moved into the embassy, and for some reason, it was determined by Ambassador Martin that we would send half of the detachment out to the Defense Attaché area out by Tan Son Nhut air base. We kept two squads at the embassy and sent two out there. That's where those two marines, Judge and McMahon, were killed. They were part of our detachment, part of those two squads sent out there.

We were briefed on the plan. The plan was pretty simple. All the Americans were told of what they called their prestaging area. There was going to be a song played on the radio. When "White Christmas" was played, everybody was supposed to go to their rally points. They would be picked up and transported to the Defense Attaché. We were going to do the whole operation out of there.

Well, before the North Vietnamese came down, before those marines were killed, we were running the air force C-130s out of Tan Son Nhut air base. We were loading up people on that like crazy, shuttling them out to the air base, putting them on Air Force aircraft, and flying them out. That didn't last too long because the North Vietnamese hit them with rockets. We were unable to use the air base anymore. They pretty much closed that down. They possessed the Tan Son Nhut air base, and what they did was, they moved their artillery up to the forward edge of the runways. I believe at that time, they had the ability to hit any place in Saigon with their artillery.

The marines were over at the air base in the DAO Compound where they were prestaging everybody. They did get most of the folks in there. They were putting them into the buildings and getting them set up and ready to go so when the helicopters came in, then they could get them on the helicopters and get them out. Helicopters were not the first choice, but rather the last choice of what they wanted to do. They wanted to use the C-130s, and I think they even talked about bringing naval vessels in to the port to get them out that way.

I understand that there was communication between the North Vietnamese and the State Department. There were all kinds of agreements and wheels and deals made, but the bottom line is, it broke down to where it was going to have to be a helo operation. What I think made that determination is when those two marines were killed in a rocket attack. Judge and McMahon were at the DAO. We got the word at the American Embassy about what had happened, and I think that was the event that determined it was time to commence "Operation Frequent Wind."

I remember a wave of helicopters coming in out of the South China Sea. I don't know how many were in the first wave, I'd say probably thirty helicopters airborne. We thought they were coming to the embassy, because at the embassy the population outside had grown so large we could no longer hold the embassy. We were losing the compound. They were actually coming over the walls, and we were no longer in a position to pick and choose who to let into the compound. We had barbedwire up there. We also had glass embedded into concrete on top of the walls. That didn't stop them. They were coming over. We had really hit a position where we couldn't keep them out much longer.

The way we got the Americans that were out there in the crowd was, we would reach over the wall and grab them by the hair on their head and drag them up and over. Ed Bradley was one of them. He was trying to climb over, and somebody reached down and grabbed him. We got a lot of them that way. We were not going to open those gates. If we had, we'd have lost the compound. Frankly, we were losing the compound. As a matter of fact, the choppers went straight out to Defense Attaché and they commenced their operation out there. That operation, from what I understand, went pretty doggone smooth. They didn't have a lot of problems. At the same time, they had brought in a EOD [explosive ordinance disposal] team. They were wiring that building to blow it. There were a lot of events going on. I believe General Gray was the regimental commander. He ran that operation out there. I don't think General Gray ever had the thought, or the plan, of bringing anybody into the American Embassy, because when we started to lose the compound, somebody got on the hook and communicated with the 7th Fleet, and for some reason, they sent us two helicopters with infantry on it. When the infantry guys got down, we were able to expand the perimeter again and really take charge of the compound. We had pretty much lost the CRA compound. We couldn't control that anymore.

We expanded the perimeter, and Captain Kean decided that the marine security guards would take care of the rooftop because we were bringing 46s on the roof and 53s on the deck. We would take care of all that and the infantry guys would take care of the exterior walls, keeping them out of there.

We got the CRA compound pretty much cleaned up, and used that as a prestage area. We were stacking and packing them there as the bird would set down. We had groups ready to go. I don't think anybody was prepared to use the American Embassy as an evacuation site to the degree that we did. They probably figured we had a few loads, and that would be it. I don't think anyone was prepared for Ambassador Martin's decision that he was going to take as many people, South Vietnamese, as he could.

He wanted to take them all. If he could have gotten them all, he would have done it. All I remember is, we didn't get any helicopters after they landed the infantry platoon for quite some time. We did get the perimeter expanded. We got everybody stacked and packed into the helo groups and everything. The weird thing was, there weren't any Americans. They were all Vietnamese. I think Ambassador Martin was holding on to the Americans because he knew as long as Americans were in the compound, they were going to keep sending choppers.

When we started getting helicopters in, one of the infantry guys was a fellow by the name of, I may be wrong on this, but I think his name was Lance Corporal Henderson. He was from the 7th Fleet. I had him on the roof because he had a radio, and I was using him to bring the choppers in. Well, he did do that for me for awhile, but I lost him. Eventually, as it got dark, he stepped off the back of that platform and fell. He went down, thank God, one story. If he had gone right or left, he'd have gone all the way. But he fell straight back. He got pretty banged up. We didn't have a doctor so I called in a helicopter and sent him out to the fleet. He ended up on the *USS Okinawa*. I got to see him later on.

After that, I had to bring one of my marines up to the roof. I brought a fellow by the name of Corporal Norman to be the helicopter support team, to bring the birds in. He did a superb job.

When we started getting helicopters in, we were getting both 46s and 53s. I remember the 53s coming in because they were landing on the ground. They went over the top of the security officer's building, and I remember the roof coming off on that. At the same time, I started bringing 46s onto the roof.

Our game plan was very simple because we were taking a lot of sniper fire up there on the roof. The game plan was, when the bird set down, we already had stacks of Vietnamese in the ladder well. Before that bird set down, we had them moving. We got that bird loaded, and they were out of there. We had to do it quickly because of the sniper fire. We didn't want to be standing up there as the bird took off, so as soon as we loaded them and the bird took off, we all laid down on the flight deck so they couldn't get a clear shot at us. It's hard to go over the time, because I don't remember how many hours it was. I just remember helicopter after helicopter.

Even as we are doing this, the crowd is getting bigger. I couldn't even estimate how many people were outside that compound. It looked like a million to me, just at the one gate. When you looked down there, all you saw was waves and waves of people. That's all you saw. I don't know where in the devil they all came from.

There was a lot of talking going on. I don't know how Ambassador Martin was communicating, because I know that after he left, we didn't have any communications with the 7th Fleet. Our batteries were dead, and all we had were quick 77s anyway. I think what he tried to do was prolong it as long as he could, hoping the President would relent and say, "Okay, land the landing force." I believe he was just going to hang on, but at that time, you have to understand, Ambassador Martin was a very sick man, exhausted. There was a point there, when you looked at him, you knew he had hit that point of exhaustion. He wasn't going to go much farther. You knew that. You could tell it by his mannerisms, his speech. He was so tired. So tired.

It had to be on the 29th. This is when a CH-46 landed on the roof. The pilot of that CH-46 was a guy by the name of Jerry Berry. He sat down on the roof and the crew chief shook his hand. He wouldn't take a load. I went over to the side and hit the button for the phone. He told me he had a presidential order for Ambassador Martin. This bird was for him, and him only, and it would set there until he got on the bird. He would take nobody out.

I went down to the ambassador's office. A staff sergeant by the name of Siguerra was his personal bodyguard. I went in and said, "Staff Sergeant Siguerra, there's a helicopter on the roof. The pilot says he has a presidential order that Ambassador Martin is to be put on that helicopter."

Martin said, "No." Period. It was not negotiable. He said, "Go up there, load it, and get it off the roof."

So I went up there, and I said to the pilot, "He said he will not go. He said I'm to load you and move you. So I loaded him. I filled him up with Vietnamese. I was stacking Vietnamese in there like cordwood. He took off, and we continued with the operation. It wasn't too much longer, probably a couple of hours, when that same helicopter came back. The pilot called me over and said, "This is a presidential order. This bird is for Ambassador Martin."

I had a little handheld radio. I picked it up and called Jim Kean. I said, "I have a problem here. This is the second time the bird set down and he's got a presidential order for Ambassador Martin to be on it, and Martin wouldn't get on it the last time." So he came up and I went down, and we met at the Ambassador's office.

Jim said, "Mr. Ambassador, you've got to go."

He went to stand up with his "No, I'm not going to leave," and I don't think he was going to make it all the way up. Staff Sergeant Siguerra was standing behind him. He reached out with his left arm and put it under his left armpit to hold him up. He said, "Mr. Ambassador, we need to go."

The next thing you know, Siguerra was dragging him out. By that time, Martin was resigned to going. Siguerra was a big boy, like 6'2" and real stocky. I remember as we were walking to the chopper, four or five people began to muster and follow him right along. I don't know who all those people were. We took him up. He had the American flag. We put him on the helicopter, and off he went. That was the last we saw of him.

Even before they sent me the Marine Corps helicopters, we had other helicopters. I was using Air America helicopters. I had the distinct honor of being the only American to put two Air America helicopters on that helo pad at the same time. We sent Ambassador Martin's wife that way, too. We sent her out on Air America.

We had been flying quite a bit with Air America to fly them out of there. The way we were getting so many people on, was we would get them up to the staging area and take everything off of them. We took their suitcases. We took their weapons, because some of them would take weapons like you wouldn't believe. There were M-16s, AK-47s, grease guns, machine guns, frag [fragmentation] grenades, 45s, 9-mms, any weapon assortment you can think of showed up. We had a guy show up with a baseball bag which you carry the baseball bats in filled with frag grenades. We took all that off these people, and throwing that on the roof. At the end of the operation that whole roof was covered three feet deep in weapons. We knew the more we could get off of them and get rid of, the more bodies we could get on the helicopter. They were doing that down below also. The fact is, one time we loaded a 53 with so many people, it couldn't take off. So we had to take some off, but my philosophy was to load as many as we could get on there until he could get into the air. We would take away all the suitcases, because they were trying to take everything.

Out on the gate there were people who offered us gold. There were people who offered us diamonds to let their families in. But we didn't do it. We were offered money. You name it, they were offering. But they were desperate. I am sure there were some folks who probably had money and gold taped to their bodies and got on, but we didn't care about that. Our only concern was getting the bulky items off them. That's all we did.

We weren't making the decision on who went or who stayed initially. The State Department Visa Section was making that decision. But I will tell you, as this operation rapidly progressed, whatever criteria they were using to make this selection went out the window. It was pretty much whoever you have in here, get them on the birds and get them out. Even if they weren't going to go, if they were in the compound, you weren't going to let them out because we weren't going to open the gates. We sent quite a few out of that compound. I don't know the exact amount, but I would guess twenty five hundred maybe.

Let me tell you, those chopper pilots knew their business. They were superb. Of course, it was scary at night with them coming in, because right before they set down, they had to turn that spotlight on. That was probably the worst part of the whole thing. I didn't like it, but we didn't want the choppers to stop either. We wanted to get them all on.

After we got Ambassador Martin out of there, we still had a few people in the compound to get out. We did that. Then Captain Kean said what he wanted to do was get all the marines, including the ground force. That made 120 of us. We had to get them into the compound and on the roof. We had to secure the roof and start moving marines out.

I was on the roof and got to see this. This is something I don't know if you are really going to understand. We had a lot of people in the compound who weren't going to go. They knew that. There were South Vietnamese soldiers all around the compound who weren't going to go, and they knew that. So now we have about a hundred marines on the ground that we've got to get into the compound through one main door and up eight flights of steps. So they started sending them in piecemeal, and they'd run right on up to the roof. Then they got down to about the last twenty-five. To the right of the front gate was a white building. That was the old security office. Down the road on the right was the embassy building. The doors to the embassy were probably forty feet high and twenty feet wide. They were made of solid oak and weighed a ton. The twenty-five guys formed a semicircle right there, and they are backing up to that door. They started to rush them. I'll never forget this Navy Seabee. I don't know who this guy is, I really don't. I don't know how the hell we had a Navy Seabee there, but he picked up this huge 2x4 and started swinging it around his head to keep them off of them. Everybody got inside, and he dropped it and turned around and ran inside. They slammed those oak doors shut and threw the bar down on the inside. They thought they were looking pretty good. Just a nice little walk up eight flights of steps. They went to the two ground elevators and threw frags in there and blew them up so they couldn't be used. They started walking up the ladder well, and the South Vietnamese, who were in the compound, got the fire engine we had at the embassy and drove it through the door. Instead of a nice easy walk up the stairs, they had three or four hundred South Vietnamese right on their asses. So they're running. It's a race up that ladder well. Well, when you get to the top of the roof, there's only one way in. It's a regular door. When they came through there, we slammed that door shut. On the left side of that door was a thin plate of glass. We punched that out and started throwing CS-gas and mace down the ladder well. We took a wall locker and threw it up against there and had five or six guys holding that door shut. We threw the CS-gas down there, and you'd figure they'd turn around and run the other way, but here's what happened. They had Vietnamese packed in that ladder well eight flights up. The ones at the bottom were pushing the ones on top. They weren't going anywhere. So they're stuck in there. We just maced them.

Well, we're on the roof now. We've got about 120 of us up there with the marine security guards and the ground forces. Jim Kean made the decision on how we were going to do it. He decided that we would get the ground forces out of there first, then we would start with the marine security guards. Jim was the one who decided who the last ones were going to be. Why he chose who he chose, to this day, I don't know. I don't know why he ever said, "Bennington, you'll go with me." I don't know.

As helicopters were coming in, we were sending the grunts out. We took all our flack jackets and gas masks and threw them over the side. We got rid of them because we could get more bodies on the helicopters. We wanted the hell out of there.

Things actually went pretty smooth, and we're down to where there's only eleven of us. It was starting to get light, but we told the helicopter pilot, "Don't forget, we need one more." So he takes off, and that's when there's this big lull. Nobody's been able to say if it was two, three or four hours. I don't remember. I know it was over two hours, and it felt like six, but I honestly don't remember. I remember that before the bird came in to get us, Jim Kean asked us what we wanted to do. He wanted to know if we wanted to go down below and give up, or if we wanted to climb down the rocket screen and head for the South China Sea. I do remember him asking that. It wasn't much longer after that we saw the spot in the air out there, which was the 46 that came to get us.

What we didn't know, and I'm really not positive today how it all worked out, but when we got Ambassador Martin out of there, from what I understood, there was a lack of communication in regards to the President saying, "Okay, shut it down," and somebody thought he really meant shut it down. So they shut it down. Then when they realized we were still there, they had to gear it back up. I'm sure they had to go back to Washington and say, "Look, we've left some on the roof. We need to go get them." We think that's where the lull occurred. It kind of makes sense, because if I was out there and the President told me to stop, I'd stop, too. Of course, I'd fight my case. I'm reasonably sure that's how that transpired. It was not intentional. They didn't really forget us, it was just a lack of communication for a short while. We're pretty much sitting on the roof, trying not to get too high because we don't want to get shot. We didn't want the North Vietnamese Army to know we were up there. We were hiding. But there was a lot of activity going on in the American Embassy compound. South Vietnamese— you had ARVNs and everybody in there, carrying weapons. It was like the shootout at the O.K. Corral. Everybody was running around shooting and all this good stuff. We still had that door barricaded so they still couldn't get to us. I do remember one trying to climb up the rocket screen. A staff sergeant by the name of Sparks picked up a fire extinguisher and threw it down on him and knocked him off the rocket screen. The rest of them decided they didn't want to try that. We pretty much hung up there. We stayed up there, and were as quiet as we could be. We watched the firefights going on. We could see the North Vietnamese Army. We could see some of the tanks and everybody forming up. We didn't want to get in any firefight. They had a lot bigger stuff than we did, and we knew the last thing we wanted to do was get in a firefight. If we hadn't seen the chopper when we did, if it had waited fifteen minutes, we'd have probably climbed down the rocket screen by that time because we were all pretty convinced we could make it to the South China Sea. We did know the city of Saigon quite well. We knew how to get to the harbor. We figured we'd probably break off in teams, two to a team, and some of us would make it. That's pretty much what was going through our minds.

All I remember was it was light when they came and got us. I know that it was 0759 on 30 April—one minute before the North Vietnamese Army commenced its major assault. We were in the air while they were assaulting.

Chapter 27

Fear, Rumors, And Panic

"They offered me Vietnam," journalist George Esper says of his superiors at the Associated Press. He realized in the summer of 1965 that the war would be a big story. He stayed in Vietnam until September 1966 and then returned to New York City. The war fascinated him, however, and he accepted another assignment in Saigon, remaining until he was expelled by the communist government in June 1975.[1]

Esper vividly recalls the scene outside the American Embassy as the communists approached. Panic was evident and Esper suggests that some of this panic was produced by our own Central Intelligence Agency which spread the rumor that the arrival of the North Vietnamese would trigger a bloodbath. While this bloodbath did not occur, thousands of southerners were sentenced to re-education camps. As a journalist, Esper chronicled the transition from Saigon to Ho Chi Minh City.

In Saigon, in April 1975, there was despair, a panorama of human emotions. There was resentment, of course. The Vietnamese felt in the final evacuation that the Americans were abandoning them, leaving them exposed to communist atrocities and harsh policies. Indeed, some of the Vietnamese tried to stop or interfere with the American evacuation because of the resentment.

The fear was so great that during the final evacuation from the U.S. Embassy some of the Vietnamese were taking their children and handing them over the wall to any westerner saying, "Take my children. The communists will slaughter them." Entire families were separated. There, also, was great panic, unbelievable panic. The day before the final American evacuation, on April 29, the embassy was mobbed with thousands of Vietnamese pressing against the fence trying to get inside, trying to get aboard the American helicopters because they feared a communist bloodbath. And, actually, the people who started the bloodbath rumors were the U.S. government, the CIA. They did this to try to spur Congress into appropriating more funds. They were saying, "If you don't appropriate funds, the South Vietnamese government will fall and the blood will be on your hands."

Well, Congress didn't appropriate the funds, but that is the story the CIA was trying to sell to news organizations. At the AP, we didn't buy it. Two CIA agents came into the AP office three weeks before the fall of

Saigon. They said, "The communists are committing atrocities on the central coast." So, I said, "Fine. We'll send a reporter up there or I'll go myself." They said, "No, you can't do that because it is too dangerous. The victims won't talk to you because action would be taken against their relatives." I asked, "Well, can we quote you?" They wouldn't let us quote them. I led them out the door. I knew it was a phony thing. But the rumors got back to the Vietnamese. There was tremendous panic with the Vietnamese trying to get out on the helicopters, threatening to stampede the gates. As a matter of fact, they endangered the marines so much that in one pathetic scene there at the embassy the marines were beating the Vietnamese with rifle butts. Some Vietnamese were climbing the fence and they were being kicked and hit with rifle butts to knock them off. The panic was incredible. This rumor about a communist bloodbath certainly caused hysteria.

The soldiers and civil servants who worked alongside the Americans and were unable to escape in the final evacuation were sent to prison camps. The communists called them "re-education camps." Some of them spent up to fifteen years in the camps under harsh conditions. But there wasn't any communist bloodbath.

I think the U.S. did a really poor job in evacuating the Vietnamese. They held off evacuating too long because Ambassador Martin didn't want to pull the plug sooner because he felt it would cause panic if the Americans evacuated. But it didn't matter because there was panic anyhow. Martin didn't order the evacuation sooner because he felt it would send the Vietnamese the message that Americans were abandoning them.

Another thing: Martin, foolishly I think, felt an agreement could be reached with the communists. Some kind of coalition government could be set up with Saigon partitioned off. He felt until the very end that the communists were going to agree to some kind of cease fire with Big Minh— with the communists holding a two-thirds majority in the coalition. That was unrealistic. Why would the communists do that? They had Saigon surrounded. They were going to win. It made no sense. Of course, Martin had personal pride. He did not want to acknowledge that Vietnam was going down the drain. He finally had to be ordered out by Washington—twice.

After the evacuation ended, there were still hundreds of Vietnamese milling around the embassy. They hoped there would be further American helicopters arriving, which there weren't. Then the southerners fell into a huge despair which was to last until the 1980s, fourteen or fifteen years.

I noticed as the communists did enter the city, the southerners, who are very adept at making accommodations, cheered them. But I don't think it was a sincere cheer. The Saigonese feared the communists but what choice did they have? They suddenly changed sides and on the surface appeared to be cheering the new communist government. But they didn't believe in them, didn't want any part of them because they feared this would be an end to free enterprise. They turned inward becoming very tentative. The mood was dark. There was no happiness. The northerners ignored them, letting them live in poverty as second-hand citizens.

In the first couple of days after the takeover, it was very quiet. It was a situation where the communists had great difficulty converting to a civilian government. They never quite made that transition. It was very awkward. They acknowledged that, "We were good at winning the war, but not good at managing the country." Finally, they made the switch in the later 1980s.

The Saigonese, who now lived in Ho Chi Minh City, became very poor. They really had no part in the government. And were just shunned, treated with great distaste. The worse thing was the imprisonment of thousands in the re-education camps. Some of those folks have only been released in recent years as relations improved with the U.S.

Another thing that gives you an indication as to why the communists won the Vietnam War was the dedication and sense of purpose they had. As Saigon was falling and the U.S. was evacuating, those final days in 1975, South Vietnamese military and civilians went in and were looting buildings, carrying away typewriters, stereos, tape recorders, anything they could get their hands on. Here's a country falling and they aren't interested in defending it. They are interested in making money, taking all these leftovers and trying to sell them on the black market.

The communists, I must say, came into Saigon very well-trained and disciplined. They never threatened westerners. They didn't do any looting whatsoever. Here's the conquering army respecting property and the South Vietnamese concentrating on looting instead of putting up a last stand.

As the country was falling, the South Vietnamese just gave up. They knew they were beaten. When Big Minh announced an unconditional surrender on that morning of April 30, the Saigon troops just marched in and stacked their weapons. They were so humiliated. They stripped their uniforms and hoped the communists would not know they once fought with the Americans. So they tried to disassociate themselves from the military. City blocks were littered with the uniforms and boots of the South Vietnamese army that had been discarded.

The evacuation ended shortly after 8:00 a.m. on April 30. The Saigon government announced its surrender around 10:00 a.m. Around noon the North Vietnamese and Viet Cong marched into the city. They had waited because they had guaranteed the United States a safe evacuation. They certainly had the city surrounded. There was an informal agreement that had been broadcast over the Hanoi radio. They ordered the Americans out and the Americans complied.

I left on June 5, 1975. The place was chaotic. The communists couldn't seem to organize a civilian government. I think because they were going to herd the South Vietnamese into prison camps the communists didn't want the press around. So, they started expelling us, a few of us one week, then some more the next week, and more the following week. At first the communists went after the political people, then the senior military officers. Tens of thousands were sent to the camps.

Conclusion

Once more unto the breach, dear friends, once more;
Or close the wall with our English dead!
In peace there's nothing so becomes a man
As modest stillness and humility;
But when the blast of war blows in our ears,
Then imitate the action of the tiger;
Stiffen the sinews, summon up the blood,
Disguise fair nature with hard-favored rage;
Then lend the eye a terrible aspect.

-William Shakespeare, "Henry V"

In Asia, 1975 was the "Year of the Cat." Certainly, the collapse of South Vietnam displayed feline characteristics. Cunningly, the communists observed the slow movements of American supplies (oil, for example) to our South Vietnamese allies. The Paris promises of 1973 had been swatted aside by a wide range of domestic and international problems: the Watergate scandal, war in the Middle East and a punishing oil embargo, generational dislocations, resignations of Vice-President Spiro Agnew and President Richard Nixon, an anemic economy propped up by a simplistic "whip inflation now" plan, an assertive Democratic Congressional majority, and a political—impotent unelected president advised by foreign policy counselors more interested in other regions of the world. A *Time* magazine photograph of President Gerald Ford and Secretary of State Henry Kissinger, attired in tuxedos on the night of the evacuation, speaks volumes. The leadership was all dressed up with somewhere else to go. As Colonel Ed Pelosky succinctly explains, "They didn't want to hear."

Policymakers were inattentive, napping while South Vietnam's needs went unheeded. In our interviews, we were repeatedly told that Americans in Saigon sensed the coming collapse months before it actually occurred. They also described the repeated attempts that were made to awaken the powers-that-be in Washington to the dangers that seemed so clear to them. Yet, the U.S. Congress seemed unwilling to allocate additional resources to our ally. The investment had soured, in spite of 58,000 American lives having been lost, and the account had been closed. And, by early spring, President Ford seemed resigned to the end of America's longest war, regardless of how ignominious that end might be. No wonder President Thieu, before he flew (on an American airplane) safely into exile, lashed out at us, voicing his anger at betrayal and abandonment.

Whether it was the erstwhile Vietcong captain, the members of the South Vietnamese and American military, the intelligence gatherers, or the officials in the American Embassy, all agreed that the resignation of President Nixon was a watershed event in the struggle for South Vietnamese independence. While Henry Kissinger acceded to a flawed peace accord in Paris in 1973, he did so knowing that his president, Nixon, would be true to his word should the north invade in force. The American armed forces in the region, Air Force warplanes in Thailand and the Seventh Fleet in the South China Sea, were ready and willing to respond to a presidential order to defend our ally with tremendous firepower. The North Vietnamese feared most of all the return of those B-52s that had brought them back to the negotiating table after the 1972 Christmas bombing of Hanoi and Haiphong. But by the spring of 1975, Richard Nixon no longer held the power to send these forces to the aid of the south's defenders. His successor, Gerald Ford, failed to frighten the communists.

Thus, the communists clawed their way down the peninsula. While some Americans (the CIA Station Chief, for example) were convinced that a coalition government could be installed, the cat was hungry for the entire meal. And when the voice of Bing Crosby singing "White Christmas" floated across Radio Saigon's airwaves, those Americans on the scene braced themselves for history's largest evacuation since Dunkirk. "Operation Frequent Wind" mirrored our total experience in Southeast Asia. Courage, confusion, dedication, greed, duplicity, anger, pain, joy, zeal, stupidity, hesitation, and gallantry were all on display during that April, a quarter century ago, as the tiger pounced, swallowing the complete offering.

Once the United States responded to the North Vietnamese aggression at Phuoc Long in December of 1974 with only feeble protests, the communists were convinced that the door to complete victory was open. Then, as Democratic Congressmen cut the financial support for the South Vietnamese and concerned themselves about whether or not the prisoners of war in the south were being treated in strict compliance with the Geneva Conventions, the armies of the north crossed the DMZ in massive numbers. It was the communists who imitated "the actions of the tiger." And while the ARVN struggled against overwhelming odds, American politicians snoozed.

A question that needs to be addressed by our society as it enters the twenty-first century, bereft of "the evil empire" of a Cold War Soviet Union is the role that we intend to play in the era of small, mostly ethnically inspired, civil wars. While television images of the victims of these wars will always bring cries for action overseas and here at home, America's leaders must only respond if they are willing to "stiffen their sinews—with hard-favored rage." And then "enter unto the breach" only if they are determined to persevere until the clearly described objective of the effort has been achieved. The disastrous outcomes experienced in Vietnam, Lebanon, and Somalia can be expected to recur any time the United States enters a war with less than the ferocity required to bring about success as quickly and completely as possible. To paraphrase Tran Trong Khan, the ex-Vietcong officer we interviewed, the most important thing in achieving the objective of inserting our military into wars like those of Vietnam, Lebanon, and Somalia, is force. If you do not win on the battlefield, you cannot win at the negotiating table.

Notes

Introduction

1. "Presidential Press Secretaries: A Roundtable Discussion," sponsored by the Public Broadcasting System and aired September 24, 1989.

2. Frank M. Snepp, III, *Decent Interval* (New York: Random House. 1977), 279; 579; interestingly, Snepp was successfully sued by the CIA for violating a secrecy agreement and forfeited all royalties from *Decent Interval*.

3. Snepp, *Decent Interval*, 565 and 580.

4. *Washington Post*, August 11, 1995; *New York Times*, August 13, 1995; *U.S. News and World Report*, January 8, 1996; the best book on America's experience in Southeast Asia remains Stanley Karnow, *Vietnam: A History* (New York: Viking, 1983); Snepp, *Decent Interval*, 580; "Frequent Wind" was the operation's code name because of the use of multiple helicopter sorties, see *Marine Corps Gazette*, February 1976.

5. In addition to works by Karnow and Snepp, we found Larry Englemann, *Tears Before the Rain: An Oral History of the End of the Vietnam War* (New York: Oxford Press, 1991) to be helpful in ascertaining the details of "Operation Frequent Wind."

6. Interview with Haney Howell, April 10, 1995, Rock Hill, South Carolina.

7. Interview with Lawrence Chambers, April 27, 1995, Reston, Virginia; interview with Larry Grimes, May 2, 1995, Pensacola, Florida.

8. Interview with Bung Ly, April 8, 1995, Orlando, Florida; see also the Fall 1993 edition of *Foundation* magazine for Chambers' account of the rescue of Bung Ly.

9. ibid.

10. Interview with Haney Howell; interview with H. C. Haynsworth, April 4, 1995, Rock Hill, S.C.

11. Interview with Chambers; interview with Grimes; interview with Adam Komisarcik, April 17, 1995, Reston, Virginia; *Midway*'s "Ship's Log," entry for May 3, 1975.

12. Stanley Karnow, *Vietnam: A History*, 669-670.

13. Karnow, *Vietnam: A History*, 668; a detailed analysis of the *Midway*'s log reveals the flurry of activity by the crew during late April and early May, 1975; Harry G. Summers, Jr., "The Bitter End," *Vietnam Magazine*, April, 1995, 38.

Slow Strangulation

1. In 1966, Congressman Ford had criticized President Johnson's "shocking mismanagement" of the Vietnam War which featured periodic cessations of bombing; at that time, Ford, minority leader of the U.S. House of Representatives, favored a more aggressive approach to the air war; see Gerald Ford, *A Time To Heal* (New York, Harper & Row, 1979) 82-83.

2. Interview with Alexander Haig, March 6, 1997, New York, N.Y.

More

1. Brady continues to move easily among Washington's powerful people; his office features a framed portrait of President Bill Clinton and himself after a game of golf; the inscription reads "Thanks for a great round."

2. Interview with Jack Brady, January 10, 1996, Washington, D.C.

Oil And Money

1. Interview with Tran Trong Khan, August 12, 1996, Washington, D.C.

Dunkirk

1. Colonel Pelosky shared with us his "Letters To Lois," correspondence with his spouse; in these letters Pelosky constantly expresses his affection for Vietnamese who he encountered during his travels around the country.

2. Interview with Edwin Pelosky, January 9, 1996, Denton, Maryland.

In The Alleyway

1. As the war ended, CBS News sent Ed Bradley to Saigon to help report the unfolding drama.

2. Interview with Haney Howell, June 27, 1996, Rock Hill, South Carolina.

Setting The Record Straight

1.General Smith inherited an assignment where he served as chief logistician; he had the challenge of keeping supply lines open while the U.S. Congress shut off the flow of materials promised to the doomed South Vietnamese military under the Paris Peace Accords.

2. Interview with Homer Smith, January 2, 1997, San Antonio, Texas.

3. One of the best examples of the South Vietnamese Army's tenacity occurred at the crossroads city of Xuan Loc, forty miles east of Saigon on highway QL-1, where the 18th ARVN Division, commanded by Brigadier General Le Minh Dao, held its ground against a much superior force for over a week. The ARVN soldiers received a grudging compliment from North Vietnamese Senior General Van Tien Dung when his advance was virtually stopped short on April 9 by what he called "the enemy's stubbornness." Over 5,000 northern soldiers died and thirty-seven tanks were destroyed before Dao's forces retreated toward Saigon. See Harry G. Summers' *Historical Atlas of the Vietnam War* (New York; Houghton Mifflin Co., 1995), and Stanley Karnow's *Vietnam: A History* (New York; Viking, 1983).

Their Country, Their War

1. General Murray is not alone in his disdain for the Joint Chiefs of Staff; for a recent indictment of the joint chiefs, see H. R. McMaster's *Dereliction of Duty: Lyndon Johnson, Robert McNamara, The Joint Chiefs of Staff and the Lies That Led To Vietnam* (New York: Harper Collins, 1997).

2. Interview with John Murray, August 13, 1996, Fairfax, Virginia.

3. For a description of General Jean de Tassigny's tactics in this battle, see Harry G. Summers' *Historical Atlas of the Vietnam War* (New York: Houghton Mifflin Co., 1995), 52.

A Done Deal

1. Interview with William LeGro, January 8, 1996, Washington, D.C.; several times during this interview, Colonel LeGro mentions that some of his observations on the war were deleted by the U.S. Army Center of History in his book *Vietnam From Cease Fire To Capitulation* (Washington: U.S. Army Center of Military History, 1981).

"Nobody Told Martin"

1. Thomas Polgar has been criticized harshly for believing the Hungarians' assurances concerning the possibility that a coalition government could be installed in Saigon; see Frank Snepp's *Decent Interval: An Insider's Account of Saigon's Indecent End Told By The CIA's Chief Strategy Analyst In Vietnam* (New York: Random House, 1977) and the interviews in this book with Homer Smith, John Murray, and Richard Armitage.

2. Interview with Thomas Polgar, November 25, 1996, Orlando, Florida.

Leaving A Pregnant Lady

1. See the aforementioned *Dereliction of Duty*.

2. Interview with Richard Armitage, August 14, 1998, Arlington, Virginia.

"Politics Is An Evil Thing"

1. Interview with John Guffey, July 23, 1996, Shawnee, Oklahoma.

Underground Railroad

1. For a vivid account of the earlier underground railroad see John W. Blassingame's *Slave Testimony: Two Centuries of Letters, Speeches, Interviews, and Autobiographies* (New York: W.W. Norton, 1977).

2. Interview with William Estep, July 23, 1996, Oklahoma City, Oklahoma.

The Fall Guy

1. Interview with Ann Hazard, July 26, 1996, Las Cruces, New Mexico.

2. Obtained through the Freedom of Information Act, the document that follows Ms. Hazard's comments sheds light on the final resolution of the money question.

An Ad Hoc Plan

1. For a glimpse of Captain Herrington's 1975 service on the Hanoi-Saigon commission, we have included one of his memoranda.

2. Interview with Stuart Herrington, August 14, 1996, Carlisle, Pennsylvania; for additional insight we suggest Colonel Herrington's *Peace With Honor?* (Novato, California: Presidio Press, 1982).

Another Plan

1. The French defeat at Dien Bien Phu is placed in a wider context in North Vietnamese General Vo Nguyen Giap's comments in the aforementioned *Major Problems In The History Of The Vietnam War*; Giap writes, "in the end the French and U.S. imperialists would certainly meet with a bitter failure" (124).

2. Interview with Leon Nguyen, August 21, 1996, Charlotte, North Carolina.

3. In an interview for the History Division of the United States Naval Institute, Vice Admiral George Steele, the Commander, Seventh Fleet in 1975, describes the circumstances for these unusual changes of command as follows: "As [the South Vietnamese Navy ships] got closer [to the Philippines], the problem grew more immediate of what we were going to do with the ships. Or could we get them in at all? [President of the Philippines Ferdinand] Marcos didn't want them in with a Vietnamese flag on them. So I proposed that just outside Subic that we reassume them. They were military assistance ships anyhow. We would put an American CO on each one to raise the American flag and take them back into U.S. custody."

Not A Teheran Situation

1. A declassified plea from the embassy to the State Department is included in this chapter; clearly, Ambassador Martin and Deputy Chief of Mission Lehman warned Washington about the deteriorating situation in South Vietnam eight months before the collapse.

2. Interview with Wolfgang Lehman, August 13, 1996, Washington, D.C.

Atop Two Walls

1. On April 23, 1975, a week before the final evacuation of Saigon, President Ford, speaking at Tulane University, remarked that there was no benefit in "refighting a war that is finished."

2. Interview with Glenn Rounsevell, August 12, 1995, Falls Church, Virginia.

3. The publication in 1995 of Defense Secretary McNamara's memoir *In Retrospect* (New York: Harper & Row) ignited a firestorm of anger from Vietnam veterans who considered McNamara's confession concerning his early doubts about the war to be "too little, much too late."

"A Fruitless, Terrible, and Tragic Fiasco"

1. Interview with Joseph Gildea, July 29, 1996, Hollidaysburg, Pennsylvania.

Mary's Place

1. Interview with Mary Vu, August 7, 1996, Rock Hill, South Carolina.

Self-Preservation

1. Interview with Donald Berney, July 30, 1996, San Diego, California; Mr. Berney's personal files contain the refugee totals which are found at the conclusion of our interview.

Giving Away A Country

1. Interview with William Ryder, August 27, 1996, Indian Harbor Beach, Florida.

Last Woman Out

1. Interview with Sally Vinyard, July 28, 1996, Fallbrook, California.

Not Normal

1. Through a Freedom of Information Act request we gained access to the complete monograph; a heavily edited version of the study had been made available by the Air Force in 1976; a chart documenting the refugee totals has been attached.

2. Interview with Arthur Laehr, July 22, 1996, Pensacola, Florida.

"Please Move Your Helicopters"

1. Interview with Bung Ly, November 30, 1996, Orlando, Florida.

Out On A Limb

1. Interview with Richard Carey, July 9, 1996, Plano, Texas.

2. Two excellent examinations of the operation which support General Carey's impressions are the one prepared by Major J.E. Rhodes at the Marine Corps Command and Staff College in 1979 and the earlier study by Urey Patrick for the Center for Naval Analyses.

0759, April 30

1. Interview with Terry Bennington, July 2, 1996, Quantico, Virginia; obviously, opinions vary concerning whether or not the marine squad was "left" behind.

Fear, Rumors, And Panic

1. Interview with George Esper, July 1, 1996, New York, N.Y.

A Note On Sources

There are over 900 secondary sources which examine the various aspects of the conflict in Vietnam. A few of the books which supplemented our use of interviews, private collections, and government documents are:

Butler, David. *The Fall of Saigon*. New York: Simon and Schuster, 1985.

Colby, William. *Lost Victory*. New York: Simon and Schuster, 1989.

Dawson, Alan. *55 Days: The Fall of South Vietnam*. Englewood Cliffs, N.J.: Prentice Hall, 1977.

Dung, Van Tien. *Our Great Spring Victory: An Account of the Liberation of South Vietnam*. New York: Monthly Review Press, 1977.

Englemann, Larry. *Tears Before The Rain: An Oral History of the Fall of South Vietnam*. New York: Oxford Press, 1990.

Herrington, Stuart A. *Peace With Honor?: An American Reports On Vietnam, 1973–1975*. Novato, California: Presidio Press, 1982.

LeGro, William E. *Vietnam From Cease Fire To Capitulation*. Washington: U.S. Army Center of Military History, 1981.

Pilger, John. *The Last Days: America's Final Hours In Vietnam*. New York: Vintage, 1975.

Snepp, Frank. *Decent Interval: An Insider's Account of Saigon's Indecent End Told By The CIA's Chief Strategy Analyst in Vietnam*. New York: Random House, 1977.

Terzani, Tiziano. *Giai Phong! The Fall and Liberation of South Vietnam*. New York: Simon and Schuster, 1976.

Chronology Of Major Events

December 31, 1971: The American war in Vietnam is ending; 156,800 U.S. troops remain. There were 1,380 KIAs in 1971. As the Americans withdraw, the communists intensify their attacks in Laos, Cambodia, and parts of South Vietnam. U.S. morale continues to deteriorate. Vietnamization is not working and the Paris talks remained stalled.

February 21–27, 1972: President Nixon makes his historic visit to China. The North Vietnamese fear that China and the United States will make a deal behind their backs (i.e., the U.S. abandoning Taiwan in exchange for peace in Vietnam).

March 30 to April 8, 1972: A major NVA offensive begins as communist forces attack South Vietnamese towns and bases just south of the DMZ. The communists open a second front with a drive into Binh Long province about seventy miles north of Saigon. Communist forces open a third front with drives into the central highlands. The fighting in South Vietnam between GVN and communist forces is the most intense of the entire war.

April 10, 1972: America responds with air attacks. B-52s strike targets in North Vietnam for the first time since November 1967. B-52s and tactical bombers also strike targets in South Vietnam. America is waging an air war over all of Vietnam.

May 8, 1972: Nixon announces that he has ordered the mining of all North Vietnamese ports.

May 20, 1972: The summit conference between President Nixon and Leonid Brezhnev takes place on schedule in Moscow. Both sides are unwilling to risk détente over the Vietnam War. Nixon's Soviet visit is the first ever by a U.S. president.

June 28, 1972: President Nixon announces that no more draftees will be sent to Vietnam unless they volunteer.

August 11, 1972: The last U.S. combat unit is withdrawn from South Vietnam. There are now 44,000 American servicemen in South Vietnam.

August 16, 1972: U.S. aircraft fly a record 370 sorties against North Vietnam. Most American aircraft fly from carriers in the Gulf of Tonkin or from bases in Thailand.

September 15, 1972: ARVN forces recapture Quang Tri City. The fighting destroys most of the city, which formerly had a population of 300,000. Most of these people now reside in squalid refugee camps.

October 8–11, 1972: Lengthy secret meetings in Paris between Henry Kissinger and Le Duc Tho produce a tentative settlement of the war. The substance of the agreement is a ceasefire, to be followed by both sides working out a political settlement.

October 22, 1972: President Thieu rejects the proposed settlement.

November 7, 1972: Richard Nixon is re-elected president by a landslide margin. He promises that he will achieve "peace with honor" in Vietnam.

November 11, 1972: The U.S. Army turns over its giant headquarters base at Long Binh to the South Vietnamese, symbolizing the end of the direct American participation in the war after more than seven years.

December 14, 1972: The U.S. breaks off the peace talks with the North Vietnamese that have been going on since Nixon's re-election.

December 18–29, 1972: President Nixon announces the resumption of the bombing and mining of North Vietnam. The most concentrated air offensive of the war begins, aimed mostly at targets in the vicinity of Hanoi and Haiphong.

December 28, 1972: Hanoi announces that it is willing to resume negotiations if the United States will stop bombing above the 20th parallel. The bombing ends on December 29.

December 31, 1972: At year's end there are about 24,000 U.S. troops remaining in South Vietnam. 312 Americans were killed in action in 1972.

January 8–18, 1973: Henry Kissinger and Le Duc Tho resume negotiations in Paris, and they reach an agreement that is similar to the one that had been rejected by General Thieu.

January 19–26, 1973: There is heavy fighting in South Vietnam between GVN and communist forces as both sides try to gain as much territory as they can before the ceasefire.

January 21, 1973: Under great pressure form President Nixon, President Thieu reluctantly agrees to the Paris Peace Accords.

January 23, 1973: Nixon announces that the Paris Accords will go into effect at 7:00 P.M. EST. He says that "peace with honor" has been achieved.

January 27, 1973: The draft ends. For the first time since 1949, America has no conscription.

February 12–27, 1973: American POWs begin to come home.

February 21, 1973: A ceasefire formally ends the twenty-year war in Laos.

March 29, 1973: The last U.S. troops leave South Vietnam. Only a Defense Attaché Office (DAO) contingent and marine embassy guards remain. About 8,500 U.S. civilian officials stay on.

June 4 to August 15, 1973: The Senate blocks all funds for any U.S. military activities in Indochina. The House concurs. The Nixon administration works out a compromise agreement with the Congress to permit continued U.S. bombing in Cambodia until August 15. The cessation marks the end of twelve years of American military action in Indochina.

November 7, 1973: Congress enacts the War Powers Act over President Nixon's veto. It requires the president to report to Congress within forty-eight hours after committing American forces to combat on foreign soil. It also limits to sixty days the time that the president can commit soldiers to foreign combat without congressional approval.

December 31, 1973: The war in Vietnam continues without U.S. involvement. Most of the provisions of the Paris Accords are not observed by either side. During the year, there were 13,788 RVNAF KIAs and 45,050 communist KIAs.

August 5, 1974: Congress makes sharp cuts in the amount of military aid going to the South Vietnamese government.

December 31, 1974: During 1974, 80,000 people, both civilians and soldiers, have been killed in the war. This is the highest total for any year since the war began in 1945.

January 6, 1975: NVA forces overrun Phuoc Long Province. When the Americans do not react, Hanoi concludes that America will not reintroduce its military forces to save the GVN.

January 7, 1975: Phuoc Long Province falls.

January 7–24, 1975: NVA pressure on Tay Ninh Province; refugee exodus follows. NVA convoy traffic up in MR II. Airborne and marines begin shift to reserve status in MR I.

January 20, 1975: Sappers destroy Pleiku ammo dump.

January 29, 1975: GVN disarms Hoa Hao Militia in MR IV.

February 5, 1975: Lieutenant General Toan becomes MR III Commander.

February 14–28, 1975: RVNAF preemptive operations against NVA buildups in MRs I, II and III.

March 1–7, 1975: Communist spring-summer campaign opens in MR I and MR II.

March 4–5, 1975: Interdiction of QL-19 east of Pleiku.

March 6, 1975: Interdiction of QL-14 south of Pleiku.

March 7, 1975: Overrun of Thanh Man District Town (Phu Bon).

March 9, 1975: Overrun of Duc Lap District Town (Quang Duc), and the assault on Ban Me Thuot begins.

March 10, 1975: Overrun of Hau Duc and Tien Phuoc Districts (Quang Tin Province).

March 12, 1975: Contact lost with Ban Me Thuot City.

March 13, 1975: Overrun of Tri Tam District Town (Binh Duong).

March 15, 1975: Evacuation of Northern Highlands begins.

March 16, 1975: Evacuation of Son Ha and Tra Bong Districts (Quang Ngai Province).

March 17, 1975: Overrun of Phuoc An District (Darlac Province). Order given to evacuate Pleiku and Kontum.

March 19, 1975: Overrun of Cheo Reo City (Phu Bon). Airborne redeployed from MR I to Saigon. Quang Tri City occupied by NVA.

March 20, 1975: Evacuation of Quang Tri City. Overrun of Hoai Duc District Town (Binh Tuy Province).

March 22, 1975: Evacuation of Quang Duc Province. Overrun of Khanh Duong District (Khanh Hoa Province).

March 23, 1975: Overrun of An Tuc District Town (Binh Dinh Province) and Dinh Quan District Town (Long Khanh Province).

March 24, 1975: Quang Ngai Province abandoned. Contact lost with Hue City. Overrun of Tam Ky City. Decision made to abandon the northern part of MR I entirely.

March 25, 1975: Evacuation of Quang Ngai Province.

March 27, 1975: Overrun of Chu Lai airfield. Evacuation of Tam Quan District (Binh Dinh Province).

March 28, 1975: Evacuation of Lam Dong Province.

March 30, 1975: Contact lost with Danang City. The city falls completing the collapse of MR I.

March 31, 1975: Overrun of Phu Cat air base.

April 1, 1975: Second Corps headquarters in Nha Trang evacuated. Contact lost with Qui Nhon and Tuy Hoa cities. Central Highlands fall to communist control.

April 2, 1975: Second Corps moves from Nha Trang.

April 3, 1975: Contact lost with Nha Trang and Dalat cities.

April 4, 1975: U.S. Air Force C5-A "Babylift" aircraft crashes near Saigon. Contact lost with Phan Rang air base and Cam Ranh City abandoned.

April 9, 1975: Xuan Loc comes under attack.

April 16, 1975: Phan Rang falls to NVA forces.

April 18, 1975: Phan Thiet City, capital of Binh Thuan Province, falls. Conquest of MR II complete. Binh Thuan falls.

April 21, 1975: President Thieu resigns and is succeeded by Vice President Tran Van Huong.

April 22, 1975: Xuan Loc falls after a ferocious defense which resulted in over 5,000 NVA KIA.

April 23, 1975: President Gerald Ford gives a speech at Tulane University in which he states that the war in Vietnam "is finished as far as America is concerned."

April 27, 1975: Vice President Huong succeeded by Dong Van (Big) Minh. Ba Ria falls.

April 28, 1975: Tan Son Nhut bombed by former VNAF pilots. At Bien Hoa, III Corps staff ceases operations.

April 29, 1975: Cu Chi overrun. Bien Hoa lost. Vung Tau occupied. Major rocket attack on Tan Son Nhut airfield. All remaining U.S. personnel evacuated in "Operation Frequent Wind."

April 30, 1975: President Minh surrenders unconditionally and orders all resistance to cease. Communists quickly occupy and control Saigon. No further combat.

Glossary

ARVN: Army of the Republic of Vietnam. The regular South Vietnamese national armed forces.

Charlie: GI slang for the Vietcong, a short version of Victor Charlie, from the U.S. military phonetic alphabet for VC.

Chinook: CH-47 transport helicopter.

CIA: Central Intelligence Agency.

CINCPAC: Commander-in-Chief, United States Pacific Command.

Cobra: Bell AH-1G fast attack helicopter, armed with machine guns, grenade launchers, and rockets.

COMUSMACV: Commander, United States Military Assistance Command.

Corps: Two divisions assigned to defend a military region.

COSVN: Central Office, South Vietnam, the headquarters controlling all Vietcong political and military operations in southern Vietnam.

Counterinsurgency: The guiding doctrine of U.S. military forces in Vietnam during early 1960s; its fundamental purpose was to win the allegiance of the people, not destroy the enemy's armed forces. Inspiration for the phrase "winning hearts and minds."

DAO: Defense Attaché Office, an agency that was part of the U.S. mission sent to South Vietnam following the January 1973 Paris Accords that ended the American war; was a replacement for MACV, DAO administered the U.S. military assistance program to the GVN, 1973–1975.

Dien Bien Phu: Site in northwestern Vietnam next to the Laotian border where the French suffered a major defeat in 1954 that led to the end of their power in Vietnam.

DMZ: Demilitarized Zone.

DOD: Department of Defense.

DRV: Democratic Republic of Vietnam (North Vietnam), created by Ho Chi Min, September 2, 1945.

Eagle Pull: Code name of the U.S. evacuation of Phnom Penh in April 1975.

FMFPAC: Fleet Marine Force, Pacific Command.

Frequent Wind: Code name of the U.S. evacuation of Saigon in April 1975.

GVN: The Government of South Vietnam.

Huey: Nickname given the UH-1 series helicopter.

ICC: International Control Commission, created by the Geneva Accords (1954) to supervise the implementation of the agreements.

ICCS: International Commission of Control and Supervision. Agency responsible for administering the January 1973 Paris Accords.

JCS: Joint Chiefs of Staff.

JGS: Joint General Staff, the South Vietnamese equivalent of the U.S. Joint Chiefs.

JMC: Joint Military Commission, consisting of members from North Vietnam, South Vietnam, the Provisional Revolutionary Government (Vietcong), and the United States, responsible for implementing the military provisions of the Paris Accords.

JMT: Joint Military Team, consisting of members from North Vietnam South Vietnam, the Provisional Revolutionary Government (Vietcong), and the United States, responsible for accounting for all prisoners-of-war and MIAs.

Kampuchea: The name given Cambodia in 1975 by the victorious Khmer Rouge.

Khmer Rouge: Members of the Pracheachon, a left-wing revolutionary movement that came to power in Cambodia in April 1975.

KIA: Killed in action.

LINEBACKER 1: Code name for U.S. bombing of North Vietnam, resumed in April 1972 in response to the Nguyen Hue Offensive.

LINEBACKER II: Code name for the U.S. bombing of North Vietnam during December 1972, the so-called Christmas Bombing.

LST: Landing Ship Tank, a large, shallow-draft cargo-hauling and landing craft.

LZ: Landing Zone, for helicopters.

MAAG: Military Assistance Advisory Group, the forerunner of MACV, 1955 to 1964.

MACV: Military Assistance Command, Vietnam, formed in 1962, lasted until 1973.

MARS: Military Affiliate Radio Station.

MIA: Missing in Action.

Montagnards: "Mountain dwellers," the indigenous tribal populations of Vietnam, who generally inhabited hilly and mountainous terrain.

MR: Military Region, formerly a CTZ, a Corps Tactical Zone.

NVA: North Vietnamese Army.

NVN: North Vietnam or North Vietnamese.

OB: Order of Battle, a comprehensive arrangement and disposition of military units deployed in battle.

Pentagon Papers: Secret Department of Defense studies of U.S. involvement in Vietnam, 1945–1967. The papers were stolen by Daniel Ellsberg and Anthony Russo in 1971 and given to the *New York Times*, which published them that same year.

PF: Popular Forces, South Vietnamese militia.

PLA: People's Liberation Army of South Vietnam, the military wing of the Vietcong.

POW: Prisoner-Of-War.

PRG: Peoples Revolutionary Government/South Vietnam (Vietcong).

RF: Regional Forces

RVN: Republic of South Vietnam.

RVAF: Republic of Vietnam Armed Forces, all South Vietnamese military forces including the ARVN, Regional Forces, and Popular Forces.

Sortie: An operational flight by one aircraft.

SVN: South Vietnam.

Tet: The Vietnamese lunar New Year and their most important holiday.

USAID: United States Agency for International Development.

VC: Vietcong, a derogatory contraction meaning a Vietnamese who is a communist.

VCI: Vietcong infrastructure, the political leaders of the Vietcong, also responsible for logistic support of the military forces.

Vietminh: A coalition political party formed by Ho Chi Minh in 1941 dominated by Vietnamese communist leaders; it came to power in Hanoi on September 2, 1945.

Vietnamization: The word was coined by Secretary of Defense Melvin Laird to describe Nixon's policy, inherited from Johnson, of withdrawing U.S. forces from Vietnam and transferring their responsibilities to the RVN forces.

VNAF: South Vietnamese Air Force.

VNN: South Vietnamese Navy.

WIA: Wounded in action.

Maps

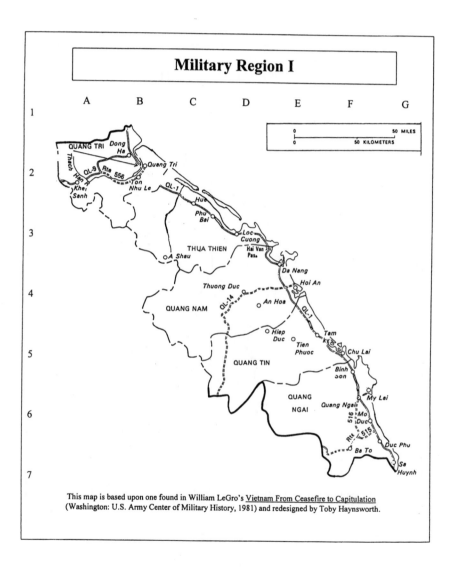

Military Region I

A   B   C   D   E   F   G

0   50 MILES
0   50 KILOMETERS

QUANG TRI Dong Ha
Quang Tri
Thach Han
QL-9 Rte 556 Ton Nhu Le
Khe Sanh
QL-1
Hue
Phu Bai
Loc Cuong
THUA THIEN
A Shau Hai Van Pass
Da Nang
Hoi An
Thuong Duc
QL-14
QUANG NAM An Hoa
QL-1
Hiep Duc Tam Ky
Tien Phuoc Chu Lai
QUANG TIN
Binh Son
QUANG My Lai
NGAI Quang Ngai
Rte 516 Mo Duc
515 Ba To Duc Phu
Sa Huynh

This map is based upon one found in William LeGro's <u>Vietnam From Ceasefire to Capitulation</u>
(Washington: U.S. Army Center of Military History, 1981) and redesigned by Toby Haynsworth.

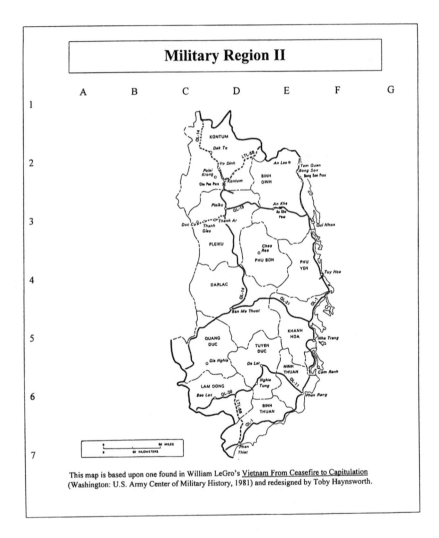

Military Region II

This map is based upon one found in William LeGro's <u>Vietnam From Ceasefire to Capitulation</u> (Washington: U.S. Army Center of Military History, 1981) and redesigned by Toby Haynsworth.

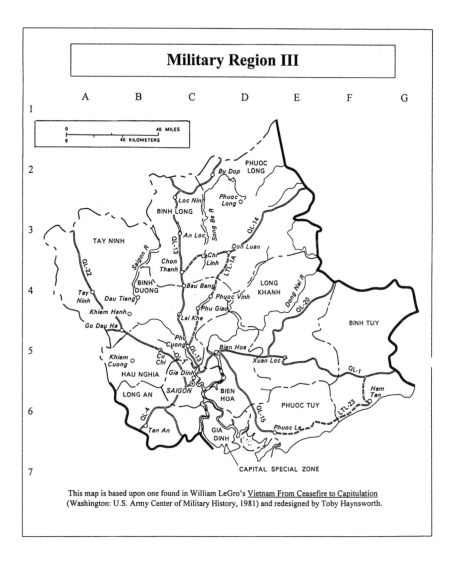

Military Region III

This map is based upon one found in William LeGro's <u>Vietnam From Ceasefire to Capitulation</u>
(Washington: U.S. Army Center of Military History, 1981) and redesigned by Toby Haynsworth.

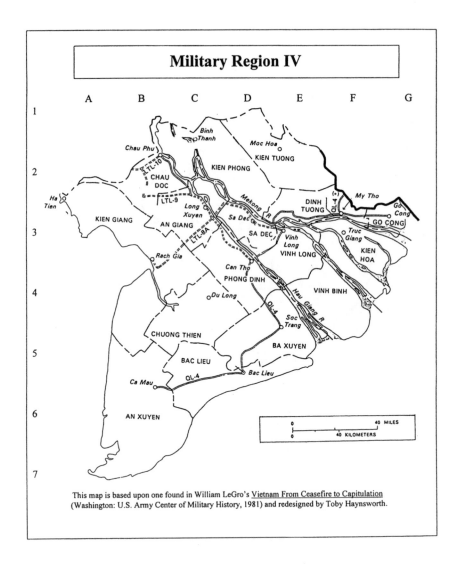

Military Region IV

	A	B	C	D	E	F	G
1							

Binh Thanh

Chau Phu

Moc Hoa

KIEN TUONG

TL-10

CHAU DOC

KIEN PHONG

LTL-9

Long Xuyen

Ha Tien

My Tho

DINH TUONG

Go Cong

KIEN GIANG

AN GIANG

Sa Dec

Mekong R.

GO CONG

LTL-8A

SA DEC

Vinh Long

Truc Giang

Rach Gia

VINH LONG

KIEN HOA

Can Tho

PHONG DINH

Hau Giang R.

Du Long

VINH BINH

QL-4

CHUONG THIEN

Soc Trang

BA XUYEN

BAC LIEU

Ca Mau

QL-4

Bac Lieu

AN XUYEN

0   40 MILES

0   40 KILOMETERS

This map is based upon one found in William LeGro's <u>Vietnam From Ceasefire to Capitulation</u>
(Washington: U.S. Army Center of Military History, 1981) and redesigned by Toby Haynsworth.

Index

Ellis, Brian, 38
"Enhance Plus," 18
Esper, George, 217
Estep, William, 88, 93, 94
Fenwick, Millicent, 11, 13
Flint, John, 11
Francis, Albert, 20, 24
Ford, Gerald, 1, 2, 7, 8, 9 ,10, 69,
    74, 108, 112, 139, 140, 149,
    152, 153, 178, 182, 221
Four-Party Joint Military Team, 15
"Frequent Wind," 2, 6, 51, 128,
    185, 193, 209, 222

G, H

Gayler, Noel, 75, 152
Giap, 52
Gildea, Joseph, 149
Graham, Danny, 54
Gray, Alan, 210
Grimes, Lawrence, 3, 4, 5
Guffey, John, 87
Green Wave, 169, 170, 171
Hai Van Pass, 19, 20, 21, 25, 48,
    49
Haig, Alexander, 6, 7, 60
Haldeman, Bob, 81
Hanoi, 2, 8, 9, 126, 222
Haynsworth, H.C., 4
Hazard, Ann, 95
Herrington, Stuart, 107
Hey, Earnest, 25
Hilgenberg, John, 191, 193
Hilsman, Roger, 16
Ho Chi Minh, 88
Ho Chi Minh Trail, 52
Hoi An, 20
Howell, Haney, 3, 4, 37
Hue, 19, 22, 25, 47, 72
Hull, Terry, 20
Humphrey, Hubert, 61

I, J, K

Indochina Resource Center, 12
International Commission of
    Control and Supervision
    (ICCS), 16
Johnson, Lyndon, 7, 9, 12, 56, 60,
    178
Judge, Darwin, 110, 209
Karnow, Stanley, 5
Kean, James, 205, 208, 210, 214,
    215
Kennedy, John, 12, 60, 178
Kennedy, Robert, 13
Kingston, Robert, 56
Kissinger, Henry, 1, 8, 9, 51, 61,
    63, 69, 70, 75, 77, 79, 81,
    84, 93, 107, 108, 109, 114,
    143, 182, 192, 203, 204,
    221, 222
Kontum, 46
Korea, 7, 13, 19, 52, 56, 72, 73,
    113

L, M

Laehr, Arthur, 191
Le Duc Tho, 63
LeGro, William, 53, 57, 58, 61, 65,
    71
Lehman Wolfgang, 61, 80, 125
LeMay, Curtis, 55
Ly Bung, 3, 4, 5, 197
MacArthur, Douglas, 52
Mansfield, Michael, 59
Marshall, S.L.A., 53
Martin, Graham, 1,2, 11, 13, 14,
    39, 57, 58, 59, 61, 62, 65,
    67, 68, 69, 71, 76, 80, 87,
    106, 108, 123, 125, 129, 131
    144, 171, 206, 208, 209,
    211, 212, 214